THE GOVERNOR

Rod Blagojevich

ISBN-13: 978-1-59777-646-2

Book Design by Sonia Fiore

Printed in the United States of America

Phoenix Books, Inc.
9465 Wilshire Boulevard, Suite 840
Beverly Hills, CA 90212

10 9 8 7 6 5 4 3 2 1

To Patti, Amy, and Annie
You have my everlasting love.

To our friends who stood by us and to all the people
who sent us letters of support and kept us in their prayers
You have our never-ending gratitude.

CHAPTER ONE

THE EYES OF THE WORLD WERE ON WASHINGTON, D.C. ON JANUARY 20, 2009. On a cold and sunny day, and under a bright blue sky—a sky many hoped signified that change had arrived and brighter days were ahead—Barack Obama was sworn in as the 44th President of the United States. A generation after Dr. Martin Luther King's historic "I Have a Dream" speech and nearly 200 years after the birth of Abraham Lincoln, our nation, conceived in liberty and dedicated to the proposition that all men are created equal, was about to see the first African-American president in our nation's history sworn into office.

What a day! The kind of day you want your kids to see. The kind of day, if you were there, you would one day tell your grandchildren about.

Everyone was there. From political leaders to Hollywood stars, from labor leaders to corporate CEOs. Aretha Franklin was there; she sang "My Country 'Tis of Thee." Oprah was there. And so were millions of ordinary citizens from all over America, making the trip to witness history and see President-elect Barack Obama.

I first met Barack Obama about 14 years ago. A mutual friend took me to the law firm he worked in. He was a young lawyer, a state senator, and a guy many saw as a rising star. I was a young lawyer, a state representative preparing to run for Congress, and also a guy many saw as a rising star. In fact, it was not long after that first meeting that he and I began our climb up the political ladder in Chicago that would one day make me governor of our state, and on this day, make him president of our country.

Washington, D.C. was indeed the place to be. But a number of miles away in Chicago, where it was cold and sunny too, the streets were empty. It seemed like everyone had gone to Washington; pilgrims making the journey to celebrate and indulge their pride in their hometown hero; to be there and be part of ushering in a new era in American history.

Everyone, that is, except me. Moments after the new president took his oath of office, I was at the federal courthouse in downtown Chicago getting fingerprinted by a deputy U.S. marshal.

On that day, the new president heard the sound of brass bands playing. He heard a twenty-one gun salute and "Hail to the Chief." He heard the multitudes roar with approval at his historic speech. Everyone is with him.

No one is with me. I'm alone. I'm hearing the sound of a heavy metal iron door unbolting, opening the lockup, and then the sound of it closing. It's a loud crashing sound—like a thunder clap—when you hear it and you're in it—it shakes you. It's a sound that says you are losing your freedom, and the world out there has now been closed off to you. It's a terrifying sound; an ominous sound. A sound, I hope, I never have to hear again.

The Governor of Illinois, the fifth-largest state in the United States, the first governor in America to endorse Barack Obama for president—he's there doing that, I'm here doing this. He's now the President of the United States, like Zeus in Greek mythology, on top of Mt. Olympus. I'm Icarus, who flew too close to the Sun. And I crashed to the ground.

On that historic day, the whole world listened to the new president as he spoke to it. On that same day, that world was closed off to me. And it felt like it was closing in.

I was arrested in the early morning hours on Tuesday, December 9, 2008. I didn't anticipate it or expect it. I had no idea it was coming. It came out of nowhere—a nightmare that was hard enough to live through as it happened and, quite frankly, is hard to relive now.

I went to bed the night before feeling good about things. I had just put in a long and productive day. Early Monday morning over the phone, I had informed my chief of staff that I had selected my first choice to be the next U.S. Senator from Illinois, filling the vacancy left by President-elect Barack Obama. I directed him to reach out to the parties involved and see if we could work out the deal. A deal that, if it happened, would do great things for the people of Illinois.

That Monday morning started, as did most weekday mornings, with a call probably between seven and eight in the morning to my personal assistant Mary Stewart to track down John Harris, my Chief of Staff. I'd routinely call him the first thing in the morning to talk about things and to give him direction. He would update me on things I was interested in and fill me in on what he was hearing.

Prior to joining me as my Chief of Staff at the end of my first term, John worked for Chicago Mayor Richard M. Daley. He served in a lot of big roles for the City of Chicago, the Chicago Police Department, and O'Hare Airport. The son of Greek immigrants, and a product of Chicago public schools, he and I shared similar life experiences and similar values. Like my older brother Rob, John was an officer in the United States Army. He was a prosecutor in the Judge Advocate General's office. And his style and habits remind me of a disciplined, organized military man. An early riser, he was someone you could always find when the day started. Where most of my top staff called me Governor, or Rod, he addressed me as Sir. This is not to suggest that he was in any way obsequious or a sycophant. Just the opposite is true. As a contemporary, with years of experience in administering government, including directing big government budgets, he oversaw the operations of state government. I had a great deal of respect for his experience, and I counted on him to make sure my administration operated effectively, honestly, and always within the rules. I relied on him to tell me what we could and could not do.

As I recall, that Monday morning I directed him to work out the details regarding my first choice for the next U.S. Senator from Illinois and see if we could get it done. He briefed me on some of the conversations he recently had with other involved parties. I explained my aim and how I preferred it done. We then had a game plan to appoint a United States Senator. And even though neither one of us liked my choice, he was going to work to execute it.

I went to bed that night sometime after 11 p.m. in good spirits. My plan was to get up the next morning at 6 a.m. and go for a morning run. Like a lot of long-distance runners who plan for an early morning run, especially in the cold and darkness of winter, it helps psychologically to lay out the running clothes you plan to wear the night before. Getting up and quickly getting into those winter running clothes is a good first step to get out the door, out on the street, and out on your run. I generally run 6 ½ miles to 8 ½ miles three to four times a week. But sometimes, when you're the Governor, things come up, and the run suddenly has to take a backseat to more pressing business, or to the intervention of circumstances beyond your control that consequently require your immediate attention. My plan for December 9th was to run in the morning. As it turned out, I never got it in.

The alarm clock went off promptly at 6 a.m. As my wife Patti hit the off button, I moaned to her, "five more minutes" and went back to sleep. Before the five minutes were up, the telephone rang. It's not a good sign, generally speaking, when the telephone rings at six o'clock in the morning. As I reached to pick up the phone, thoughts started crossing through my mind. What happened? Did somebody die? Was a loved one or friend in an accident? Did a storm, a flood, a tornado hit? Did a bridge collapse? Was a state trooper killed in the line of duty?

When the phone rings that early in the morning, your life experience instinctively prepares you to brace yourself for bad news. But never—not in my wildest dreams—did I expect what I heard when I answered the phone that morning.

In a sleepy haze, I picked up the phone. The guy on the other end of the line identified himself as Agent Grant of the FBI. He said he was in front of my home armed with a warrant for my arrest. At first I wasn't sure I had heard him right. When he repeated the purpose of his mission, I asked him if this was some kind of joke. I honestly thought, for a fleeting moment, that someone was actually playing a practical joke on me. I was quickly trying to gauge the voice and run through my mind who might be doing it. Which one of my friends could this be? My staff? Would they play a joke on me like that? State Senator Jimmy DeLeo, a lawmaker and a friend, and a guy known for his sense of humor—could this be him? For a moment I thought it was him.

As those questions raced through my mind, the FBI agent on the other end of the line insisted it was no joke and asked me to come to the front door and let them in. At that point, one of the leaders of my executive detail got on the phone to assure me that this call was not a joke. What was happening was real. And that, in fact, the FBI was at my front door with a warrant for my arrest.

I quickly put that call on hold and then, on another phone line, reached out to find Bill Quinlan, legal counsel to the governor. As that happened, the FBI agents began ringing the doorbell and knocking hard on the front door.

By this time Patti was up and aware of what was happening. She was as shocked and confused as I was. She went downstairs to let them in, and I returned to the phone line to resume the conversation with the agent in charge. He was urging me to hurry up. With that, I got dressed as quickly as I could, putting on the running clothes I had laid out the night before since they were right there and ready to go. As I was dressing, one of the agents was already on the second-floor and in our bedroom telling me to hurry up. I greeted him and noticed that Annie, our five-year-old, caught his attention. It's not uncommon for our little one to sometimes call out for her mother in the middle of the night, and Annie sometimes climbs into bed with us for the last few hours before it's time to wake up. It so happened she was in our bed that fateful morning. But, fortunately, she didn't wake up and slept through the whole ordeal.

And while it's hard to be thankful to an uninvited FBI agent who shows up in your bedroom at six o'clock in the morning to arrest you when you haven't broken the law, I will say that to the credit of the agent, once he saw Annie was there, he was very careful to whisper and not wake her up. In fact, I really believe that had he known she was there, he would've probably waited for me downstairs. Maybe I'm wrong, but I like to think so.

Our older daughter Amy, who is twelve, was still asleep in her bedroom with her door closed as this was happening. But as we began to walk downstairs, her alarm clock went off. Fortunately, before she got out of bed and opened her door, she called out to her mother to ask if she could sleep in a little longer. Patti quickly said yes, and Amy, too, was spared witnessing the scene where FBI agents were in her home escorting her father away.

I was now well on my way to being placed under arrest. I used to be a prosecutor myself. I spent a lifetime without having a criminal record. The fact that I was now being arrested, and for the first and only time in my life about to be charged with a crime, and that it would happen only after rising to the highest office in the state, was an irony not lost on me at that moment.

We left the house out the back door and through the backyard. It was dark outside, and a light drizzle was falling. Patti walked me out, and when the agents insisted that I be handcuffed, she incredulously said something like, "You have to handcuff him?" It was at this point that I told her not to worry. That everything would be all right. I kissed her goodbye. I told her I loved her. And I reminded her not to forget to get a hold of my lawyer.

With that, I took a backseat in the car the FBI agents were driving. I recall it being black. I was told by the agent in charge what to expect for the rest of the day: where we were going; what would happen there; about a scheduled court appearance in the early afternoon; and roughly what time I might expect to be home. I sat back, quiet for most of the ride, handcuffed and steeling myself for a day I never imagined I'd ever have to face.

"When you walk through a storm, hold your head up high, and don't be afraid of the dark." These are the opening lines from the inspirational song, "You'll Never Walk Alone." I thought about the words to that song as I was being driven by the FBI agents to their processing facility. Already informed about the day ahead, I began envisioning what else was likely in store for me as the day unfolded. A tsunami-like media frenzy was an absolute certainty. So was the political firestorm that was about to start. Calls from my political adversaries for my resignation and impeachment were probably only hours away. And as I was anticipating what was about to happen, I was also trying to figure out what it was that I allegedly did that violated the law and justified this arrest.

After all, who arrests sitting governors in their homes in front of their families at six o' clock in the morning? When does that ever happen? What do they think I did that warranted this arrest? Do they think I killed someone? Or was about to kill someone? Did they think I was planning to run away? What was this? It just had to be some kind of mistake. How else could this be happening?

And what are my supporters going to think when they hear the news? What would the people think? I was mortified at the thought that the people would think ill of me, or worse, that they would think I broke the faith, breached their trust, or let them down. I was devastated at the thought of that.

That last thought really bothered me. Criticism by the press or unfair and inaccurate stories by them is nothing new. I was used to that. It's an occupational hazard and goes along with the territory. Attacks and vilification from political enemies—however hypocritical, partisan or self-righteous—were also nothing new. That, too, comes with the territory. Those things, while irritating at times, and something you might, on occasion, vent to your staff about, are not something I ever lost sleep over.

But what really troubled and concerned me were those times when I feared I might be losing the people. Now, I'm not talking about approval ratings in polls. They can't determine whether the people have a sense that you are on their side. Polls merely test the general mood of the public and are more a reflection of the times when the survey is taken and of the hardships the people may be facing. No, I'm talking about something else; something deeper; something that can't be measured in a poll. It's more instinctive than it is scientific. It's kind of like Justice Powell's famous definition of obscenity: "You can't define it. But you know it when you see it."

It is something you can sense. You can feel it when you're out among the people. It's an instinct I always trusted. And I was grief-stricken at the thought that the people would see me as yet another phony politician who talked a good game but, yet again, was only in it for himself. That thought really bothered me. The thought that the people might think of me in that way cut me to the core and filled me with a real sense of sadness.

There might have been a light drizzle outside while we were driving to the FBI facility, but I was literally in the middle of a storm. This was a disaster. I was facing a crisis the likes of which I had never faced before. It wouldn't be long before I learned that I wasn't the only one of my team visited that morning. I would soon learn that my Chief of Staff, John Harris, was also arrested. And that my deputy governor Bob Greenlee, legal counsel Bill Quinlan, and my brother Rob were also visited. It was like the scene out of the movie *The Godfather, Part One* when Michael Corleone, who has agreed to be godfather to his sister Connie's baby, is at the baptism and actively participating in the ceremony. Just as he expressly renounces Satan, he is simultaneously wiping out all of his enemies.

That is what happened to me. With my top staff incapacitated, I had no choice but to walk through the storm, face this disaster, and handle this crisis alone without them.

Adversity can either break or make you. As we were driving down to the FBI facility that morning, I thought about that too. So much of who you are as a person, the strength of your character, your mettle, your integrity—all of these characteristics are tested when you're forced to face a crisis. Do you run from it? Hide in a corner? Whine and whimper about your fate? Are you paralyzed by fear? Do you look to others to get you out of it? Does fear compel you to lie? Will you sell out your principles, your friends, or both to save yourself? In the end, do you handle it like a coward? Or do you face the crisis like a man? Are you true to yourself and to the truth? Do you face it honestly, forthrightly, straight up, and head on? Embrace the truth as you know it. Face it, with the values your parents taught you. Face it like the heroes you read about in history books.

I've lived my life finding inspiration from reading about great men and women in history. How would Teddy Roosevelt handle this? Or Abraham Lincoln? Mandela, Gandhi, and Dr. King all knew what it was like to be arrested. How did they keep their dignity? I'm not saying I'm like any of them, but I thought of them—to get perspective and find inspiration and to remind myself of something I learned from years of reading history—from years reading about the lives of brave men and women who down through the ages subordinated themselves and their happiness and comfort to a higher principle, a higher purpose, and to a larger cause. They faced untold hardship and the deprivation of their liberty. And many of them faced death itself. But they faced those things bravely—with strength, and resolve, and courage.

You can read about these things in books or see them played out in the movies. You can read about these people and be inspired and moved by their example. And I'm sure you like to think if you are ever faced with a crisis like that, that's how you would handle it too. But it is one thing to read about it in the comfort and safety of your favorite chair at home, or watch it on the big screen at the movies or on TV. It is quite another when you have to face it in real life. When it's not about someone else you're reading about in a book or watching in a movie. When it's you. When it's no longer abstract but real; when it's here and now, and you have to deal with it. It's a prize fight. The bell just rang, and it's round one. And it's you and him. Now let's see what you're made of. How are you going to face this moment of crisis and peril? How are you going to approach what Teddy Roosevelt might call your crowded hour? Is this an opportunity where, when the chips are down and the stakes are high, you stand tall, you hold your head high, and be like those heroes you so long admired and read about?

Here's your chance. What are you made of? Who do you want to be? What are you going to do?

The next several hours were spent being processed and waiting for my lawyer to arrive. The law firm where I had spent nearly two million dollars had to withdraw its representation of me because they had a conflict with another client, and because we believed we were going to be fine regardless of the ongoing federal probes of the past four years, I did not, at the time, have a legal team in place. Instead, I relied on an old and dear friend, Sheldon Sorosky, to monitor the situation. I've known Shelley longer than I've known my wife Patti. I first met Shelley nearly 23 years ago when I was a brand-new lawyer just starting out. He was then, and is now, a great criminal defense attorney. He's been doing it for more than thirty years. I had cases with him when I practiced law. But more important than that—far more important than that—he's a friend. And in a world where it's hard to find people you can trust, I trust Shelley. I know he is interested first and foremost in what's best for me and for my family.

The arraignment in federal court was scheduled for 1:30 p.m. at the Dirksen Federal Building in downtown Chicago. I was taken there sometime around noon. Prior to changing venue, I passed the time waiting with Shelley. He had a chance to review the charging document, albeit in a cursory manner. When we had a chance to talk privately for the first time, I pulled him aside and asked him what all this was about. He confirmed what the FBI agent in charge had said hours before on the drive down after leaving my home: the charges concerned the selection of a United States senator to replace President-elect Obama. I immediately told Shelley, "These charges are nonsense."

I spent most of that time by myself waiting for court to start in a holding cell. The cell was small, maybe 6' x 8'. Nothing was in it except for a metal stool that was bolted to the floor, right in the middle of the cell. Without a book to read, there was nothing to do but wait. I did some push-ups to pass the time.

I had a lot of time on my hands to think. I was thinking to myself, how did I end up here? Just the day before, I had a productive day that led to helping a lot of people. The kind of people I always fought for as governor. Working people. And I took on the big powerful Bank of America to help them.

Republic Windows is a company located in the North Side of Chicago. The company announced that they were going out of business and relocating their operations. The real-life consequences of that decision meant that a large number of workers would not only lose their jobs but also be deprived of their severance pay, which they are entitled to under their union contract and/or federal law. The purpose of my appearance at Republic Window the day before my arrest was twofold: first, to stand with and show support for the workers and their families, and, second and more significantly, to help. I was there to announce that I was ordering every agency under the control of the governor, which is most of state government, to stop doing business with the Bank of America until it agreed to provide a line of credit to the Republic Window Company that would provide the severance pay to the workers.

I showed up sometime around ten in the morning. The first order of business was to meet with the workers who had organized a sit-in and a boycott. They resolved not to leave the plant until their grievances were met. And they were not alone. They had some powerful allies. Over the weekend, the Reverend Jesse Jackson visited to show his support. United States Congressman Louis Gutierrez championed their cause—organizing, negotiating, and leading the effort to raise awareness of the plight of the dislocated workers.

After meeting with the workers, I went outside to talk to the media. I was accompanied by union leaders and some of the organizers of the boycott and sit-in. It was a cold day, and there was a lot of media present. After announcing the action I was taking, I had, what, in hindsight, was perhaps my first glimpse of what was coming my way.

I was asked a question about a published news report that my former congressional chief of staff, John Wyma, whom I considered a close friend of mine, had agreed to work with the FBI and wear a wire, presumably to set me up. After the story broke, his lawyer issued a statement saying that the report was untrue and that his client had not in fact worn a wire to set me up. I answered the question by saying something to the effect that if my telephone lines were, in fact, wiretapped—as I was soon to learn they were—and you heard the conversations, what you would hear was a governor who might use words in private that you wouldn't hear him use in public. But that you would also hear a governor talking endlessly about the people and working tirelessly on their behalf.

Little did I know that some of my telephone lines were, in fact, tapped. They had been for over a month. And the conversations I was having that presumably were private were instead being listened to by government agents.

When the whole story of the wiretap conversations is heard, in its proper context, the characterization I gave on that day will be shown to be essentially accurate: of a governor working to try to get things done for the people around cynical political gridlock, working through the frustrations of a process that, I feel, all too often puts personal politics above the interests of the people.

After the Republic Windows event, I spent most of the rest of the day working in my downtown Chicago office. Congressman Jesse Jackson Jr. had an appointment to meet with me in the late afternoon. After that meeting, I attended a small fundraiser held for me that evening at a downtown Chicago club. When that ended sometime between 8:30 and 9 p.m., I went home.

My day wasn't over. My deputy governor Bob Greenlee briefed me on the progress of negotiations that we were participating in on behalf of the workers of Republic Windows. These talks included United States Congressman Gutierrez and representatives from the union representing the workers. Bank of America was involved in the negotiations that were taking place throughout the day. I was told by my deputy governor that progress was made but a resolution had yet to be reached. But my deputy governor was confident that an agreement with a fair result for the workers was likely to be reached when the talks resumed the next day. I felt great about that. Here's a situation we learned about only a few days before–workers facing the loss of their jobs, their severance pay, and a situation where they couldn't support their families–but we were able to intervene in a real and meaningful way to bring leverage to the negotiations and hopefully produce a good outcome for workers and their families. It was my expectation that I would quite possibly join my deputy governor in those discussions the next day to do everything we could to earn the workers a good and fair result.

I also spoke later that night with the counsel to the governor, Bill Quinlan, to get updates from him. It was a full day; a good day. I was optimistic that a good result was likely to occur for the displaced workers at Republic Windows, and I was feeling good about the prospects of success on some other issues, including the matter I directed John Harris to work on when the day began. If we could pull that off, it could bring real and meaningful results to hundreds of thousands of people across Illinois.

I appeared before Federal Magistrate Nan Nolan at approximately 1:30 p.m. I had never seen her before. But I thought to myself, oh my God, what does this respected judge think of all of this? As she was conducting the court proceedings and speaking to the lawyers, I noticed on one or two occasions she glanced at me. As she was doing this, I felt her silently saying to me, "How could you get yourself in this position?" I had this powerful urge to jump up on the table and tell her I didn't do anything wrong–that this must be some kind of mistake.

As expected, the courtroom was packed with the media. These are the kinds of things they just love. Good news; forget about it. Real and meaningful results that you accomplished for people, that touched the lives of people, that helped them–okay, sure–we'll write about it. Let's see. There's room on page 27.

This was going to be a great day for them. This is what they live for. The misfortune of others is a mother lode of fortune for them. And in a mad dash to write about the bad news, they're so busy tripping over each other and trying not to get scooped by the competition that the search for the truth is a casualty. It's collateral damage. Newspapers need to be sold. Deadlines have to be met. There's no time to lose, not even time to catch your breath. Not even time to ask the right questions. Aren't they supposed to challenge the information; to be objective; to probe? Isn't that what a vigorous and free press is supposed to do? The fourth estate is supposed to check the unfettered power of the government. It's supposed to act to check the abuse of power, wherever it exists. And when they fail to do so, our democracy is undermined, and our freedoms are threatened.

In the frenzy surrounding my arrest no one in the media took a second to reflect on the presumption of innocence and the right to a fair trial. Nor did the media bother to ask whether the unprecedented arrest of a governor was necessary. And when the United States Attorney held a press conference where he said, "Abraham Lincoln would roll over in his grave," the media was virtually silent about the prosecutor's flagrant violation of his ethical responsibilities. The man bringing the accusation violated every canon of ethics that governs how prosecutors are required to behave, and the media said nothing.

Well, of course not. This was too good a story to let the truth get in its way. Nor was there even time to search for the truth. It's a rat race out there. It's a rush. It's a rush to beat the competition. It's a rush to sell newspapers. It's a rush to judgment! Screw the truth. Edward R. Murrow would roll over in his grave.

When the clerk called the case, I saw my co-defendant John Harris for the first time that day. He was dressed in a suit and looked like his usual professional self. There was discussion earlier on whether I should change into a suit or not. While I was being held, after Patti saw our daughters off to school, she frantically brought a suit and tie down to the lawyer's office so I could change into it before court. In the wake of being prevented from showering or shaving that morning, I chose to stay in the running clothes I was wearing when I left the house. I felt it was a more honest depiction of what was happening.

So there we were. John Harris and I. Co-defendants in the federal criminal court. Standing together before a judge hearing the case called against us: the United States versus John Harris and the United States versus Rod Blagojevich.

Here I was. The son of an immigrant father; the product of the American dream; a neighborhood guy made good. A guy who loved his country. A guy who served his country as a prosecutor and in public office. A guy with a strong sense of patriotism and love of country. Here I was, before a federal judge answering "Not guilty" to charges that I did things against the best interests of our country—a country I loved for the opportunities it gave me.

I didn't have a chance to talk to John before court. In fact, except for a brief exchange moments later, we hadn't talked since all this happened. It's not appropriate when facing criminal charges because you want to be sure to avoid even the appearance of obstructing justice.

After we entered our "not guilty" pleas before the judge, I had a second to talk to John. I teased him and said something like, "Let me ask you a question. Now, who would you rather work for? Mayor Daley or me?" John and I had previously talked about who was harder to work for. Without hesitation, John would laugh and say that it wasn't even a close question. It is well known that Mayor Daley has a reputation for being hard to work for, and John didn't do anything but confirm that perception. As for his response to me that day in court? He just laughed. But sadly, there was no joy in that laughter.

I left the courtroom not long after pleading "not guilty" but not before I approached one of the federal prosecutors to say hello. I met her one evening a little before my reelection campaign in 2006 after I was leaving a fundraiser at a downtown Chicago restaurant. I remembered her. I remembered introducing myself that night and asking her to vote for me. I didn't know then that she was a prosecutor. In court that day, I approached her, shook her hand, and reminded her that we had met. She remembered. I then went on to tell her that it was my hope that this was one case she was going to lose.

Among the many thoughts I had as the day unwound was what I was going to say when I addressed the media. I just assumed there was no way out of the federal building that day without having to deal with them. In the lockup, I visualized in my mind what it might be like. Hoards of reporters buzzing and hovering around me like a swarm of bees, shouting out stinging questions–all venom, no honey. Teams of cameraman holding their heavy cameras, fighting each other for position to get the shot, pushing and elbowing each other like power forwards under the basket, fighting to get the rebound.

As I was leaving the courtroom, I began to think about it again. I was told that after appearing in court I would be free to leave. So I figured the rendezvous with the media was right around the corner. I began thinking about what, if anything, I might say. In matters like these, lawyers advise you to say nothing. And that's what most people facing a situation like this generally do. But I'm a governor of the state. Twice elected and hired by the people. I work for them. They deserve an explanation. And I believed I owed them one. And even if we only had a brief glance at the charges and were not prepared to know what the nature and extent of the accusations were, I wanted to say something. To assert my innocence–I was dying to at least do that. To let the people know I didn't do anything wrong. The only issue as far as I was concerned was when. In view of the presence of the media throng that day, and my desire not to just push past them and not say a word, I thought it would be now. It turned out it wouldn't be for a number of days.

The FBI agents who arrested me that morning had made arrangements with my security detail for me to leave the federal building from the basement in the state police SUV I usually traveled in. This way I wouldn't have to directly face the media. I didn't ask for it. They just arranged it on their own.

Avoiding the media as we left the federal court building was not easy. As soon as we pulled out of the underground garage and turned left to leave, an army of cameramen and reporters appeared. When we had to stop for a red light, they began to surround the vehicle. I sat in the backseat and watched as it all happened. I couldn't wait for the light to turn to green. Just as it did, the executive security officer who was driving began to move forward. As he carefully worked to negotiate his way around the media that was blocking our way, a guy caught my eye. He was standing on the sidewalk, off to my left. He was a white male, probably in his early to mid-30s. What caught my attention was that he was holding both his middle fingers up, waving them at me as he shouted out what I couldn't hear but, by reading his lips, his body language, and the expression on his face, could only be a "f— you." Now I've heard that epithet directed at me before. I regret to say, not infrequently. This is another one of those things that goes along with the job. And I'm amused by it when it happens. But on that day, and under the circumstances that inspired it, I wasn't amused. I was filled with anguish. I felt these false charges against me made this man feel I had let him down. But I didn't let him down because the charges against me aren't true.

As soon as we found our way clear of the media, I picked up the cell phone to call Patti. I hadn't called her since kissing her goodbye early that morning. I was worried about her and our children. I feared there was a good chance the media might stake out our home. I was right. They were there; all over the place. In fact, what I encountered when I got home was something that we would have to live with, on and off but all too often on, for the better part of a month and a half. But it wasn't just us. So did our neighbors. And we felt terrible about that.

When I was first elected Governor in November 2002, Patti and I had a decision to make. It was a personal decision but one with political consequences. Do we move to

Springfield, our state capital, and live in the Governor's mansion? That's where most of my predecessors lived and that's where many people believe the governor should live. Or do we stay in our home in Chicago, in our neighborhood where we lived before I was elected?

If this decision and the considerations involved concerned only Patti and me, it would have been easy. We would have happily moved to Springfield. Why not? It's a 50,000 square foot home. I was raised in a five-room apartment. It comes with a staff of 25 people, including two chefs. I don't cook. It's a historic home–Abraham Lincoln slept there, so did Teddy Roosevelt, so did Arnold Schwarzenegger. I love history, and I love old Abe and Arnold. If it was just Patti and me, we would have moved there in a minute. But we had to consider our children. When I was elected, our daughter Amy was six, and Annie was due the following April.

As parents we have to think first and foremost about what's in the best interest of our children. I spent six years in Washington serving as a congressman. I remember taking note of the fact that at least three of my colleagues lost a child to suicide. I often wondered if some of that could have been a result of growing up the child of a politician. Moreover, both Patti and I have seen some of the ill effects that happen to the children of politicians, especially Patti. She was raised in a political family. Her father has been a prominent Chicago alderman for more than 30 years. She saw firsthand some of the things that negatively impact children. She was really sensitive about that and was determined to shield our children from as much of that as possible. Among the things we were both concerned with was doing the best we could to raise our children with the right kind of humility. Not as the governor's kids but just as kids. Like all the other kids. We didn't want our children growing up spoiled with a sense of privilege and entitlement. Growing up in a big governor's mansion, surrounded by staff, in a company town where the only business is government business, and you are the governor's kids. That's not a normal way for children to grow up. We wanted to keep their lives as normal as possible and keep them as humble as possible.

When I got home it was a madhouse. I had never seen my neighborhood look like it did. Media trucks, from every local affiliate to the national networks, from CNN to Fox, were all there. And it was only the beginning.

Told in advance by my security detail what the scene was like, I instructed the driver to forgo taking the street we live on and instead go in a back way, through the alley, so I could be dropped off at the back of the house. This would, with the coordination of the security detail, give me a little separation from the media and allow my family and me a chance to get in and out of our house without having to walk through a media gauntlet.

When I walked through the back door and into our family room, Patti was there waiting for me. She gave me a big hug and kiss. I said something like, "That was not exactly a typical day at the office. It sure is nice to be home." It was obvious she had been crying a lot. Her day was long and hard. After seeing me leave in the morning, getting the kids ready for school without telling them anything about what had just happened, and running around to get a suit and tie in case I needed it, her day only got more challenging. She had to pick up the girls from school because word of their father's arrest was starting to spread. Not wanting to alarm them, she took them out of school early. Patti wanted to be the one to break the news to our girls; to ease them into it in as gentle and loving a way as possible. To explain to them what it meant.

After Patti kissed me, our daughter Amy came up to me and said kind of nonchalantly, "Hi, Daddy." She kissed me as she usually does when I get home. I was both relieved and pleased that her greeting wasn't anything special or unusually emotional. It was just kind of matter-of-fact. Like it always is. Patti evidently did a great job explaining what happened and imparting to our daughters a sense that they shouldn't worry. What I was facing was a problem for Patti and me to deal with. We would handle it. And that both Amy and Annie should just go about being kids and focus on the things kids do.

My sister-in-law Deb was also at the house. She came over in the morning to be there for her sister. Deb has a great relationship with our children. They love their aunt Debbie, and it was reassuring to have her providing help and comfort to her sister, to her nieces, to all of us.

I saw Annie as I walked through the hallway to hang up my coat in the closet. She had been playing in the foyer, which in our home is around the corner from the hallway closet. She ran out and kissed me. She was very sweet about it. With the innocence of a child, she asked if I had been arrested. I told her yes and asked her, "Who told you?" She said, "Mommy." Before I could ask her what she was playing with, she handed me a card she made at school. Glued on the front were the letters DADDY. Underneath the letters were three baseballs, probably cut out from a magazine or a book. Also included on the front, between the baseballs, was written, presumably by Annie's teacher, *Happy Birthday!* Inside the card, also written by someone not five years old, were the words, "Dear Daddy, I hope you have a happy birthday. I love you!" The card was signed by Annie.

Now I know Annie's handwriting. It's very distinguishable to me. I guess you can say fathers know these things about their kids. It's not exactly hard to tell. After all, she's five, and so far there are not a lot of words in her arsenal that she could actually write. It was clear she signed her own name to the card and also drew a big star on the inside page.

It was a sweet moment. In a day filled with shock and the terror of all that had happened. My freedom snatched away, and my privacy violated. The world seemingly closing in and out to get me. Yet that little moment with Annie was, like the commercial says, priceless. And she remembered my birthday. I didn't. The day I was arrested was the day before my birthday.

As day turned to night, our home was plunged into darkness. With the eyes of the media, their cameras and reporters, all fixed on our house, a sort of bunker mentality settled into our home. How do you keep the world out there from getting in here? How do we protect our kids from this? How do we preserve their privacy and ours too?

The only thing we could do to keep those outside from looking in was to keep off as many lights in the house as possible and cover up as many windows as possible. And spend most if not all of our time at home in those rooms that are least accessible to the prying eyes of the media.

That first evening was spent hunkered down with Patti, our children, and Debbie. In an effort to create a mood that would insulate our kids from the circus outside and focus their attention on something positive and cheerful, Patti decided to change the schedule. Unlike most Tuesday nights, where Amy is required to do her homework, and both Amy and Annie have to be in bed by a certain time, we did something different. Why not turn a bad day into a fun night for the kids? So instead of homework and the usual routine, this was a night to decorate the Christmas tree in the foyer. Patti made an event of it. Kristin, Deb's partner, came over to help. Patti made hot chocolate and hot apple cider. Christmas music was played. Pizza was ordered for dinner. A festive atmosphere was created. The kids loved it. And while Patti, Amy, Annie, Deb, and Kristin decorated the tree, I hung back, in the family room, watching some old movie on the Turner cable network. I don't think I saw a second of it. I can't even remember what it was. But it was a chance for me to decompress. An opportunity, for the first time that day, to finally try and sort out what had happened.

Before I went to sleep that night, I made a couple phone calls. I spoke with my brother Rob who was now caught up in this. My brother lives in Nashville, Tennessee. He is a retired colonel in the United States army and in the real estate business. A Republican with no connection to Chicago or

Illinois politics except for me, he agreed, as a favor, to manage my fundraising operation only a few short months before. Because my big brother is honest and forthright, and because he is a man of integrity, and because he is clean-cut and straight-laced and not part of the political game in Illinois, and because I trust him, I persuaded him to manage my fundraising from July to December 2008.

I wanted to be extra careful that everything in the area of fundraising was done beyond reproach and without even the appearance of impropriety. My brother was reluctant at first to work on this issue. I had to persuade him. And I had to persuade his wife, my sister-in-law Julie, about why this would be a good thing for them. Patti and I now bemoan the fact that I persuaded my reluctant older brother to help out. I feel terrible I got them involved in my world. It's as if he came for a visit, leaving the safety and comfort of the affluent Nashville neighborhood he lives in (former Vice President Al Gore lives a few blocks away), and agreed to spend some time and be my guest.

The only problem is now he is in my neighborhood—the neighborhood of Illinois politics. The only problem is the neighborhood I live in is not a quiet and safe place. It is a dangerous place. It's like I told him to walk with me through a dark alley in my neighborhood one night, and we got mugged.

Before retiring to bed to get some much-needed sleep, there was one more phone call I had to make. My brother told me that Lon Monk had called and asked that I give him a call. He gave me a cell phone number where he could be reached. Lon Monk is my former law school roommate and one of my best friends. A former sports agent, he represented athletes like tennis star Ivan Lendl and Olympic skater Nancy Kerrigan. He was my campaign manager during my first run for governor in 2002. He then went on to become my Chief of Staff during my first term, only to leave to become the campaign manager for my reelection. After I was reelected, he rebuffed my offer to return to government and instead became a consultant and lobbyist. He was still a very close personal friend and was very active politically by helping me to raise campaign funds.

I called him that night. Lon has an even-tempered personality. He told me he was appalled that I was arrested. In a measured but determined way, he reassured me that this was the worst of it—and that as bad as everything seemed, this day would prove to be the low watermark. And that slowly but surely, as the truth comes out, things would only get better.

We both went on to talk about how unbelievable the whole situation was. He asked me whether I thought that the comments I made the day before at Republic Windows in front of the media, where I invited anyone to listen to my private conversations, was perceived by the federal authorities as daring them to do what they did that day. I don't know the answer to that question. I would hope not. I cannot imagine that making statements that you believe to be true and are, in fact, true would provoke federal law enforcement authorities to arrest you. This is, after all, still America. But considering what just happened to me, when Lon asked that question, I wasn't so sure about the answer.

Before falling asleep, I thought about my children, my wife, my mother, and my father. I shortened the prayer I usually say at night. I asked God to look after my family and to give us the strength we'll need to see us through the trials we now must face.

CHAPTER TWO

FOR MOST OF MY CHILDHOOD, I WAS RAISED IN A FIVE-ROOM APARTMENT IN A TOUGH, BLUE-COLLAR NEIGHBORHOOD ON THE NEAR NORTHWEST SIDE OF CHICAGO. It was a neighborhood filled with factories. Factories like the Ecko Utensils plant where my mother worked, the Good Humor ice cream plant, the Mary Ann Bakery factory, along with a lot of other smaller privately-owned manufacturing companies. It was in these factories where most of my schoolmates' fathers worked.

It was an ethnically diverse neighborhood in a large city, in a time of strict racial segregation. It was the 1960s; a time of change, of unrest, of tumult, and conflict. It was a time of great social, political, and demographic change. And the working-class neighborhood I grew up in was on the front lines of that change.

My mother and father were working people. They raised two sons; my older brother and me. At a time when most of the moms didn't work, mine did. She had to. From as early as I can remember, my mother was a working mom. Her jobs varied. They were always driven by, and subordinated to, the needs of her two boys. When we were babies, she was mostly at home but would, on occasion, work as a waitress to make a little extra money. As we got older, she began working full-time jobs, when both my brother and I were safely in school. She would supplement these full-time jobs with occasional part-time work.

I remember one job she had working on Saturday nights at a place called Grocerland, a small, independent supermarket owned by a Greek immigrant family. It was in our neighborhood and convenient to get to. The wages she earned were modest. They had to be. The profit margins in supermarkets are not very high to begin with. And the small, independent family-owned markets faced the added pressure of having to compete with the emerging corporate chains like the Jewels, and later, the Dominicks. But despite the modest wages, it was a friendly and happy place to work. Everyone knew everyone. And there were benefits too. If you worked there, you got a discount on the groceries you bought. So from my mother's point of view, working there part-time made a lot of sense. She could earn a little extra money to help her make ends meet, and she could save some money on the groceries she needed to feed her family.

Among the warmer memories I have as a child growing up were those Saturday nights when our father would take my brother and me with him to pick up my mother from work. We would get there early, a little before her shift was over. We would first visit her to say hello and let her know we were there. She worked at the delicatessen section within the store. I can still see her now—her cheerful smile when she would first see us.

She worked behind a glass counter that displayed all sorts of meats—hams and salamis, corned beef and ground beef, steaks and chickens. And if your eyes kept scanning to the left, you might see other things that made you hungry. Things like potato salad and coleslaw, macaroni salad and rice pudding. I especially remember the rice pudding. It had cinnamon sprinkled on top. Most Saturday nights, my mother would bring some home as a special treat for my brother and me.

But the best part of the night was the time we would spend with our dad. He would take us to the tavern that, like the delicatessen, was within the supermarket, adjacent to the grocery section. You could walk right through without having to open any door. It wasn't big. It had a bar in the middle and some tables and chairs off to the sides. A TV was perched above the bar for the patrons to watch. Those were the days of black-and-white television, and if it was a spring or summer night, invariably the channel was turned to either the Cubs game, if they were on the road, or the Sox game. The Sox played night games at home but the Cubs didn't. Back then, there were no lights at Wrigley Field.

The best part of it all was taking a seat at the bar with our father. My brother and I would climb up on the stools right next to our dad. We'd sit there with him, elbow to elbow with the other grown-up men. My dad would order a beer for himself and pour it into a small beer glass. He would order root beers for us, but we insisted on the small beer glasses too. I just loved it. For a brief and fleeting moment on those Saturday nights, I was able to pretend that I was like my father. I was a grown-up sitting at the bar with the other grown-ups. My father would sip his beer and talk to the bartender or the other men who were there while my brother and I would drink our root beer, watch the ball game, and occasionally ask our father to buy us a pack of peanuts and another root beer. He always would. He never said no. And because our dad was always working long hours during the weekdays and on Saturdays, and we hardly ever saw him, those Saturday nights were our time with him. They were brief moments; simple moments. But for me, they will always be special moments.

My father was an immigrant from Yugoslavia who came to America after World War II. His early life was spent in a small Serbian village. He was raised by his oldest brother, the patriarch of the family. His father died during World War I when he was either three or four. His mother died not long after. He had an older sister; she died when he was young too. In addition to his older brother, he had two other brothers. Both were older than him.

At the age of 12, he was sent off to military school to join one of his brothers—the brother he would name me after. From then on, for both boys, the village they came from was now a place they would only visit to see their family. For them, their lives were now in the military.

To understand my father you must first understand the world he grew up in. With little or no female influences in his early life, without a mother to raise him, and growing up as a teenager in a military school, my father grew up in a male-centric world. My father was a handsome man. Based on what I know of his early life in pre-war Yugoslavia, it seems he distinguished himself more for his exploits with women than he did for his exploits in battle. But to be fair, he wasn't given much of a chance to find glory in war. He was captured by the Nazis during the German invasion of Yugoslavia and would spend the next four years as a prisoner of war.

After the war, my father had a decision to make: return to Yugoslavia and restart his life there or join the millions of other refugees displaced by the war and scattered throughout Europe who didn't want to go back.

As far as my father was concerned, he didn't have a country to return to. As the Iron Curtain began to descend on Eastern Europe, the Communists, led by Marshal Tito, took over control of Yugoslavia. An ardent anti-Communist, my father spent the next three years of his life waiting in a refugee camp in Austria for the chance to come to America. Finally, in 1948, the United States Congress—a congress that his youngest son would one day join—passed a law called the Displaced Persons Act. That law gave him, and millions of others like him who came from places like Poland, Czechoslovakia, Romania, and Lithuania, a chance to move to America and start their lives over.

My father never looked back. He loved America. He saw it as the land of opportunity where you were free to say what you want, pray where you want, and be who you want. To the day he died, he believed America was the most special place on earth. A place where dreams came true. A place where, if you were willing to work hard, and sacrifice, and weren't afraid to try, you could be almost anything you wanted to be. And if you tried but failed, if you stood up and fell down, all you had to do was pick yourself up, dust yourself off, and try again. He really believed that. In fact, that was the story of his life in America. He worked long hours, dreamed big dreams, failed in small business, lost everything, picked himself up, tried again, worked long and hard again, lost again at small business, picked himself up again and, like most parents, always had big dreams for his children.

Maybe the best gift my father ever gave me was that belief in America. He believed it, he lived it, he never gave up on it. And he passed it on to his sons—a legacy far more valuable than inheriting any amount of money.

Not long after my father came to America, he met my mother. An organization named the Serbian Brothers Help, whose mission was to assist newly arrived immigrants get settled, helped him get started. Ethnic organizations like that were created to help immigrants from their native lands get situated in America. They found newly arrived immigrants a place to live, a place to work, and helped them integrate into the social life of their ethnic community—a social life that usually centered around the church.

My father's first stop was a boarding house in Waukegan, Illinois. The boarding house was owned by a Croatian woman named Magda. He lived there, sharing a room with his brother and another newly arrived Serbian immigrant. All three of them found jobs working at the nearby Goodyear Tire plant.

It didn't take long for my father to find a social life. Like most immigrants getting acquainted with a new place in unfamiliar surroundings, he gravitated to his community and found an outlet by being active at church. He was involved in a variety of social functions. And it happened that through those activities he was invited to a party hosted by a couple who were also members of the church. It was at that party that he met my mother.

My mother was American-born; lucky for me that she was. I like to joke that had my mother come from the old country as well, my first name would be as hard to pronounce as my last name—and I never would have been elected to anything in Illinois.

She was the daughter of Serbian immigrants who came to America in the first decade of the 20th century. She was the youngest daughter in a family of eleven children, nine of whom survived to adulthood. Her father was a big, strong man; a saloon keeper, who also moonlighted as a professional wrestler. Her mother died young, at the age of 36. She contracted tuberculosis and spent time in a tuberculosis sanitarium before she died. My mother's recollection of her own mother was slight. She described her as pretty and soft-spoken. And she remembered her wake. My mother was only six years old when her mother died. Back then, it was not uncommon to have a wake for a loved one in your home. Among my mother's few recollections of her mother was that as a small child, she played with other children as her mother rested peacefully in a coffin placed in the front parlor of their apartment.

My mother was a child of the Great Depression. Growing up during those hard times profoundly shaped her outlook on life. Because she lost her mother at an early age, she, her four older sisters, and her four younger brothers (two of the boys died before the age of five) were raised by her father and his brother. After her father died when she was in her early teens, it was her uncle who took over and raised his brother's children.

She grew up in a working-class neighborhood on Chicago's North Side. A large concentration of immigrants from Central and Eastern Europe settled there; Germans and Poles, Bohemians and Romanians and Serbs. They mingled with second and third-generation families of Irish, German, and Italian descent. They found jobs working in factories located along the North branch of the Chicago River. Factories like Gutman Tannery, Continental Can, Stewart Warner, and Finkl Steel. The Biograph Theater, and the alley next to it, where the famous Depression-era bank robber John Dillinger was shot and killed, is one mile to the east. In fact, my mother's oldest sister, my aunt Helen, was once at a party with the infamous "Lady in Red," who was Dillinger's date that night. She was an immigrant from Romania who had set him up.

A little farther south, about a mile and a half away, was 2122 N. Clark Street. That address is the site of the infamous St. Valentine's Day massacre. That's where Al Capone's gang dressed up as Chicago police officers and duped members of Bugs Moran's gang into compliantly agreeing to line up against the wall before they were summarily executed gangland style.

My mother never had a chance to finish high school. Like so many of her generation, she had to leave school early to work and help support her family. After the Japanese attacked Pearl Harbor, forcing America's entry into World War II, my mother was among the legions of young women who helped the war effort by manning the factories when the men were called away to fight.

She was like millions of other young women across America who were popularized by the famous Rosie the Riveter campaign—the women who produced the weapons and the parts that made America the arsenal of democracy that would eventually lead to the Allied victory in World War II.

My parents were married in October, 1950. My older brother was born five years later. Sixteen months after him, I was born. For the first three years of my life, we lived in a small apartment on the third floor of a multi-unit building. Almost all of my mother's family lived in the other apartments. The building was owned by my mother's uncle. It was located on a big and busy commercial street. My mother's brothers, my uncle Willie and my uncle Nicky, operated a storefront grill on the street level. Their grill was always open. They served breakfast, lunch, and dinner. I remember the grill as being a busy and noisy place filled with patrons who worked in the many factories that anchored the neighborhood.

I have great memories of living there. To help defray expenses, my parents took in a boarder. He was an elderly Serbian man who my brother and I called *Kum* which in Serbian means godfather. He was a very distinguished looking man with a shock of white hair. As toddlers, my brother and I would wake him up some mornings by playfully jumping up and down on him.

It was also a great place to live because most of our cousins lived there too. My brother and I are the two youngest in a family with more than twenty first cousins. We looked up to our cousins and played with the ones closest to us in age.

I never had a grandparent. My last living grandparent died during the Great Depression, before World War II. The nearest my brother and I had to a grandparent was my mother's Uncle Obren. He was the one who raised my mother and her siblings after his brother passed away. It was an extraordinary commitment. He was single and gave up a chance to marry and have a family of his own because he was now left with the responsibility to raise his brother's children. And he did. He was devoted to them; just as if they were his own. And without him, some of the younger children, including my mother, would have been sent to an orphanage.

I'll never forget his wake. I had just turned six. It was a cold night in early January. And it was the first time I can remember being falsely accused of something. Where I stood up for the truth and for what was right, and ended up getting an ass kicking for it. And I can't help but see parallels to what happened to me and my brother then and what's happening to the two of us now.

The wake for Uncle Obren was held at Muzyka's funeral home. A funeral home owned by a Ukrainian family in a neighborhood in Chicago known as the Ukrainian Village. Probably because there wasn't an established Serbian mortician on the north side of town, and because of similar cultures and religions, families from the Serbian community tended to wake their loved ones there.

The night of our great uncle's wake, my mother dressed my brother and me in our nicest "Sunday going-to-church clothes." Dark pants, a white shirt, and a clip-on tie. She took special care to make sure our hair was properly combed, even putting a little dab of Brylcreem on it—the greasy kid-stuff boys wore in the fifties and early sixties—to make sure it stayed in place. My mother was heartsick over Uncle Obren's passing. He was like a father to her, and she was going to make sure her boys showed him the proper respect.

Naturally our entire family was at the wake. All of our cousins were there. This was the first wake I remember ever going to. And I was both sad and kind of scared. I'd never seen someone who had died before.

Holding my mother's hand, we approached the casket. My great uncle was lying peacefully in an open coffin. My mother had prepared me earlier for what to expect. She explained that I would see my great uncle looking as if he were asleep. She reassured me that he had gone to heaven and was in a better place. And that going to his wake and seeing him in his coffin was our way of saying goodbye until the time we would all see him again one day in Heaven.

Wakes are a combination of mourning and socializing; a chance for family and friends to come together and see one another, to reminisce about the loved one who had just departed, a chance to get reacquainted. A lot of what happens at wakes occurs outside of the chapel and in the lounge. In most funeral homes I've ever been in, the lounge tends to be located in the basement. It was common back then, and not uncommon now, for refreshments to be served in the lounge. Not just coffee and cookies but spirits and whiskey too. That certainly is the case at Serbian wakes. And that was the case at my Uncle Obren's wake.

After viewing our uncle's body and saying the prayer my mother taught us to say, she released us to go and play with some of our cousins. We found our cousin Russell and went with him down to the lounge because he told us there was soda pop and cookies down there. There were a lot of grown-ups there and many of our older teenage cousins. Somehow somebody got the idea—I believe it was my cousin Patsy's husband Bill—that it might be funny to see if they could get my brother to drink a shot of whiskey. My brother was only seven years old. I remember several of my cousins and some of the older kids daring my brother, egging him on. Saying things like, "I bet you're not man enough to take a drink" or "You're probably too scared and chicken and cowardly to do it." Well, my brother may have been only seven, but he wasn't about to look like he was afraid. And besides, when you're that age and have older cousins, it's a natural thing to want to please and impress them. So he took the bait and decided to take a drink.

I remember seeing that shot glass of whiskey. It was full to the brim and overflowing; probably VO or Canadian Club, since that's what working class white ethnics drank back then. I can still see my brother now, taking that shot of whiskey and in one big gulp drinking the whole thing, kind of like Clint Eastwood at the bar in one of those old spaghetti westerns. As soon as my brother took the drink, it triggered a roar of laughter, approval, and disbelief from both his tormentors and enablers. I can't even begin to imagine what effect that shot had on him. But whatever the effect, he didn't have long to experience it. Maybe it numbed him a little for what was about to happen.

After watching my brother take that shot of whiskey, my nine-year-old cousin Gary decided to run upstairs to the chapel, find my father, and tell him what my brother had just done. My father followed him down to the lounge. By the time my father arrived, those same instigators who encouraged my brother to drink that shot of whiskey now betrayed him. They suddenly sold him out. Instead of acknowledging to my father that they dared him to do it, they instead took the position that my brother was acting on his own, showing off, and that they were shocked that a little kid like him would try to impress them by pouring a shot of whiskey and drinking it on his own.

Now my father was a loving man. He was easy-going. He was indulgent and a soft touch. At home he rarely, if ever, disciplined us. That was my mother's department. But on those rare occasions when my father would learn that one of his boys may have done something wrong, and if the transgression happened in public where people saw it, God help us. Somehow, in his mind, his manhood and his reputation as a father whose boys were honest, polite, obedient, and well behaved was being challenged. He couldn't have any of that. No sir. When it came to being a father, he wanted people to know he was no wimp. So in a stern and angry tone, he asked my brother whether it was true. Did he drink a shot of whiskey or not?

My brother and I never, ever, ever lied to our parents. They raised us that way. To lie to them would be an act of betrayal. It was tantamount to us not loving them. And no matter how bad the truth might be, we never did. When confronted by them, we always told the truth. Besides, even if my brother was tempted to lie, there simply was no way out. Too many witnesses were there who saw him do it. So better to just quickly answer truthfully and hope for the best. And that's exactly what my brother did. He stoically told my father that, yes, he had in fact taken a shot of whiskey. But before he could explain, my father decided to act. It apparently never dawned on my father to ask a seven-year-old why on earth he would drink a shot of whiskey. It seems that under the circumstances, a follow-up question like that would have been a reasonable and prudent thing to do. But he didn't and instead immediately took off his belt, the instrument he used to spank us. In fact, he even gave that belt a name: *Svete Ilija*, which in Serbian means Saint Eli.

The belt came off, and the spanking started. And as all of this was happening, I was frantically and feverishly trying to help my big brother and explain to my father that my brother didn't do anything wrong. That he drank the whiskey because he was told to do it by the grown-ups. That he didn't do it on his own. That it wasn't his fault. Unfortunately, my plea fell on deaf ears. As he was hitting my brother, my father then turned on me, saying something like, "Do you want some too?" And before I was given the chance to answer "no," he started spanking me too. To this day I still have no idea why I got a spanking. What did I do? I didn't drink the whiskey. I didn't tell my brother to drink the whiskey. I was just trying to explain to my dad that my brother didn't do anything wrong. But whatever the reason, I now joined my brother in getting my ass kicked.

My father had his own way of spanking. He'd grab us by one of our hands with his left hand, while he would wield the belt with his right. It was always his intention to hit us below the waist, targeting the back of the legs and our backsides as the places to strike. That's where most of the blows generally landed. But sometimes he would miss the mark. Inevitably, when you're swinging the belt at someone's butt, and the recipient on the other end is doing whatever he can to elude getting hit, there's going to be some collateral damage. You might take a hit on your back, your shoulder, or even higher up on the back of your head. This spanking was no exception.

And while the spanking stung, what really hurt was the embarrassment. We had to suffer the further indignity of it happening in front of a lot of people. Some of the people there were the ones responsible for the episode. They were the ones who instigated the whole thing. And they were laughing at us.

When my mother learned about what transpired, she immediately came to our aid. Ironically, my mother was the disciplinarian. But she would never have spanked us like that in public. Where my father would almost always say yes to us, she would say no. She set the rules and strictly enforced them. She was the parent who spent the time teaching us right from wrong. And she would explain the reasons why. My father was too busy working to do that, nor did he have it in him to do it that way. He just wasn't the type of guy who had any idea why you have to explain anything to a kid about whether he should behave or not behave. No one ever explained anything to him when he was growing up. You either behaved, or you were punished. From my dad's point of view, you just did what you were told to do and that was the end of it. There was nothing more to discuss.

When it came to raising small children, my mother just had a much better feel for it than my dad. She understood children better. Again, a lot of it had to do with differences between moms and dads, as well as their own background and life experience. But my mother was clearly much better at it than he was. First, she knew us better since she was the one who dealt with us on a day-to-day basis. Second, she had a lot more common sense when it came to kids and how they think and how they feel than my dad did. Again, it's not something unusual. I know in our home Patti has a much better understanding of our children than I do.

After my brother and I found sanctuary in the company of our mother, we spent the rest of the evening sitting by her in the chapel. We were emotionally drained. I sat there sobbing. I couldn't stop. When you go through something like that, and you're only six years old, it takes its toll on you. After all, we were raised to listen to our elders. Notwithstanding all of what had just happened and how, in your mind, you believed you didn't do anything wrong, for your father to be as angry at you as he was, and to spank you like he just did—surely, you must have done something wrong. And the worst of it was that you felt guilty that you let your father down. And you're thinking now maybe your father, who you love so much, might not love you anymore. That was the worst part of it all.

And that fear was reinforced by another adult. He was a relative who married into the family. His name escapes me, but I'll never forget him. I remember the scene as if it were yesterday. I can see him sitting there that night at the wake. He sat in the row directly in front of us. He had a swarthy complexion and wore a mustache. And what I remember about him was that up to that night, he was always nice to us. He would tease us and liked to joke around.

While I sat sobbing in the chapel next to my brother as my mother was trying to comfort us, this relative began to start in on us. He called us bums and kept saying things like "throw the bums in the alley." He was obviously joking. But we were just small children and that's not how we took it. We felt so bad; we took what he said literally and worse, as further evidence that we were no good; that we were, in fact, bums. He didn't mean to, but this relative only reinforced the sense of shame and guilt I was already feeling. It's funny how I never forgot that or how, at the same time, I never forgot how kind our uncle Nicky and aunt Millie were to us during that dark hour. What a relief it was that Uncle Nicky and Aunt Millie said that if nobody wanted us, they would be happy to take us home to live with them.

Sometime when I was three or four, we moved. My mother believed that a busy commercial street with a lot of car and heavy-truck traffic was not the right place to raise young children. So we moved to a residential street and into a second-floor apartment owned by her cousin, my aunt Daisy. At that time, Aunt Daisy was a single mother raising her daughter, Angela. After we moved in, Angela, who was two months older than me, became my constant companion. The two-flat was on a tree-lined street and had a small backyard. There were a lot of other kids who lived on the block so we had plenty of kids to play with. We lived there until I was in the second grade. And we were devastated when we were told that we were moving. Those were happy times, and I have nothing but the best memories of the three years we lived there.

And those memories include starting school. I am a product of the Chicago public school system. So was my brother. I was enrolled in kindergarten at the Henry Lloyd elementary school. My brother went to school there too. He was two grades ahead of me. Back then, if you were in kindergarten, you went to school for a half day. My mother was working full-time, so for part of the day my aunt Daisy would babysit me until my brother and Angela came home from school to join me.

We walked to school every day. The school was nearly a mile away. I would walk to school with a group of kids that included my brother and my cousin and was led by one of the older girls who lived in our neighborhood. She was in the fifth grade.

One day, I had to walk to school by myself. This was a big deal for me. My brother did it all the time. But he was older. Walking to a school nearly a mile away in a large bustling city for the first time was not an insignificant challenge for a five-year-old. From my point of view, asking me to walk the distance of a mile was like asking my father to walk the length of the city. Plus, there was some danger involved. The route to school required crossing a major intersection—not one, but two busy streets. Now I had walked this route a lot, taking it to school every day, but never alone. I felt I was up to it and couldn't wait to prove myself and make my mother proud. I couldn't wait for the chance to take my first step toward self-reliance and being more like my big brother.

My mother spent what seemed like hours preparing me for my maiden voyage. It was like I was Columbus crossing the Atlantic on the Santa Maria but without the Niña and the Pinta. Over and over again, she reminded me to look to the crossing guard before crossing the busy streets and where there wasn't one, at the small streets, to be sure to stop and look both ways before crossing. She admonished me to not talk to strangers; to go straight to school. And to stay as close as possible to any other kids I might find along the way. And she reminded me that the policeman was my friend.

My big day arrived, and I proved up to the challenge. With a few butterflies in my stomach, I left for school—a five-year-old on a mission. I was determined; I was focused. And as it turned out, I made it to school safely and on time.

Three decades later I took another walk.

I began my political journey, making my way through the mean streets of Chicago politics. It too would be a dangerous road and, in the end, I would once again be traveling all on my own.

CHAPTER THREE

I COME OUT OF CHICAGO POLITICS; OUT OF THE REMNANTS OF THE OLD CHICAGO DEMOCRATIC POLITICAL MACHINE. That machine was first built in the late 1920s and the early 1930s by the George Washington of the Democratic machine, Mayor Anton Cermak. He was the Chicago mayor killed in Miami, Florida, by an assassin who intended to assassinate President Franklin Roosevelt. Tony Cermak was of Bohemian descent, and he built a political coalition in Chicago that brought together the different white, ethnic working-class communities across the city and melded them into a formidable and oftentimes invincible political machine. That political machine was held together by a patronage system that rewarded political work like canvassing neighborhoods for votes with government jobs. It was organized not unlike the Catholic Church, where the archdiocese is the center or the hub, and different neighborhood parish churches are the spokes. In this political model, the office of the Mayor and City Hall would be like the archdiocese. The mayor would be like the Cardinal. The various ward organizations throughout the city would be like the parish churches. And the Democratic ward committeeman, who was also often the alderman, would be like the parish priest. The precinct workers, the ones assigned to canvass the voters and get them out to vote, are like the active members of the church. The largess and spoils of victory come from the mayor's office at City Hall and are doled out to the various ward organizations based upon how well they performed in the last election.

This political machine grew and was modified with the passing of time. Legendary Chicago mayor Richard J. Daley presided over its golden years with its peak being the 1960 presidential election where Mayor Daley made sure John F. Kennedy eked out a victory over Richard Nixon. With the advent of television and its commercials, the power of the precinct captains diminished in high-profile races like those for president, governor, and senator. But to this day, in lower-profile races for Congress or the state legislature, those political organizations still very much dominate the political landscape.

And those political organizations are very much like old feudal organizations from medieval Europe. In Chicago, over the years and over the generations, they've grown into patrimonies or baronies to be passed down from father to son, or father to daughter. The House of York and the House of Lancaster in old England have their equivalents in Chicago with the house of Daley, the 11th ward; the house of Madigan, the 13th ward; or the house of Stroeger, which is the 8th ward. Those organizations survive and thrive on the old patronage system. The local ward boss, the Democratic committeeman or alderman, builds a political organization based on the vote it gets out and the number of jobs it can get for its members. It's a very transactional kind of politics. If the precinct captain does a good job getting a good vote out of his or her precinct, the ward boss makes sure that he or she is given a good job in government with the chance for upward mobility. It's a system that invites people into the political process not around issues, political philosophy, or causes, but instead gets people involved in politics because that's how they can get a job, earn a living and if they are good loyal soldiers, can move up the ranks in Chicago and Cook County government and to a lesser extent, in Illinois state government. And it's no accident that the most powerful democratic political organizations are the ones that have the largest number of government jobs.

And it's not unusual for those local Democratic political organizations to clash. They might have turf wars over who is the more powerful in a certain part of town. One political organization might have a candidate for the state legislature that's running against a candidate of another political organization. No political organization worth its salt doesn't at least have a state representative who might be able to leverage state government on behalf of the organization he or she comes from. And if you're a ward boss, and you don't have a state representative or a state senator, then the perception in the political world is that yours is an organization that doesn't have a lot of clout. If you're someone who wants to get involved in politics knocking on doors with the hope of one day getting a government job, then maybe you should join another political organization that might be in a better position to help you. It was in this kind of dynamic that I unexpectedly got my first opportunity to run for office.

It was a Sunday afternoon in early January of 1992. I was in the shower having just finished running in the cold. My wife Patti got a phone call from her father, Richard Mell who was a prominent and powerful Chicago Democratic ward boss. He asked if we were free to come over to his house that night.

When we got there, Patti and I found him on his knees on the floor of his living room intently looking over some political maps. Without looking up, he said, "Ronan left me last night, and I'm looking for a candidate to run for state representative here," as he pointed to one of the maps. Al Ronan was a longtime political ally of my father-in-law. He was a state representative and kind of like the junior partner of the 33rd ward Democratic political organization. The night before, Ronan had apparently moved his furniture out of the ward office in the middle of the night and made a political deal with some of the other ward bosses in the area to run as their state representative. In the world of Chicago politics, if you're going to be a powerful Democratic ward committeeman, you can't let your state representative emasculate you like that or else you'll appear weak and vulnerable. Caught off guard by the betrayal, my father-in-law was scrambling around for candidates who he could run for the state legislature. From his point of view, I was a natural.

While not a blood relative, I was his son-in-law and therefore a member of his family. I was a lawyer. I had been a prosecutor. And I had been active in his ward organization, helping him get reelected by working a precinct and proving to be good at it. He also knew that I read a lot of history books and that if given a chance to run for office, I would probably be eager to do it. The downsides were: I was completely unknown, had a long and hard-to-pronounce last name that conventional wisdom said would be a problem, and I didn't live in the district he wanted me to run in.

But when he asked me if I was interested in running, I didn't hesitate. My only question to him concerned my freedom to take whatever positions I wanted on the issues. I'll never forget his answer. It was short and to the point and says as much about the mind-set of Chicago ward bosses as it did about him. He answered, "I don't give a fuck about that."

He had been alderman of his ward and ward committeeman for nearly twenty years. He had one of the most effective political organizations on the north side of Chicago that grew and was sustained by his ability to get his members jobs in city and county government. His organization was also successful because he had, as his junior partner, a state representative who for a dozen years was able to leverage his position as a lawmaker to get state jobs for Democratic precinct captains from Republican administrations.

That first race for state representative was, for Patti and me, the happiest time we had in politics. We were young and innocent, we were still relatively newlyweds, and we were brimming with enthusiasm and idealism. And we were a family, all working together for a common purpose. The differences I would begin to have with my father-in-law had yet to surface. Running for state representative was good for both of us. It was my chance to get into politics to run for elective office. And it was his chance to show the other ward bosses on the north side who was boss. And he had his work cut out for him.

His ward only made up about 27% of the legislative district. Every other political organization in that district was in one way or another supporting the incumbent.

By any objective analysis at that time, I should have had no chance to win. I was running against a twelve-year incumbent who came out of Congressman Dan Rostenkowski's 32nd Ward Democratic organization. At that time, they were considered the preeminent Democratic political organization on the north side. It also meant that my opponent had the support of Mayor Richard M. Daley and was the beneficiary of all the resources the mayor's political organization could provide. It was a long shot. We had no money. I didn't even have a campaign fund. We hadn't planned for this race. The only planning had been for a possible race by my father-in-law for Congress in the newly created fourth Congressional District. Everyone was against us, and even my father-in-law predicted I was probably going to lose.

But that's what made it so much fun. We were bucking the odds, and the worst thing that could happen was we'd lose an election. This was my chance to run for public office. And if I failed, then chances were I probably would not be in a position to run for office again. I could put to rest any thoughts or dreams I might have had from years of reading history books to think that I might have a chance to make something of myself politically. And then I could focus all my efforts on becoming the best lawyer I could be and building a law practice and a good quiet life for Patti and me.

But first there was a race to run. I had $25,000 to my name, and I committed all of it to that race. I was, as they say in poker, "all in." My in-laws matched that amount with a loan which Patti and I repaid after the election.

And then there was the first precinct captain meeting where my father-in-law explained to those who remained loyal to him in his 33rd Ward Democratic organization what happened and why it was so important that they all stay together. This was an important first meeting. Maybe half of the organization left and followed Al Ronan; the other half stayed with him. While personal loyalty still counted for something, for most of these precinct workers this was all about bread-and-butter concerns—their jobs and their futures. It was important to pick the winner, and it was important to make sure the meeting was full and that whatever the exodus of the Ronan loyalists might be, Mell still had a big political army left that ultimately could lead to victory. It was important for any wavering precinct captains, who weren't quite sure whose side they were going to be on, to see that we had a lot of support and a lot of volunteers, and we were going to win. To that end, I invited everybody I knew to be at that first meeting. I called all my friends and told them what I was doing and asked them to volunteer and help me out in the campaign. And I invited a lot of my clients who generally would see me during office hours on Saturday mornings. Some of them were Yugoslavian gypsies whom I represented in the criminal courts. They knew nothing about nor cared about local politics. But I thought it might help fill the room if they met me at the precinct captain meeting where I could talk to them about their cases afterwards.

Alderman Mell generally held precinct captain meetings on Saturday mornings at 9:30 a.m. at a VFW hall in his ward. That's where this first meeting occurred. It was also the meeting where he would explain to his loyal precinct workers why he chose me as the candidate to run. Now I've gone to these meetings several times before. I was active in the ward organization and had worked a precinct myself. But this was the first time I would attend one of those meetings as a candidate. And I think it's the first time I was ever asked to speak.

I have vivid recollections of the day I spoke to the precinct captains for the first time. I can't tell you that I remember much of what I said. In many ways, I was kind of like the new kid on the block. There were members in the organization that had been there for a long time who felt that it was their turn and that they should have a chance to run. Naturally there was some dissent and grumbling about my being chosen. On the other hand, this was Chicago politics, and it was not unusual for the ward boss to anoint his son or daughter or a member of his family to be the candidate to support in an election. But whatever the different feelings were among the different precinct captains and volunteers that day, they were ultimately loyal to my father-in-law. They put aside their own personal interests and worked hard for me in the election.

While I don't remember the speech I gave, I do remember what I said as I closed. I quoted from Shakespeare's *Henry V*, where King Henry was speaking before his troops on the eve of the historic Battle of Agincourt. Like us, the English were outnumbered and outmatched by the French. The smart money was on them to lose. But they had a cause to rally around, and their leader appealed to their sense of glory. So like those heroes of old England, I told them what Henry V told his troops before leading them into battle and beating the odds. I said, "We few, we happy few, we band of brothers. For he today who sheds his blood with me shall be my brother and gentlemen in England now abed shall think themselves accursed they were not here, and hold their manhood cheap while others speak that fought with us on St.Crispin's Day."

There was a pause. These were mostly seasoned Chicago precinct captains I was speaking to. They had heard a lot of speeches over the years from a lot of candidates who sought their support, but I'm not quite sure they ever heard a candidate reciting Shakespeare before. And when I went on to say, "Al Ronan never did that for you before," they responded with laughter and cheers. That was the moment that began a relationship where those hard-working precinct captains and volunteers would work hard and support me in that first campaign, as well as every other campaign I ran.

I proved to be good at campaigning. And I brought about a different kind of campaigning that really wasn't practiced much in Chicago before. It was the common practice of candidates for the Legislature who came out of and had the support of traditional Chicago Democratic political organizations to lay back and allow the precinct captains to do the talking and the walking. The precinct captain was close to his voters. If he was good at it, he would help his constituents with all sorts of services and any other help he might be able to provide. So, for example, if your teenage son got into a fight and was in trouble with the law, the precinct captain might bring the parents to see the alderman, generally on Monday nights because that's when he would hold court, and the ward committeeman and alderman would help find the family a lawyer who could represent their son in court. And in the case of my father-in-law's organization, that lawyer who was called upon to help oftentimes was me.

It is awfully hard for a candidate to win in a precinct against a precinct captain, who season after season and year in and year out, is there to help his constituents. And when a precinct captain is asking you to vote for a candidate for state representative, for an office most people don't know or care much about, most voters trust their precinct captain and will vote according to his recommendations.

A case in point: I called my late mother once before an election to ask her to vote for a friend of mine who I knew as a lawyer running to become a judge. I was a United States congressman at the time, and I called my mother from Washington. I asked her to get a pen and a piece of paper and write down the name of my friend so she would be sure to vote for him when she went to the polls on Election Day. But before she committed to following my advice, she asked me who Dennis was for. Dennis Sharkey was her precinct captain. He's been one of my father-in-law's best captains over the years. When I told my mother I didn't know who he was for, but I needed her to vote for my friend, she told me she was sorry that she couldn't do it. She was going to vote for the candidate Dennis told her to vote for.

And that was the biggest challenge of my first campaign. With all of the major Democratic organizations and their precinct captains backing the other guy, and with their territory comprising between 70 to 75% of the voters of the legislative district, the key to victory was being able to go into those hostile wards and precincts and get as many votes as possible while depending upon my father-in-law and his precinct captains to carry me big in his ward.

So I spent virtually all of my time campaigning in so-called enemy territory. Morning noon and night, from 6:30 in the morning till 9 or 9:30 at night, fourteen to fifteen hours a day every weekday, eight to ten hours a day on Saturdays and maybe six to eight hour days on Sundays, I went to bus stops and train stations, supermarkets, and restaurants. I went everywhere and anywhere where I could shake someone's hand and introduce myself. And I knocked on doors. I mostly knocked on doors. Because that's where the registered voters were. Accompanied by a volunteer marking a voter canvass sheet, we would ring doorbells and knock on doors, and I would introduce myself and explain who I was and what I was running for. I would usually start by first asking the voter if they knew who his or her state representative was. I can honestly say that I can't recall a single person that did. Then I would explain a little bit about who I was and why I was running for state representative. If I was in a precinct that had an effective precinct captain working against me, sometimes I would confront that issue head on. It's interesting and so typical of Chicago politics. Rarely would I be compelled to confront the voters by speaking about specific issues like the high cost of their electricity or healthcare or the quality of public education. More often, when knocking on doors in a ward whose organization was working against me, I would directly raise the issue of the precinct captain who those voters knew and liked and trusted. And I would say, for example,

"Now I know George is a good precinct captain and does a lot of things for you. But this is an important election and having a legislator in state government who is going to look after your interests is very important. So if you could, I'm only asking you to vote against George on just this one race. By all means feel free to vote for his recommendations on all the other races. But in this one, I'm asking you to make an exception and give me a chance to be your state representative. Give me a chance so I can fight for you."

With rare exception, the people were overwhelmingly nice and friendly, and after two months of doing this, and with the help of my father-in-law, his precinct captains, and a growing number of volunteers as well as the gentrifying of neighborhoods that brought in more young professional, independent voters, it all paid off on primary night when I beat my opponent by getting 61% of the vote.

I have the greatest memories of that first election. How great it was to work with my father-in-law and together be part of an effort where seemingly the whole world was against us—our family and his political organization against the whole political establishment—and to win. To win big. And to varying degrees, our whole family helped to make it happen. My mother-in-law ran the phone banks and did our polling. She didn't like politics, hardly if ever participated in politics, knew nothing about polling, and yet, like everything she did, she proved to be successful at it. And then there was Patti. She worked as hard as I did. She took a precinct in a gentrifying neighborhood and tirelessly knocked on doors on behalf of her husband. When precinct workers from Mayor Daley's organization were assigned to work that precinct for my opponent, she soldiered on and helped me win better than 73% of the vote in that precinct, proving, among other things, that love is the most powerful of motivations. In fact, she had the third best-performing precinct for me in the whole legislative district, beating every one of my father-in-law's precinct captains except for his two best, who had the benefit of working their own home precincts where most all of their voters had known them for years.

Primary night is one of the best memories I have. For two intense months, I immersed myself entirely in that campaign. It was hard work, but it was fun and thrilling, and while I met so many people and the response felt so good, I was new at this and wasn't sure what to expect on election night. In fact, at three o'clock that afternoon, after I had spent the previous nine hours standing in front of polling places to shake hands with voters, I spoke to my father-in-law for the first time that day. He asked me how I felt things were going, and I told him "good." When I asked him the same question, he burst my bubble. He told me turnout in the opposition wards was at record levels, and if they were voting with the precinct captains, then this was going to be a long day and, "Pal, you're going to get your ass kicked." Disheartened but undaunted, I suggested that maybe the increase in turnout was the so-called yuppie voters—the young professionals who moved into the gentrifying neighborhoods—who were independent of the precinct captains and many of them were women who were going out to vote for Carol Moseley Braun, who was on the verge of making history that day. I told him I believed those were going to be my votes and that having spent the last two months out among the voters, that this was going to be a change election, one of those where the influence of the traditional precinct captains was not going to be as significant as it had been in previous elections.

My instinct was right. As soon as the first precinct reported that night, I walked into my father-in-law's ward office, and he and his staff were already celebrating. He knew that with me breaking even in one of Dan Rostenkowski's ward's strongest precincts meant that I was on my way to victory. While I trusted his judgment, I needed to see some more of the vote come in before I started celebrating. And they were. The phones were ringing off the hook as precinct workers were calling the office reporting their results. We were doing well everywhere. As expected, we won big in my father-in-law's home ward and unexpectedly won big in every other ward except my opponent's home base, where the two of us essentially broke even.

Much to my surprise, amazement, and deep sense of appreciation for the people who placed their trust in me, I won my first election in a landslide. And as soon as I could, I called my mother with the news. I told her I had won, and she was naturally delighted. She told me how much she wished my father was still alive and how proud he would have been to see his youngest son win an election in America. She then went on to give me some advice. I love this story because it says so much about how my mother, a senior citizen and a lifelong resident of the city of Chicago, saw Chicago politics. In fact, when I ran for governor I loved to tell this story to voters all across Illinois. And considering the challenges I'm facing now, the story has an ironic twist.

Her advice to me was, "Son, now that you're going to be a state rep, whatever you do, always be for the people. Always, son, be for the people. Be on their side. Don't forget where you came from. And be honest, son. Whatever you do, promise me you'll always be honest. And, son, don't take any bribes." When I reassured her that I would be for the people and wouldn't forget where I came from, I then promised her that, of course, I wouldn't take any bribes—I wouldn't do anything illegal or do anything to shame her or shame the memory of my father. With that done, she then asked me one more thing: do you think you can get Aunt Daisy's son-in-law a job?

Well, I never broke my promise to my mother, though I regret to say, I wasn't able to get my aunt Daisy's son-in-law a job.

Looking back, it's easier to see patterns of behavior emerging that when they're happening, appear merely as isolated acts in the unfolding of events between people. The first signs that my father-in-law and I would have problems began to manifest themselves immediately after that primary election and shortly after I was sworn in as a state representative. The issue concerned my budget as a state representative and my staff. State representatives are given small operating budgets to run their offices and do their jobs. This is by design. It's done for a reason. It keeps the elected state legislator dependent on their legislative leader, the House Speaker, for their resources, their staff, and their information. Now being a new state representative who can share office space with the alderman and committeeman who was my father-in-law was a big advantage for me. It was also good for constituents. One-stop shopping. If you needed a city service, you saw the alderman. If the issue concerned the matter dealing with state government, you could see the state representative. That arrangement was good for everybody.

About a month or so into my job as state representative, I discovered that two of my father-in-law's staffers, who I thought were just volunteering and helping out, had in fact been paying themselves bonuses out of my budget. To this day, I don't like dealing with the details on the operations side of government. As governor, I left those matters in the hands of my chiefs of staff. As a state representative, I left those in the hands of the person who was staffing my state rep office. In the beginning, that happened to be one of my father-in-law's assistants. While I focused my attention on the handful of bills I was sponsoring, or spent my time out in the community among my constituents, I left matters like paying the bills and handling the budget to that assistant. Had I been asked, I would've been more than happy to pay her or anyone else who was doing work for me and for my constituents. But it was wrong and deceptive to take money out of my budget, not by asking me, but by going to my father-in-law and asking him. And what bothered me even more was that it was all done purposefully behind my back. At the time, this was not a big issue. It was more like a minor irritant that would soon be forgotten. But for the first time, I got a glimpse of how my father-in-law would try to control some things in my public office and do so in a less than forthright way. By itself, this episode was insignificant and unimportant. But it would prove to be an omen for more serious issues that would develop between us over the years.

I spent two terms as a state representative in the Illinois House. Like a lot of new experiences, at first I thought it was great. A month into the job, I made the front page of a major Chicago newspaper because I had filed a bill that sought to increase the fee gun owners pay for their firearms owner identification card. The response to my bill prompted a firestorm of protest. Mail from gun owners across Illinois poured into my office. A radio talk-show host in Springfield, Illinois, railed against the bill and called me "Representative Blowhard Bitch." I hadn't been a state rep for a month, and already I was caught up in a controversy. I valiantly defended my bill and argued that the sacrifice I was asking of law-abiding gun owners was for the purpose of funding the police and hospital trauma centers. The irony is, it wasn't even my idea. The bill was brought to me by one of the House Speaker's staffers. In any event, my bill went down in flames. I'm glad it did. It was a stupid idea. And looking back I learned a valuable lesson. That bill was likely initiated by a lobbying group that purported to be fighting against handgun violence and for reasonable gun control laws. But rather than push reasonable and sensible legislation banning assault rifles and making it tougher for gangbangers to get guns, they used their bill and they used me as a way to polarize the debate by pushing a bill that went after law-abiding citizens who lawfully owned guns instead of going after criminals and the kinds of guns they use.

It didn't take me long to see how the game was played in Springfield. In the Illinois House, the Democratic members were like pawns in a chess game. Mike Madigan was the House Speaker back then. Like now, he had the power to call or not call any bill for consideration. It didn't matter how meritorious the bill might be; if he didn't want it, he had the power to simply not call it. And nobody challenged him. Most of the members abdicated their authority to him. He raised all their money, he ran their campaigns, he appointed the committees, he gave them more money by giving them committee chairmanship, and in exchange for that they supported him for speaker, and they asked few if any questions. They just took orders. And so there wasn't a lot of real work to do if you were a House member. And that explains why so many of them spend all their time during the legislative session being wined and dined by lobbyists, partying, and carousing, fraternizing with each other or with staff members, and drinking, drinking, drinking. I hate to say it, but a lot of the men and some of the women who make the laws in Illinois are hungover when they're doing it.

Sometimes I would try to organize a few of my colleagues to challenge that dictatorial authority. For example, over dinner and with a couple of beers in them, they could sound like Patrick Henry, or John Hancock or Paul Revere—suddenly they would become revolutionaries and patriots—and then you would leave them and go to bed, thinking that maybe they will stand tall, and we could actually change some things and have more of a voice in the process and do good. But then, by the next morning, when I saw them in committee or would follow up with them on the House floor, now suddenly the ardent revolutionary spirit they exhibited the night before disappeared, and they no longer had the appetite for it. Where the night before they were gulping their beers and drinking their spirits, intoxicated with revolutionary fervor, invariably I would find the next day that they had slept it off. They were no longer drunk—and they were no longer intoxicated with the revolutionary spirit. Sobriety and reality set in. They were, after all, content to just going back to doing what they were told, and when the session for that day came to an end, to start the cycle all over again where they would caucus over beers and bourbon some lobbyists paid for.

By the middle of my first term, I was already eyeing a run for the United States Congress. Congressional giant Dan Rostenkowski was under federal investigation and would soon be indicted. As a consequence, he would lose his reelection bid to an unknown, unemployed lawyer by the name of Michael Flanagan.

There was a lot of competition in the 1996 Democratic primary for Congress in the fifth Congressional District. Whoever the Democratic nominee was, he or she had a very good chance of defeating the Republican incumbent, Congressman Michael Flanagan.

And before the Democratic primary field was set in 1996, there was a lot of positioning and coalition building that was taking place.

Nineteen ninety-four was a big Republican year. The Republicans took over control of the House of Representatives. Newt Gingrich and his Contract with America fed into an electorate that was fed up and hungry for change. Congressman Flanagan was elected largely because of Dan Rostenkowski's legal troubles, but he also benefited by the mood for change that permeated the electorate.

That desire for change among the people was still very much alive in 1996. But where two years before the voters blamed President Clinton and the Democrats, with the emergence of Newt Gingrich and a lengthy government shutdown at the federal level, the people's anger was now more directed at Gingrich Republicans than it was at Bill Clinton and the Democrats.

The Democratic primary for Congress in 1996 was hard-fought and very competitive. After all the maneuvering and positioning, it ended up being a three-person race. State Representative Nancy Kaszak was my principal opponent. She and I were elected together in 1992 as insurgent candidates against the machine. She represented the legislative district directly to the north and east of mine. In 1992, she received a lot of help and support from my father-in-law, who supported her run against his former ally Al Ronan. It was an added bonus when she surprisingly won. But we were never close, and it wouldn't be long before it was obvious that she had her eye on the same Congressional seat I coveted.

She was a formidable opponent. In a legislative district where better than 60% of the registered voters were women, and being of Polish descent, which is the single largest ethnic group in the fifth congressional district, she was considered by many political pundits as the favorite. She was also viewed as being independent and as having a successful legislative record to run on. And as the only woman in the race, and with the help of Emily's list, a national organization with a network of Democratic women contributors, she proved to be a fundraising machine, raising hundreds of thousands of dollars in campaign contributions from women all across America. In fact, she ended up raising and spending more money in that campaign than me.

My other opponent was an attorney by the name of Ray Romero, who worked for one of the big utility companies. He was an impressive person with a good educational background and an impressive resume. He was also Hispanic, which meant that he would likely take votes away from me because I had a strong base of support in the Latino community.

In this race, like my first race for state representative, my father-in-law worked hard to help me. Part of our tragedy is that our best times together were when he and I were joined together, taking on and fighting a common adversary. Those were the times we got along the best. It's very strange. And it's very sad. Because from my point of view, those were great times together.

With my father-in-law's help, I was able to build a coalition of support that included every regular Democratic political organization in the congressional district. He also helped me get the support of Mayor Daley. It was the reverse of what the political landscape was for us years before when I ran for state representative. Back then, I was the insurgent candidate challenging the regular organizations. Now I was the candidate of the regular Democratic organizations, and those were the organizations who since 1958 had, every two years, helped to reelect Dan Rostenkowski to the Congress.

But I also had a progressive record as a legislator and had built a lot of support among progressive activists, particularly among female legislative colleagues, who supported me against Nancy Kaszak. Where the eastern end of the district that includes the lakefront tends to be more progressive and has more independent-minded voters, notwithstanding the predictions of the pundits, I ran stronger than expected there.

Running and campaigning for Congress was in many ways similar and in many ways very different from running for State representative. First, a congressional district is six times larger than a state legislative district. Second, this race involved former Congressman Dan Rostenkowski's congressional seat that was being held by the David who slew Goliath. So unlike the race for state representative, the media was interested in this race and that meant we needed to put together a more sophisticated campaign team. Third, it costs a lot more money to run for Congress, and the rules are different. Federal campaign finance laws have restrictions on the amount of campaign contributions individuals and political action committees can give. At that time, there were no restrictions in state legislative races. So there was a fundraising component to this race for Congress that didn't exist when I first ran for State representative. And fourth, in this congressional race, radio and television ads would be purchased by the candidates. Voters could be reached through the air by TV and radio commercials. This meant that the role of the traditional Chicago precinct worker was, to some extent, marginalized. Because if you had the financial wherewithal, you didn't need a precinct captain to deliver your message to the voter. You could do it yourself through paid advertisements .

So this was going to be a different kind of campaign than the one I ran four years before. I needed time to raise money. And under the federal rules, that meant making phone calls to potential supporters, asking them for contributions, or meeting prospective supporters and asking them to help by either making a contribution and/or by raising money themselves.

It was during this period when I was raising money for the Democratic primary for Congress that I met Tony Rezko. To help me raise money, I hired a woman by the name of Kathleen Murray who had a fundraising business. She was recommended to us by one of Mayor Daley's aides. Part of what her firm did was provide a list of Democratic donors who contributed to other Democratic candidates. Those donors would be called and solicited. At that time, I didn't know a lot of them and part of what we did was to make appointments for me to visit them and introduce myself to make the case on why I would be a great congressman and why they might want to consider supporting me. One of those donors was Tony Rezko, who agreed to support my campaign. This began a relationship that I would have with him over the next several years that I believed was based on friendship and on his belief that I was a rising political figure who he wanted to know because he believed in me and the things I represented. And it wouldn't be long after I met him that he took me to a law office in the River North area of Chicago where he introduced me to a young lawyer by the name of Barack Obama, who he also saw as a rising political leader with a bright future.

I approached the Democratic primary for Congress in the same way I approached the Democratic primary for State representative four years earlier. I was going to pour my heart and soul and everything I had into it. Because a congressional district is so big, it's a bad use of time to knock on doors and reach voters one by one. So going door to door like I did in the State rep race was not something I was going to do. Instead, I would replace that form of retail campaigning by shaking hands with voters at the elevated and subway stations every morning before they went to work. This way, I could literally meet hundreds, and at some of the busy train stations, thousands of voters every morning. I would get up every morning at 5 a.m. and would be at the train stations before 6:30 a.m. before the early morning rush. Our primaries in Illinois are during the winter. So, I began this regiment in early January when Chicago is coldest. And it was cold. I remember the winter of 1996 as a particularly cold one. One morning, the wind chill was something like 23 below zero. But I took pride in my ability to tough it out and stand there shaking hands. I figured the colder it was, the more the voter would appreciate how prepared I was to sacrifice to be a congressman. And if that commitment didn't persuade the voter, then maybe if he was undecided when he was making his decision at the voting booth, perhaps he might remember that cold day and that might tip the scales in my favor.

We had a routine. It was important to get it right. I had it down to a science. I called it the shake and pass. First, I would shake the hand of a commuter, and a volunteer standing right beside me would pass the literature. Shake first, pass the literature second. Any other sequence ruined the flow and meant I would have fewer hands to shake.

Every weekday morning from the day I started, which was January 8, Elvis' birthday—I picked it because as a big Elvis fan I liked the karma of starting on his birthday—through the morning of primary day, I went to train stations every morning to campaign. And I went to supermarkets. I visited every supermarket across the entire congressional district several times over the span of the two-month campaign. That's how I would spend the early evening hours between 5 p.m. and 7:30 p.m. I would stand with a volunteer and do our version of the shake and pass. After the supermarkets, most weekday nights I would visit some senior citizen bingos and finish campaigning by shaking hands in bowling alleys. In short, I went everywhere and anywhere where I could find a lot of people who were likely to live within the congressional district I was running in.

And what about the actual workday between the hours of nine to five? That was the time I spent raising money. I would go to the campaign office and make fundraising calls, or I would meet with potential contributors who were on the schedule for a visit on that particular day.

I didn't get any major newspaper endorsements in that campaign. For some reason, I never really was very good at that. Ray Romero got the endorsement of the *Chicago Tribune*, which carried a lot of weight along the lakefront in the eastern end of the district. Nancy Kaszak won the endorsement of the *Chicago Sun-Times*, which was more the newspaper of the working class. I won the endorsement of the people—and that's the one that matters. I won the primary with 50% of the vote, Nancy Kaszak finished second with 38% of the vote, and Ray Romero finished third with 12%. Of course, I felt great about it. I now had a chance to be elected congressman and represent the neighborhoods I grew up in. All that was left to do was to run hard and win the general election. And while looking back now it doesn't seem like that should have been so hard, as far as I was concerned I had a big challenge ahead. There was going to be no letting up. I was determined to run as hard as I could and for as long as I could. Victory was in my grasp, and I wasn't about to let it get away.

I won the November general election, winning 64% of the vote. I campaigned in the fall exactly as I had during the winter. I did the same regimen of train stations, supermarkets, senior citizen bingos, and bowling alleys as I had during the primary. The only difference was that fundraising was easier. I was now the Democratic nominee, and Democratic contributors were happy to help me win a seat back for the Democratic Party.

It wasn't all about campaigning that year. Between the primary and the general election, Patti and I were blessed with something far better than winning elections. On the night of August 3, at 11:36 Central Standard Time, our daughter Amy was born. I was there of course. She was beautiful, a precious gift from God. I greeted her not with the shake and pass, but with gentle kisses and a profound sense of joy.

Our baby Amy was baptized on a Saturday, just four days after I was elected to the Congress. Strains between my father-in-law and me had already surfaced. He attended the baptism but wasn't speaking to me. He was angry because I wouldn't commit to hiring all the people he recommended to my new congressional staff until I first had a chance to attend an orientation in Washington, D.C. for new members of Congress. I was prepared to and ultimately did hire every one of his recommendations. But that happened only after he angrily ordered me to move out of his office, and we spent a cold and uncomfortable Thanksgiving together.

Here again was a foreshadowing of things to come. In the immediate aftermath of victory, where my father-in-law was a substantial contributor to that success, before we could even savor the achievement, tensions developed around what was in it for him. Like before, we got through this and worked it out. But a pattern was starting to emerge. The bigger the office I was elected to, and the greater the success, the bigger the expectations and demands from my father-in-law and, correspondingly, the greater the problems between us.

David Axelrod, who is now a senior adviser in the Obama White House, helped me find a chief of staff for my congressional office. David was my media consultant in that race for Congress, and I had a lot of respect for his judgment. The first candidate he presented to me was a young man by the name of David Plough. Plough would go on to become Barack Obama's presidential campaign manager. I offered him the position, but he turned it down. He said he had other plans, and whatever they were, they must have been good ones.

Another candidate for the job who David Axelrod introduced to me was John Wyma. John would take the job and serve as my Chief of Staff until the end of my second term in Congress, when he left me to run the office of New York Senator Chuck Schumer. He would return when I decided to run for governor, and after I won would go on to develop his lobbying and consulting business in Illinois.

I was sworn in as a member of the United States Congress on January 3, 1997, almost fifty years after a previous Congress passed a law that allowed my immigrant father a chance to live and build a life in the United States of America. My father never lived to see that day, but as I was taking my oath of office and holding our five-month-old Amy in my left arm, I started to choke up a little. I thought about what my father would think if he were alive to see this. This was a day where everything my father believed about America came true. And as far as I was concerned, it wouldn't have been possible without his hard work and sacrifice.

CHAPTER FOUR

IT WAS A WEDNESDAY NIGHT IN APRIL OF 1999. I was on the floor of the United States House of Representatives, giving a speech that warned my colleagues and the 37 people across America who were watching on C-SPAN that Serbian president Slobodan Milosevic wasn't bluffing. And that if NATO followed through with its threats to start bombing Serbia over his refusal to sign an agreement that would cede sovereignty to a part of his country, that he would do in Kosovo what he did in Bosnia. He would expel innocent people from their homes and create untold misery for tens of thousands of people.

The breakup of the former Yugoslavia was painful if predictable because it had all happened before. Where diplomacy failed, violence prevailed. As it turned out, the Balkan wars of the 1990s were like every other Balkan war in history. They turned into wars of ethnic cleansing. Whoever was stronger did more of it to the one who was weaker. That's what those wars were all about. And when the leaders in charge of the different parts of the country that are breaking apart happen to be old-school, Soviet-style Communist dictators, then that's a recipe for the barbarism and cruelty the world witnessed.

I was the only Serbian-American member of Congress during our war with Yugoslavia over Kosovo. I opposed the decision to bomb Yugoslavia. I spoke against it. I thought NATO's decision to bomb Yugoslavia over Milosevic's refusal to sign the Rambouillet agreement was wrong. The night I spoke in opposition to the bombing, I warned that the moment it began, Milosevic would unleash the 40,000 troops he had amassed at the border and begin the wholesale ethnic cleansing of innocent civilians that the experts from the State Department claimed he would never dare to do.

But he did. And I was right, and they were wrong. Or were they? Were they so cynical that they figured once the bombing started, that would predictably trigger a massive response from Milosevic in the form of an ethnic cleansing campaign, the scale of which was never before seen by a world that was watching because of the twenty-four hour news cycle? The world could watch around the clock as Milosevic's forces ruthlessly kicked innocent civilians out of their homes. The world could witness first hand as Milosevic began his onslaught against innocent civilians. And the world would be shocked and appalled. And world opinion would be so outraged that the NATO forces would be able to sustain the bombing of a sovereign nation and achieve their objective of taking a part of that nation away.

Putting aside the morality of it for a second, I've always thought that Milosevic stupidly played right into their hands. Being the brutal dictator that he was, human life meant nothing to him. And the men and women who ran our foreign policy, and those who decided the foreign-policy at NATO, also knew that to be true. So they calculated that they could achieve their goal of removing a portion of this country's territory either by forcing this dictator to sign an agreement that gave it away or, more likely, by forcing his hand and putting him in a position where his natural instinct led him to respond with brute force, which, in turn, would create such an outcry against him that the NATO forces would then be able to achieve its objectives through the use of force.

The only problem with that thinking was that tens of thousands of innocent people would get killed. Innocent civilians would suffer. Families would be displaced. For a lot of these Ivy League educated State Department bureaucrats, innocent civilians like those in Kosovo were just pawns. Sure it was foreseeable that innocent men, women, and children would be thrown out of their homes, or killed, or tortured, or taken captive. It wasn't only foreseeable, it was almost certain to occur. And yes, there would be untold cruelty and horror perpetrated on innocent people. But from their point of view, that was the price that had to be paid to take a part of one nation away and use it to build a new one.

I didn't agree with the policy of my country concerning the war with Yugoslavia. I thought it was wrong for the international community to hold a gun to the head of a sovereign country and tell them that if they didn't voluntarily agree to give up a part of their country then they would blow their brains out. That was the policy of the United States and NATO. If the Serbs didn't agree to give up Kosovo, which was as much a part of their country as Texas is to ours, then they would take it away from them through the use of force. I opposed the policy because the United States was going to war over an issue that had nothing to do with our nation's national security. And we were going to war over an issue that had nothing to do with our vital national interests. And from a personal standpoint, I shared with my fellow Serbs that same sense of betrayal that they would so often express. How could the United States of America do this to Serbia, a country that in both world wars was an ally of the United States?

That night, I felt I gave a good speech arguing against that war on the floor of the House of Representatives. Unfortunately, I didn't change a lot of minds—at least the minds that mattered. In fact, my speech was so ineffective that the very next day, the bombing started. Incidentally, the day the bombing started was the last day that Congress would be in session until the expiration of a two-week Easter break. And just as I predicted, immediately after the United States and NATO forces started bombing Yugoslavia, Milosevic then began kicking innocent civilians out of his country.

My country was now at war with the country my father came from. But however I might disagree with the policy, I was for my country. And now that we were at war I would do whatever I could to support my country's efforts to make sure we won that war. In Congress I would support the appropriations to pay for military operations. I would speak against the deplorable ethnic cleansing that Milosevic was perpetrating against innocent Kosovar civilians. And I would incur the wrath of a lot of my fellow Serbian-Americans who felt that I should, as the only Serbian-American member of the Congress, speak out more forcefully against the policy of my government. I understood their point of view, but once the shooting started, and America was at war, I may not have liked it, but I was going to serve my country however I could.

And my chance to serve in some meaningful way presented itself not long after the war started. The day before we started bombing Yugoslavia, I had a visitor in my congressional office in Washington D.C. This visitor claimed he was an official of the Milosevic government in Yugoslavia. I was kind of skeptical. It's not uncommon for some people to purport to be something they are not. I'll refer to this man as Mr. Gajic. I believe he came to my office to gauge whether I thought the United States was bluffing and would actually start the bombing we were threatening if Milosevic refused to sign the Rambouillet agreement. I told him it was not a bluff. It was a real threat. And that if Milosevic didn't sign the agreement, the United States and NATO would begin to bomb Yugoslavia just as they promised. I told him I hoped I was wrong, but unfortunately I knew I was right.

I remember asking him if Kosovo was worth it. I said something like, "Look, I'm an American, I know my dad and a lot of other Serbs see Kosovo as a historic and sacred part of old Serbia. I know all about Vidovdan, the annual celebration of that famous battle where the Serbs lost to the Turks back in 1386, but is it worth going to war over? A war where the whole world is against you? A war you can't win? And over a place that's been nothing but a headache for you and will continue to be nothing but a headache for you? Is this a war worth fighting?"

He said it was. And the next day the war began.

That weekend, I was with my in-laws at their home in Lake Geneva, Wisconsin. I turned on CNN. And as I was watching, a news clip came on that showed Slobodan Milosevic meeting with his top advisers in what appeared to be a kind of war council at his presidential palace in Belgrade. As the camera scanned the room, low and behold, there seated at the table was the man who only a couple of days before was in my office. Mr. Gajic was for real. I now knew I had a contact in Milosevic's government.

I spent that weekend in Lake Geneva trying to figure out what, if any, role I might be able to play as the only Serbian-American member of Congress to help my country succeed and help bring about a peaceful resolution to this war. It sounds kind of presumptuous that I would be thinking like that. After all, I was a junior member of Congress, in the middle of my second term, and my only real accomplishment to date was the naming of a post office after a slain Chicago police officer. And it wasn't like I had established any foreign-policy bona fides. But then again, most of the other congressmen hadn't either. In fact, the overwhelming majority of them hardly even knew where Kosovo was. I did. I actually knew a lot about this issue, and I would write an op-ed that was published in the *Washington Post* that called for the partition of Kosovo, not unlike what was done with India and Pakistan in 1948, or with some of the territorial disputes between the Israelis and the Palestinians.

About a week after the bombing began, three U.S. soldiers were taken prisoner by the Serbs. Their names were released to the media but little else was known about where they were or how they were doing or if they were even alive. The Red Cross was not given permission to see them.

David Axelrod was my media consultant back then, and he took an active part in advising me during my years in Congress. It was his idea to see if there might be a role for me to play in helping to negotiate the release of our three soldiers.

He rightly believed that I could draw on my contacts in the Serbian-American community and use my unique position in Congress to open up a line of communication with people in the Milosevic government. I immediately embraced his idea and was excited that I might now be useful.

But trying to be useful wasn't as easy as it might seem. There were two governments to deal with; the Yugoslavian government and my own. It was decided that before I reached out to anyone connected to the Yugoslavian government, I would first seek to offer my help to high-ranking officials in the Clinton White House. So the first thing I did was place a telephone phone call to President Clinton's national security adviser Sandy Berger. He was unavailable when I first called so I left a message. When he didn't call back after a couple of days, I placed a second phone call and left another message. I was a member of Congress who sat on the armed services committee, and while I wasn't surprised that I hadn't gotten a phone call back right away, I did expect that sooner or later somebody from the national security adviser's office would return my phone call. After a week went by and my phone calls were still unanswered, my Chief of Staff placed a phone call to Sandy Berger's Chief of Staff, whom he knew personally. I want to say that I think I remember his name as being Miles Lackey. Not an inappropriate last name for a guy working as an aide to another guy. My top staffer was told the secretary had a long list of calls he needed to return but that my name was on the list, and I should expect a call back. It never came.

Undeterred, I then reached out to President Clinton's Chief of Staff John Podesta, someone I had something in common with. Like me, John Podesta came from Chicago. He called back right away. When I explained the purpose of my call and how I thought I might be helpful in obtaining the release of the soldiers, he told me he would run it up the flagpole and get back to me. He was positive and very upbeat. Unfortunately, nothing ever came of it, and after two weeks of trying to work with the Clinton White House, it started to become clear that they had other plans. They didn't want to work with me. My sense was that they didn't want the soldiers released at that time. Their public relations campaign was doing a good job demonizing Milosevic as a genocidal maniac. Anything that might make him and the Serbs appear less barbaric would undermine those efforts and their ability to sustain the bombing of Yugoslavia.

So with that dead end, the next question was what do I do next? Where do I go from here? I wasn't sure. But then an opportunity presented itself. During this time, I read in the newspaper that the Rev. Jesse Jackson refused an invitation from the Yugoslavian government to inspect the damage NATO bombing was doing to the civilian population of Yugoslavia. Former United States Attorney General Ramsey Clark had already visited, but Rev. Jackson took the position that any inspection be conditioned on him being able to visit and see our three U.S. servicemen. At a meeting in David Axelrod's office, it was agreed that partnering up with Rev. Jackson might be a way to help our soldiers in a meaningful way.

In many ways, it was a perfect pairing. Disappointed but undaunted that the Clinton White House was turning a blind eye to my overtures, I was still determined to find a way to help our soldiers. Here again, I was up against Ivy League policy wonks from the State Department, young bureaucrats who come from the so-called best families, who went to the best schools, who sit in the safety and comfort of their offices and conference rooms, pursuing their careers, where they might hope to become the next Dean Acheson or the next Henry Kissinger as global chess players. Except in this chess game, their pieces are real people like our very own soldiers—pawns in a real life game with real life consequences. There were our soldiers, sacrificing and putting at risk their lives and their liberties serving their country, and here are these bureaucrats with their callous and snobbish indifference to their well-being and justifying that indifference with a smug intellectual rationalization about their plight. The men and women who serve in our Armed Forces—young people from the inner city, or from the farm, or from small-town America—they fight our wars, they risk their lives. And if the elites from the best schools who decide our foreign policy see them as only cannon fodder, then at least congressmen, elected directly by the people to represent the people, should see them differently. The congressman's job should be to look after the well-being of those soldiers. That's how I saw my role. Let those elitist snobs at the State Department play their geopolitics with their detached indifference to the plight of our soldiers. That might be their job. My job, as I saw it, was to inject myself into the equation as someone who was going to try to help those soldiers and help their families.

And the way I could be most helpful was to pair up with Rev. Jackson. By myself, there was only so much I could do. As a junior congressman whose father came from the country we were at war with, the Clinton White House and the State Department would easily be able to squeeze me and prevent me from negotiating a release of our soldiers. They could portray me as a meddling Congressman with conflicting loyalties. They could create a political drumbeat that could cause political problems for me in my next election. They could put pressure on me by using the Democratic leadership in Congress to discourage me from even trying to help. The State Department could easily deny me whatever visas I might request to go to Yugoslavia to try to negotiate in person the release of our soldiers. By myself, I could easily be silenced and squashed.

But not with the Rev. Jesse Jackson. Not with the political and religious leader who happened to be President Clinton's personal spiritual adviser during the Monica Lewinsky scandal. How could the Clinton White House or the State Department silence him? And with a history of having successfully performed these missions in the past, securing the release of Navy Lieutenant Robert Goodman in Syria in 1983 and the release of 22 Americans from Cuba in 1984, there was no way they could keep Rev. Jackson from getting involved.

But Reverend Jackson's problem was he couldn't get the guarantees from the Yugoslavian government to even visit the U.S. servicemen, much less negotiate their release. And he had already publicly stated that he wasn't going to entertain a visit to Yugoslavia unless he could at least visit with our three captured soldiers.

That's where I came in. I could reach out to my contacts in the Serbian-American community and to Mr. Gajic, the member of the Milosevic government who had been in my office, and see if I could make a visit possible. I could serve as a liaison to representatives from the Yugoslavian government. They could trust me more than some other American Congressman because my father came from their country. And the fact that I spoke the language, albeit not perfectly, was an added bonus that would make them feel more comfortable with me. That's how I could help Rev. Jackson be in a position to help our soldiers.

So the tactical imperative was clear. But how do I hook up with Rev. Jackson? The answer was obvious. The road to Rev. Jackson was through his son, my colleague in the Congress, Congressman Jesse Jackson Junior.

Jesse Jackson Junior and I had a good relationship when we served together in Congress. He was elected to Congress about a year before me in a special congressional election to fill a vacancy. I didn't know his father. I met him once at the airport and introduced myself as a Congressman who worked with his son. He couldn't have cared less and acted like he didn't have the time of day for me. That came as no surprise. I came from a part of town that didn't have a strong opinion of him to begin with, so it didn't bother me when he brushed me off. The problem though, was that experience led me to think that if I directly reached out to him, he might give me the brush off again.

So I went to Jesse Junior. We returned to Congress after two weeks in recess. The war was already in full swing. And the soldiers were already captive for more than a week.

The first thing I did when I got back to Washington was reach out to Congressman Jackson. I found him on the House floor during our first vote of the day. It was a Tuesday morning, and I took a seat next to him as the house conducted its business. I remember this conversation well. I told him that I'd read in the newspaper that his father wanted to go to Yugoslavia but that he wouldn't go unless the government promised to let him visit our soldiers. I then went on to tell him that I had some contact with some people who purported to be connected to the Yugoslavian government. And if I could arrange with those people a visit to see our soldiers, did he think his dad would be interested in going? He immediately answered, "absolutely." And he then promptly suggested that I, and I'm quoting him, "Call the Reverend now." I said I wasn't comfortable with that. I hardly knew his dad, and I would feel a lot better if he would call him first. Before he could answer, I then asked him quizzically, "Do you call your dad Reverend?" I was struck by that. By the formality of it. Jesse Junior not calling his father dad, or daddy, or father, or Papa or even old man. I found it very interesting that instead he called his dad Reverend.

It was decided that he would first call his father to gauge his interest. And as soon as he did, he would call me, and if his father was interested, I would then call him. That's exactly what happened. Within twenty minutes, Congressman Jackson called me at my office and told me his father was excited and that I should call him immediately. He gave me his cell phone number. I called it, and one of Rev. Jackson's aides answered the phone. I told him who I was and asked to speak to Rev. Jackson. Moments later he came to the phone. He spoke in a low voice, and it was hard to hear him. It was my first experience talking on the telephone with Rev. Jackson. He is such a forceful and powerful speaker in public, but is very soft-spoken and speaks with almost a whisper on the telephone. Before I explained to him why I was calling, I mentioned that the subject matter was kind of sensitive and asked if there was a hard line I could call him on. He said there wasn't. He told me he was at a voter registration drive in Mississippi and couldn't leave. But he wanted to talk. So he then went on to ask me to talk to him in, and I'm quoting, "code."

Now here I am. I don't know Rev. Jackson. I met him once, and he basically blew me off. Now I'm on the phone talking to him about possibly freelancing around the president of the United States and the State Department, and he's asking me to talk to him about these things in "code." What did that mean? What code? I didn't know any code.

But I did the best I could. I told him that I had some contacts in the "operation over there?" I was referring to the Yugoslavian government, and I said it in the form of a question. Rev. Jackson didn't say anything except, and I'm quoting, "understand." I went on to say that if these guys were the real deal I might be able to arrange a visit to see our soldiers. He said, and I'm quoting again, "understand." I then went on to say that before these contacts could commit to a visit, they would have to get approval from, and I quote, "the big cheese." I was referring to Milosevic. He again said, and I quote, "understand." I told him that if all went well, they would have an answer for me by the next day somewhere around 5 p.m. Washington D.C. time. If the answer was yes, I asked him, would he be interested in going? For the first time he answered one of my questions with a word other than "understand." He said "yes." I then asked him how soon he would be able to go. He answered that he was tied up in Mississippi until Friday, but if the answer was yes, then by Saturday of that week he would be willing to, and I quote, " Move on." He said that last phrase with great enthusiasm. He then went on to say that if I pulled this off, if I could help make this happen, he was going to take me with him. Now I found that interesting. After all, I was playing a significant role in putting this whole thing together. As far as I was concerned, it went without saying that I was going with him.

Before approaching Congressman Jackson and talking to Rev. Jackson, I had made contact with the vice president of Yugoslavia, a man by the name of Vuk Draskovic. He was a political rival of Slobodan Milosevic, but he was presumably a part of a coalition government. He assured me that he had the authority to speak on behalf of his government. I believed him. Prominent Serbian-Americans who knew a lot more about the politics in Yugoslavia than I did confirmed that to be the case. His name was also consistently mentioned in news reports during that time. We discussed not just a possible visit to see the soldiers, but about the possibility of actually negotiating the release of our three soldiers. He liked the idea of me reaching out to Rev. Jackson to see if he might want to participate in these efforts. And he gave me a timetable that I passed along to the Rev. in my subsequent conversation with him. It was in this phone conversation that Mr. Draskovic made it abundantly clear that all roads lead to Milosevic. And if any of this was going to happen, he would have to be the one to personally sign off on it.

Apparently he did. Because the next day at the appointed time I spoke to Mr. Draskovic, and he told me that his government would be extending a formal invitation to me and Rev. Jackson. Now it was up to us to figure out when we were going and how we were going to get there.

We were traveling to a war zone. When the word got out that we were planning to travel to Yugoslavia to visit our soldiers, the Clinton administration and the State Department made it very clear that we were doing so at our own peril. Under no circumstances were they prepared to in any way modify or change their bombing schedule. If we were choosing to travel to a country that was being bombed, that was our problem. They had no intention of stopping or pausing the bombing. Nor should they. They had a plan that was presumably carefully prepared by the military. To ask them to change it for us would be foolhardy. If we were choosing to go, we should assume the risk. It was our responsibility. Our challenge was to find a way to get to Yugoslavia, and once there, to move around Yugoslavia without getting bombed. As far as I was concerned, we had no right to ask our government to change its military plans to accommodate us. All we asked was that they didn't stop us from going.

But they were trying. First they were trying to discourage us from going. And when that didn't work, they actually took steps to make it difficult for us to get there.

My first meeting with Rev. Jackson concerning our trip to Yugoslavia took place at his Rainbow Push offices in Georgetown. When I arrived at his office, I discovered that he wasn't planning on traveling light. He was taking an entourage with him. He had assembled what he called an interfaith delegation of multi-denominational religious leaders from around the country. There were, among others, a Methodist minister from Mississippi, a Jewish rabbi from Los Angeles, a Muslim imam, a Russian Orthodox Bishop, a Roman Catholic priest who taught conflict resolution at Boston College, and a woman named Dr. Joan Brown Campbell who was the head of a national organization of liberal-minded churches.

I discovered something else when I first got to that meeting. Rev. Jackson was wearing a microphone, and what I thought was going to be a private, preliminary meeting to discuss our strategy to free our soldiers was instead a meeting that was being filmed by HBO. Apparently, Rev. Jackson had arranged beforehand that this upcoming adventure might make for a good documentary. I think it explains, in part, the warm response the Rev. gave me when I walked into that meeting. Unlike the first time I met him at the airport, this time he quickly got up and much to my surprise embraced me. Caught off guard, I said something like, "How come your son doesn't treat me like that?" And then I felt the microphone around his belt, and I realized why he was giving me so much love. I also realized that there was a camera in the room, and this private meeting had now become reality TV.

It was at this meeting that Rev. Jackson informed the assembled group that he was told by high-ranking officials in the Clinton administration that if we chose to go to Yugoslavia they could not guarantee our safety. That the Yugoslavs might choose to take us all hostages and that NATO had no intention of pausing the bombing to accommodate our travel plans. “We ain’t going to no beach party,” he said.

And he wanted everyone who intended to travel to know this upfront so they could back out if they felt it was too dangerous. So he put the question to the group that maybe we should consider the warnings of the Clinton White House and scrap the whole idea because of the danger involved.

Now I don’t want to appear too cynical, but I found the whole discussion about whether we should go or not as being contrived for the camera. It was all shtick. There was no way Rev. Jackson was not going to go. And of course it was possible that once we got there Milosevic could take us hostage or that we could get blown up by our own country’s bombs. This was possible, but I believed the odds of either one of those things happening were remote. And I believed everyone else in that room did too. And besides, we knew all of this before this meeting. No, this whole scene was being staged for the camera.

So I figured, what the heck, “when in Rome, do as the Romans do.” I’m going to get myself on HBO too. So at the first opportunity, I climbed up on my high horse and spoke up saying something like, “Reverend, we owe it to those boys to get them out, whatever the cost to us. Now I can’t speak for the rest of you, but I can sure speak for me. I want to go, and I want to go now.” And then I directed this bromide to Rev. Jackson, “If the Clinton administration wants to bomb you, then let’s dare them to do it. Let’s play Russian roulette. I’m betting there’s no bullet in the chamber. I can’t see the Clinton White House bombing President Clinton’s personal religious adviser.”

It took us a couple of weeks before we could actually leave. Rev. Jackson was in charge of arranging the travel. Originally, the plan called for us to leave on a Saturday and fly directly to Belgrade on a World Airlines jet. Rev. Jackson had arranged to get us that plane. He is amazing that way. This is among the things I learned about him from this trip. Rev. Jackson lives off the land. I don't think Rev. Jackson carries any money, but he doesn't have to. He has this amazing ability to get what he wants. At a moment's notice, he can get a jet plane for his personal use. I don't know if he drives or not, but he could, at the last minute, decide to travel anywhere in the world and end up in the place he wants to go. And he has this way, if he chooses, of sweeping people into his vortex. Where one minute you have plans and a schedule to follow like voting on the floor of the Congress, and then all of a sudden you're around him, and the next thing you know you might find yourself in Mississippi missing those votes and wondering how you got there.

The morning of our scheduled departure for Belgrade on the World Airlines jet, I got a call saying the trip was delayed for a day. Apparently, the CEO of the airlines contacted Rev. Jackson and told him that after the State Department learned he was providing the plane for our trip, they told him that there wasn't going to be any pause in the bombing and that his plane was flying into a war zone. The CEO informed Rev. Jackson that because of that call, he needed to get a war insurance policy on that plane. When later that day, Patti saw that I wasn't leaving, she asked me what happened. I told her our departure was delayed for a day because the plane needed to get a war insurance policy. It was like a bell started to ring. For the first time, the reality dawned on Patti that I was voluntarily flying into a war zone. And being practical minded, she then immediately called our insurance agent to ask if my life insurance policy covered me if I knowingly traveled to a war zone. It turns out she did not have to worry. I was covered under my life insurance policy.

Reassured, a cheerful and carefree Patti then kissed me on the cheek, wished me luck, said goodbye, and told me to call her when I got home.

We were never able to take the World Airlines plane. We learned the next day that the war insurance policy was just too expensive, and the plane was no longer available. So then an itinerary was planned where we would take one of the two direct flights from Rome that were still flying directly to Belgrade. After we learned that this was our plan, suddenly NATO intervened, and the two commercial flights from Rome to Belgrade were abruptly canceled.

We finally got to Yugoslavia by using a third option. We flew from Washington, D.C. to Frankfurt, Germany, and then got on a connecting flight to Zagreb, Croatia. Once there, we took a bus and traveled through Croatia and across the border into Yugoslavia. Once in Yugoslavia, we traveled for about two hours before reaching our destination, the Hyatt Hotel in Belgrade.

It was surreal. There was a big crowd waiting at the hotel–mostly the international media. But a lot of other people started to assemble. In the crowd I noticed a familiar face I had seen on the television news. It was Arkan, reputed to be Serbia's most notorious war criminal. He was the most wanted war criminal of the Balkan wars, and the United Nations and NATO wanted to bring him to justice. But to the Serbs who were fighting these wars, it was them against everyone, and Arkan was a national hero. You could see posters of him all around Belgrade dressed in paramilitary fatigues and holding an assault weapon the way you might see posters of Michael Jordan holding a basketball around Chicago. And he was there with his girlfriend who was a beautiful Serbian movie star. You couldn't help but notice her, and God bless Rev. Jackson, he did too. It was only natural that he would. In fact, as he was about to say hello to her, I pulled him aside and told him who that guy was next to her and that a camera shot or photograph of him with the notorious Serbian war criminal was the wrong way to begin our visit.

Exhausted from the travel and suffering jet lag, there was no time to rest. Rev. Jackson and I were scheduled to meet with the Yugoslavian Foreign Minister, the equivalent of their Secretary of State, later that night. It was a dinner meeting at around midnight at another hotel in Belgrade called the Intercontinental. The purpose of the meeting was to begin a dialogue with the decision-makers in the Yugoslavian government. I would soon learn that there was a pattern to the NATO bombing of Belgrade. It would generally begin around midnight and last until about four o'clock in the morning. There was something humane about our bombing schedule. It was a kinder and gentler form of bombing. I believed it to be by design. We were bombing this big city but the people in it could plan their day around it. They could go about their business during the day and the early evening, knowing they would be safe from the bombs that wouldn't start falling until after midnight. Yes, we were bombing a sovereign country and a city with a large civilian population, but we were doing it in a way where we would try to avoid casualties and minimize the suffering of the people.

The Intercontinental was a surreal scene too. This big, five-star-type hotel was a ghost town. It was empty. There were no guests as the hotel was considered to be a likely target for NATO bombs. Because that night's bombing was about to start, all the lights at the Intercontinental Hotel were turned off. Only a small, designated area in the restaurant was kept lit, and even those few lights were turned down low. Most of the light was provided by candles. We were served an elaborate midnight dinner by waiters dressed in tuxedos. I think I remember a guy playing "Oche Chornia," a classic Hungarian song, on the violin. And along with our multi-course dinner, we were served an angry diatribe by the Foreign Minister condemning the NATO bombing and the policies of our government. Several times during the dinner we would be interrupted by the sound of air raid alarms signaling the appearance of planes and the dropping of bombs. The dinner and the diatribe lasted for several hours. We didn't get back to our hotel rooms till around 3:30 in the morning.

I can't remember what floor my hotel room was on. I do remember it was one of the upper floors. And as soon as I got to it, I could see from the window our bombs falling in the distant horizon. It was perversely fascinating. I've never seen bombing before. There would be a pause, and then the night sky would flash red or white, not that dissimilar from a fireworks display. And then periodically a white light would appear and move in a direction toward our hotel, like an airplane approaching, and then drop out of the sky and presumably hit its target. One of those lights actually appeared to be moving so rapidly in the direction of my hotel window that I felt compelled to move away and get down on the floor. The next day we visited the apartment that was hit by that bomb. It was just across the Danube River, less than a mile from our hotel. The unlucky guy who was sleeping in that apartment was blown out of his bed and out of his apartment landing on top of a car that was parked directly outside. His apartment was in charred ruins when we saw it at about 11 o'clock that morning. The alarm clock that was set for 6 a.m. was still intact and beeping because its owner never had a chance to hit the off button. The guy apparently survived the bombing. His legs were broken, and he suffered other injuries, but amazingly he lived to see another day.

I didn't get to sleep that first night in Belgrade until well after four in the morning. I had a wake-up call set for 6 a.m. because we were scheduled for a full day. I decided to lay down and try to squeeze in an hour or two of sleep. I was quickly in a deep sleep when suddenly the phone rang. I figured this was my wake-up call. When I answered the phone, it was Patti. I had tried to call her before to let her know I had arrived safely but with the seven hour time difference, she wasn't home. And she wasn't home when I tried to call her after I returned to my hotel room in the wee hours of the morning. I planned to call her when I woke up, but she beat me to the punch. When I heard her voice on the line, I was stunned and asked her how she got this number. She said it was easy. She just called 1-800 Hyatt Hotel. I'm in a war zone where just an hour before I could see bombs falling outside of my hotel window. Directly across the street from the hotel is the shell of a high-rise building that only a day before had been gutted by an American smart bomb. And here's Patti calling me on the phone and easily reaching me at that place by doing something as simple as calling directory assistance.

Our first full day in Belgrade was filled with a whole series of public appearances. Those appearances included viewing some of the places that had been bombed. Rev. Jackson and I were accompanied at all of our public appearances by the members of the interfaith religious delegation who traveled with us. And everywhere we went, the American media and the international media followed. We also met with religious leaders from Yugoslavia, including the patriarch of the Serbian Orthodox Church. While these public events were going on, I would busy myself making the case to officials in the Yugoslavian government that it was in their interest to allow Rev. Jackson and me to see the soldiers. While our visit to Yugoslavia was preconditioned on a promise to see our soldiers, the Yugoslavian Foreign Minister was noncommittal about it at the dinner the night before. Now, something we thought was a certainty was no longer certain. What a disaster this could be. We agreed to travel to Yugoslavia and in exchange for a promise to see our soldiers, we agreed to see the damage caused by our bombing. But if the Serbs don't keep their end of the bargain, and we don't get to see our soldiers, they would have duped us and used us for the purposes of propaganda, and we would have nothing to show for it. It would be embarrassing for Rev. Jackson. It would be devastating for me. After all, I was the only one in our delegation who could be unelected by the voters.

And I was already on the hot seat. David Axelrod had faxed to my chief of staff, who was with me in Belgrade, a *Chicago Sun-Times* editorial entitled "Blagojevich's Folly." It criticized me for meddling in foreign policy and compared my visit to Yugoslavia with Senator Carol Moseley Braun's visit a few years earlier to Nigeria. They couldn't have been more wrong. Senator Braun's trip to Nigeria was linked to her boyfriend who was lobbying and being paid on behalf of the Nigerian government. She wasn't risking her life traveling to a war zone or trying to secure the release of Americans who were being held captive. I was. And furthermore, there was obviously no financial benefit to me, or my family, or any friend of mine. In fact, because my trip to Yugoslavia was unofficial, I chose to pay for it myself. Personally. I didn't use taxpayer money. I paid for the trip myself as if I were a private citizen.

Mr. Gajic turned out to be very helpful when we got to Yugoslavia. During one of the public events where Rev. Jackson was speaking, he and I met in a hallway to discuss the status of the soldiers. He told me that he would be seeing Milosevic later that day and promised to try to convince him to not only agree to let us see the soldiers, but also to agree to grant us a meeting with him so we could make the case directly on why he should allow us to take our soldiers home with us.

I don't know if it was Mr.Gajic who convinced Milosevic, but in the end he agreed to allow Rev. Jackson and me to visit the soldiers at an undisclosed location the next day. And we began to get a sense that Milosevic might be willing to meet with us too.

I learned something about religious leaders who are involved in politics that I didn't know before. And it's that some of them can be just as egocentric and driven to the spotlight as any politician. Because once the word got out that Rev. Jackson and I were the only ones allowed to visit with the soldiers, a controversy broke out in the ranks of the religious delegation. Some of them were angry because no one from their group was invited to go. Soon the pressure would be put on me to give up my spot to one of the religious leaders. The first wind of this came in a conversation I had with Rev. Jackson in the backseat of the Mercedes that was driving us in between public appearances.

Rev. Jackson started thinking out loud about the upcoming visit to see the soldiers. He asked me if I had a lot of experience interacting with religious leaders. I told him I had some, though I confessed, I should probably go to church more often. He then went on to tell me that I would find that a lot of religious leaders were just as ego driven as the political leaders I was more familiar with. I told him that I thought he made an interesting observation and that I was just now starting to get a glimpse of that. He then started to move the conversation to its real purpose. He told me that there was a lot of grumbling among members of our interfaith religious delegation. They were unhappy that nobody from the religious sphere was invited to visit the soldiers. And that some were threatening to leave if a spot wasn't found for them. I knew exactly where Rev. Jackson was going with this. But I decided to play along. After all, I told him, what do they take you for? Chopped liver? You're a Reverend. He responded by saying that the religious leaders in the interfaith delegation saw him more in the "political sphere" and not in the religious one. I told him I thought they were selling him short, and then I cut to the chase. I said respectfully, that if this conversation was about me giving up my spot to see the soldiers, my answer was no way. I was setting up these meetings, I was doing the work, I developed a bond with the Serbs that was proving to be instrumental in helping us make progress, and I reminded the Rev. Jackson that I was the one who was sticking my neck out. I was the only one in our delegation who was an elected official, and if this trip was a failure, I might have to answer to the voters. I then went on to tell him about the *Chicago Sun-Times* editorial. When I told him that, he startled and said, "They what?" I repeated that the *Sun-Times* was comparing me to Carol Moseley Braun and her controversial trip to Nigeria.

He then proclaimed that editorial as being racist. I told him I didn't know about that, but I did know I wasn't giving up my spot to see the soldiers. When he saw that I was determined, he quickly retreated and said something like, well this is, after all, about the soldiers and not photo ops for the religious leaders. "So fuck 'em." After that, Jackson never brought the subject up to me again.

But there was still one thing left to do to lock in my position. I hate to say it, but I didn't completely trust that Rev. Jackson wouldn't try an end run around me and go to the Serbian officials and convince them to give my spot to one of the religious leaders. He was being besieged by them, and I was afraid he might try to undermine me. So at the next public event, after I was approached by Dr. Joan Brown Campbell to give up my place to see the soldiers, I asked her to join me and approached the relevant Serbian officials to see if they would be willing to expand the number of visitors to see the soldiers to include her. I spoke to the Serbian officials in the Serbian language. And I reminded them that I was Serbian like they were and that my dad came from this country. I was playing up our common Serbian heritage. Dr. Campbell was standing right next to me and couldn't understand what we were saying. I asked in good faith if they would be willing to allow an additional visitor. I was genuinely trying to get her in. But they emphatically said no. They said that the military was already upset that the Rev. and I were being allowed a visit. And that under no circumstances could they ask for another person to be granted access. I then asked if it was possible for either Rev. Jackson or me to be substituted. They asked if that was something I was interested in doing. When I told them absolutely not, that I was concerned Rev. Jackson might quietly screw me and get them to agree to substitute my place with the woman standing right next to me, they laughed and reassured me that they would not do anything without first talking to me. When I went on to say that if it ever came down to it, and it was between Rev. Jackson and me, who would they choose?

They laughed and without hesitation said, "Of course, you. You're the Serbian John Kennedy." After that, I didn't worry about a thing. I knew my home boys had my back.

It was amazing when we finally got to see the soldiers. They were being held in what looked like a local jail somewhere in the city of Belgrade. Before they were brought in, we waited for them in what looked like a very small courtroom. Along with Rev. Jackson and me was a CNN cameraman and a *New York Times* reporter. Rev. Jackson and I sat at a table to the right of the door. I sat to his left, closer to the door. The Serbian officials sat to our right and were elevated above us. A member of their military who may have been a judge conducted the proceedings. There was a court reporter there, and the Serbs had their own cameraman in the room.

Suddenly, Sergeant Stone appeared. He was a young soldier from Michigan who left behind a young wife and a baby. He looked scared. He saw me first. And probably thought to himself, just some guy in a suit. Then when he looked a little to the left, he gasped as he saw the familiar face of Rev. Jackson.

The Serbian military authorities began rushing us. They were obviously uncomfortable with the whole episode. In a few minutes, the air raid sirens started to sound, and the Serbs became even more anxious to rush the process along. In fact, they wanted to end the visit right then and there. Rev. Jackson was adamant. We weren't leaving until we saw all three of our boys. And he insisted that we see them all together. As the air raid sirens continued to bellow, the Serbs kept pressing to shut the whole thing down. But to his credit, Rev. Jackson was immovable. He kept repeating something like, "We're not going to flee, until we see all three." And he was remarkable. With the power of his personality and the audacity that makes people either love him or hate him, he was now controlling the agenda.

Think about it. Here we were. Visitors in a country our government was bombing, and while we're in one of their military facilities, our bombs start raining down again and there's Rev. Jackson, refusing to leave and conducting what is the equivalent of a sit-in. And the best part of it is he is going to get his way! The Serbs relented and despite the air attack, we saw all three of our soldiers. In fact, we would learn that this would be the first time any of them had seen each other since being taken prisoner.

Rev. Jackson was amazing the next day too, when we met with President Slobodan Milosevic at the Presidential Palace in Belgrade. When we heard the news that our request for a meeting was granted, I knew that we were going to get to bring our boys home. Unless we insulted Milosevic or screwed up in some other way, I believed all we had to do was reassert the reasons and make the same arguments we were making to the other Serbian officials directly to him. They had evidently been doing it. All we needed to do was make the same case to him.

We arrived for our meeting at the Presidential Palace. President Milosevic formally greeted us in a receiving line with other high-ranking officials, including the Foreign Minister. I was struck by how tall he was. He was much taller in person than he appeared on the television news. Rev. Jackson was the first to greet him, then me. When my time came, I introduced myself and said, "How are you?" in Serbian. I found it interesting that he didn't answer or say anything. He just limply shook my hand. In fact, he was cold and aloof, purposely standoffish. I believe he adopted that posture to send a message. Sentimentality was going to have no bearing on him.

Before we took our seats at the conference table in the room that CNN or MSNBC would show almost nightly on the evening news, Rev. Jackson immediately seized the initiative and took control. He grabbed Milosevic by one hand and me by the other, and before Milosevic had any idea what hit him, the Reverend said, "Let us pray." He then proceeded to lead us in prayer. I was fascinated by the scene. During the prayer, I stole a glance at Milosevic to watch his response. It was incredibly amusing. Here was this hard-core Marxist, Communist dictator, accused of genocide and ethnic cleansing and all sorts of acts of brutality, and he's holding Rev. Jackson's hand praying in a circle that includes other high-ranking officials in his government. We are praying, and all of it is being captured by cameras from around the world.

After the prayer, we all sat down to business. As expected, Milosevic sat at the head of the table. Rev. Jackson sat to his immediate right; I sat to his immediate left. The Yugoslavian Foreign Minister sat to my left, and right next to him was an English interpreter. The rest of the seats around the table were filled by members of our interfaith religious delegation and by other officials in the Yugoslavian government including Mr. Gajic. Refreshments were served: Turkish coffee, which is an espresso popular in the Balkans, some carbonated lemon and orange drinks, and some cookies. Milosevic nervously chain-smoked cigarettes throughout the meeting and consumed several cups of Turkish coffee.

And he spoke fluent English the entire time. After the pleasantries were concluded, and before Rev. Jackson could begin to make his pitch, Milosevic went on a mini-filibuster where he decried what the United States was doing to him. I found his identification of himself as a victim very interesting and very telling. He was so egomaniacal that what the innocent Serbian people had to endure wasn't something he felt even merited mentioning. His complaint was that the war and the bombing were being done to him. The United States and NATO were bombing him. And he couldn't understand how the leaders in the United States could be so wrong to believe what he claimed were lies and propaganda against him. Amazingly, he denied the reports of ethnic cleansing. He simply denied that it was happening. That was shocking to hear, that a leader of a not-insignificant European country would so blatantly deny the obvious and lie about it with the kind of conviction he was showing. He suggested that all the images being shown on the television news of civilians being forcibly removed from their homes weren't real. They were, he asserted, productions used for the purposes of propaganda. It was remarkable to witness. And as he was saying these things, I couldn't help but think about the thousands of displaced refugees I had seen only a few weeks before in a camp in Macedonia

The only time he employed the services of his interpreter was after Rev. Jackson concluded his opening appeal and invited me to join him in making the case on why our soldiers should be released to us. Rev. Jackson turned the floor over to me by saying, "Now your home boy would like to say a few things to you." Before I could begin, Milosevic turned to his interpreter and asked, "Vhat is home boy?" The interpreter didn't know. He was unfamiliar with the vernacular in the African-American community in America. I guess they don't teach that when learning English in Yugoslavia. In any event, the interpreter was struggling to interpret "home boy." And as he was stumbling and stammering, and with an impatient Milosevic glaring at him and waiting for an answer, I started to fear for this poor guy's life. I started to think. Would Milosevic have him executed if he couldn't interpret the word? It sounds outlandish, but who knows? Whatever the case, I intervened. I leaned over to the interpreter and whispered to him, "Tell him a home boy is a neighbor from your village." When the interpreter did that, Milosevic slowly nodded his head and turned his attention to me.

My case was simple. I told him my father was a Serbian immigrant and that, growing up, I was raised in the Serbian community through the Serbian Orthodox Church. I told him how my father was an officer in the Yugoslavian army during World War II. And how ironic I found it, that the last time my father saw Belgrade, Nazi bombs were being dropped on it. And that the first time I ever saw Belgrade was when my country's bombs were falling on it. I told him how proud my father was of being Serbian; and how he used to tell me all about the old country. And how sad it was for those of us who were Serbian-Americans to see what was happening to the country our parents came from. And that the kind of things the Serbs in Yugoslavia were being accused of were very painful for those of us who were Serbian Americans. I shared with him the sentiments of Serbian-Americans I had spoken to who couldn't understand how the United States could join an alliance against their old ally in two world wars by siding with some of those who fought us in those very wars. And that a lot of the things Serbs in Yugoslavia were saying to me were exactly the kinds of things Serbs in America believed as well.

But the reality of the situation was that the American people believed the allegations against the Serbs made by the international community. They believed that innocent civilians from Kosovo were being ethnically cleansed and removed from their homes. How could they not believe those things when every night on the evening news that is what they were being shown? They were seeing images of innocent people, tens of thousands of them, being forced to live in refugee camps in places like Macedonia because they had nowhere else to go.

And I told him that the simple reality was that the United States would never stop this war until those innocent civilians were allowed to go back home. And that he was so demonized that nobody would believe him if he sought a negotiated solution until he did something that was real. So I suggested he do something real. And something meaningful. Something that would be interpreted as an overture that would signal that he truly was interested in negotiating an end to the war. Releasing the three U.S. servicemen to Rev. Jackson and allowing him to bring the soldiers home would be seen by the American people as a genuine gesture and a step toward peace talks that could lead to the return of the Kosovar refugees and an end to the bombing.

Several hours after our meeting with Milosevic, we were summoned to meet with the foreign minister. He had an answer for us. Reading from a prepared statement, he told us that his government had decided to release the three U.S. servicemen to our delegation. He asked that we embargo the news of this decision for at least one hour so that his government could break the news first. Respecting his wishes and being extra careful that no one from our delegation leaked the news, we stayed at the Foreign Minister's residence for over an hour before returning to our hotel.

When we got back, the news was out. It was a media frenzy in the hotel lobby. Rev. Jackson's aides were busy gathering members of our delegation into one corner before any individual member of the delegation spoke to the media. Evidently, Rev. Jackson wanted to do all the talking by himself. As I was working my way around reporters who were shouting questions at me, I noticed that Rev. Jackson was crying. He was surrounded by some of the more sycophantic members of our delegation who were consoling him. I hate to sound cynical, but I was amused by the whole scene. We heard the good news more than an hour before, but the only time I saw anybody crying was when the cameras were on.

A Fox TV news reporter was trying to interview me as I was working my way toward our delegation. She was describing the scene for her viewers, and her description was filled with hyperbole. This will come as no surprise, but this is what the media likes to do. They exaggerate and overdramatize. She was describing how members of the delegation were hugging each other and crying. She then introduced me to her audience by saying something like, "I'm here with Congressman Blagojevich, a member of Rev. Jackson's delegation. He's in tears. The entire delegation is in tears. Everyone is hugging, and everyone is crying. Congressman Blagojevich, how do you feel?"

Well, I was feeling great. I was thrilled and elated, and I felt a deep sense of satisfaction that we were successful in our mission to bring our boys home. But I wasn't crying. I was nowhere near crying. And I wasn't about to pretend like I was.

The whole crying jag some members of our delegation were on struck me as ridiculously contrived. So the first thing I said when I answered that reporter's question was something like, "First of all, let me say, I'm not crying. But, I'll tell you something. I feel great. I feel great!" I then went on to answer her questions and explained how it all happened and where we were going from there.

We left Yugoslavia the next day. We went back the same way we came. We boarded a bus and drove from Belgrade, crossing the border into Croatia. The only difference this time was we had three new passengers with us. The Serbs gave us our soldiers to take home. And unlike the day before, I started to choke up as I was saying goodbye at the border to the Serbian officials who had been so helpful to us. Their lives were only going to get worse. Once we left, I was certain President Clinton would immediately begin to intensify the bombing. He couldn't allow the Serbs to think that he was going to go easy on them. I told my Chief of Staff what was going to happen next. I predicted that the war would be over in a month, but first Clinton would bomb the crap out of the Serbs. I told him, correctly it would turn out, that bringing our soldiers home was the beginning of the end of the war with Yugoslavia. But that in the immediate aftermath of our soldiers' release, the Clinton administration would talk tough, intensify the bombing, and cause more destruction, while at the same time back-channel talks with the Yugoslavian government that would lead to the return of the civilians and an end to the bombing. And that Milosevic would eagerly cut a deal along those lines as long as he is allowed to stay in power. In the meantime, the Serbian people would continue to suffer more intense bombing, and the innocent Kosovars would have to wait longer before they were able to return home.

When we returned to the United States, Rev. Jackson and I and some members of our interfaith delegation were invited to the White House to debrief President Clinton. Reverend Jackson was carrying with him a confidential personal message from Milosevic that he personally gave to the President. That evening, we met with the President, along with Vice-President Gore, Secretary of State Albright, and National Security Adviser Sandy Berger in the Roosevelt room in the White House.

Earlier in the day, we had arrived in D.C. We flew back to the states on a military plane from Germany and landed at Andrews Air Force Base where we were greeted by our families. I hadn't seen Patti or Amy for nearly two weeks, and to my great surprise they were waiting with the Jackson family for me at Andrews Air Force Base. Amy wasn't yet three, and her hair was naturally curly, giving her a little bit of a Shirley Temple look. In fact, Patti and Amy joined members of Rev. Jackson's family for a visit to the White House before our meeting started. I'll never forget President Clinton seeing Amy and asking me if she was my daughter. When I told him she was, he said, in that classic Clinton way, a sort of wistful look in his eyes that so many of his critics characterize as slick, "She's a beautiful child." Now I don't care what his critics say. How could you not like a guy who says that about your little girl?

Mission accomplished. It was risky going to Yugoslavia to free our soldiers. There was risk in voluntarily going into a country that was at war and being bombed. There was risk in voluntarily going into a country and dealing with that government and its leader who were considered international outlaws. There was risk that we could be taken hostage and used to negotiate an end, or at least a pause, in the bombing. I was aware of those risks going in. But I never felt that those risks outweighed the benefits of what I thought was a realistic chance to successfully secure the release of our soldiers. The more realistic risk was political. I was a relatively junior member of the United States Congress, acting on my own and negotiating around the wishes of the president and his administration. If I took part in a highly publicized visit to Yugoslavia and failed to bring the soldiers home, I could pay a steep political price for doing it.

Before we left for Yugoslavia, Congressman Henry Waxman from California expressed concern about the political risks of me going. He was doubtful that we had much of a chance to get the soldiers out. He warned me that I would be the one to bear the brunt of the blame of a failed mission. That I would be portrayed as a meddling Congressman who had no business getting involved in something like this. That I was being used by the Serbs for the purposes of propaganda, and he concluded by saying that Rev. Jackson couldn't possibly be a plus in my congressional district.

The concerns Henry expressed to me were genuine. He was sincerely trying to dissuade me because I believe he had my best interests at heart. I sincerely believed that as he was trying to convince me not to go. And I appreciated him for that. But I told him that I felt that, notwithstanding the risks involved, what would Teddy Roosevelt do if he were in this position? Would he be afraid to go because he was afraid to fail? Or would he dare greatly? I really believed we had a chance to succeed and bring our soldiers home. And I just couldn't look myself in the mirror if I didn't take that chance because I was afraid I might fail and would have to face the consequences for trying. I told him I didn't become a Congressman to just vote and press the yes or no button on the floor of the Congress. If that was all I was there to do, then it would be better if I ended up doing something else.

In many ways Rev. Jackson was a lot of what I thought he was before I got to know him better. But he was also a lot more than I thought he was after I had a chance to work with him to free our soldiers.

Of course he was shameless when it came to self-promotion and the use of the media. There was a P.T. Barnum quality surrounding our whole trip. I could cite dozens of examples during my Yugoslavian experience with him to prove that point. He was a media hog who jealously and tirelessly worked to keep the attention all to himself. I like to joke that on that trip with him, whenever there was a camera around he would position, and muscle and throw elbows around like he was a power forward fighting for a rebound. If you wanted to get on TV you better figure out a way around him. But I don't think I am saying anything new that most people don't already think. And besides, it's precisely that self promotional quality that is a major part of what makes him so successful in missions like these. He's a master at using and manipulating the media to help him succeed in achieving his objectives. It was precisely because Rev. Jackson was able to put the spotlight on our soldiers that we were successful in securing their release. And it was precisely because Rev. Jackson was the leading actor in the drama that it succeeded. For a brief moment, the eyes of the world were on Rev. Jackson as he became the central figure in a human interest story during a war the whole world was watching. And it was the attention he was able to garner that was the single biggest factor in successfully bringing our boys home.

And I saw another side to Rev. Jackson that I didn't know about. Sure, I believe he turned the tears on and off for the camera when the word was out that we were bringing the boys home. But I was with him long enough during that trip to see that he really cared about our soldiers. He was tireless in his efforts to secure their release. And I really believe that he would've stayed as long as it took and done whatever it took to bring them home. At our meeting with Milosevic at the presidential palace, Milosevic pulled Rev. Jackson aside and initially offered to give him one of our soldiers to take home. If Jesse Jackson's motives were solely about self-promotion, he would've jumped at the offer, met with the press, declared a huge success that nobody expected, and basked in the glow of bringing home another American captive. But he rejected that offer and made it very clear that all three came together, and he wasn't going to leave until he brought all three home.

And while the Reverend may not be very generous when it comes to sharing the spotlight in public, in private he is actually very different.

A case in point. Our delegation left the former Yugoslavia with our soldiers and flew to the Ramstein Air Force Base in Germany. It was there that we returned our soldiers to the designated American military officials. Before leaving the next day on a military plane for the United States, we spent the night at the Air Force base. Each of us were given our own room. Rev. Jackson was given a nice, simple room with a bed in it. I noticed it only because I was given a place to sleep too. They gave me, as a United States congressman who sits on the armed services committee, a nine-room suite that is reserved for the use of visiting generals. Somehow my accommodations didn't feel right, especially when Rev. Jackson was only given a single room. He was the general of our delegation. If anyone was going to have the general's quarters, I felt it should be him and not me. So when I offered to swap it for his room, he refused. He could not have cared less about the nine-room suite. If it were nine cameras, maybe it would have been a different story. But a nine-room suite, he was more than happy to let me have it.

CHAPTER FIVE

I ANNOUNCED MY CANDIDACY FOR GOVERNOR ON AUGUST 12, 2001, AT A RALLY AT THE FINKL STEEL COMPANY WHERE MY FATHER WORKED. I chose the Finkl Steel Company as the location for my announcement because it underscored why I wanted to become governor. I was going to champion the cause of working people like my parents.

The rally was a huge success. Thousands of people attended. The crowd was filled with people from diverse backgrounds. This was before the Barack Obama phenomenon. And while the crowd was nowhere near as big as the crowds he would later draw, for that time and for a gubernatorial race, it was unprecedented. And it was a great day. I spoke about both of my parents in my speech and got a little choked up when I recounted how hard and long my father worked in the very place his youngest son was announcing his race for governor. Patti looked beautiful. Amy was five and so cute. There was great promise ahead. I was filled with high hopes and optimism. I felt that way even though I was, at that time, considered a long shot by most of the political pros, pundits, and prognosticators.

And I was rolling the dice. Running for governor meant I couldn't keep the seat I was elected to in Congress. I had to voluntarily give up a seat in the United States Congress. A lot of people didn't believe I would. It was a seat that carried a certain prestige. A seat that was held before me by the legendary Dan Rostenkowski. A congressional seat that, if I gave it up, former Clinton aide Rahm Emanuel was likely to run for and win. A seat that was probably mine for life, if I wanted it. In fact, former U.S. Commerce Secretary Bill Daley told a friend of mine that I was making a big mistake to give up what he described as "a safe, lifetime seat."

And Bill Daley's observation had merit. The polls showed me running last or next-to-last in a field that included several potential candidates at the time I announced. Outside of my own congressional district and in places around Chicago, I was mostly unknown. I was told that no Congressman in modern Illinois political history had ever successfully run for governor directly from Congress. And I was considered by some of the pundits as a third-tier candidate.

So why did I decide to run for governor and risk losing what I had?

First, contrary to the conventional thinking among the professional political class, I never saw myself as being a lifetime member of Congress. Don't get me wrong, it's a great job. The pay is good. You have staff who work for you. Like U.S. Senators, you can see the world by taking so-called fact-finding missions. And when you do, you travel with great convenience. You're away from home a lot, generally 30 to 40 weeks a year, but you are home a lot too. And when you're in Washington doing your job, you're doing it in one of the most magnificent workplaces in the world. And the work involves important and interesting issues, and the resources are there to help you learn and master them if you want. You can give speeches on the floor of Congress. And people across America, all 47 of them, will see you do it on C-SPAN. You can literally sit in seats John F. Kennedy or Tip O'Neill once sat in. And while I believe most congressmen are not very recognizable back home, on Capitol Hill everybody knows you, and everybody kisses your ass. It's what I call the political industrial complex. The lobbyists and the staffers, especially the career staffers who are working their way up for different congressmen, hoping to climb the ladder to one day work for a senator or become a lobbyist, they are obsequious in the attention they give you, especially the lobbyists. They'll hold the door open for you, they'll hold your coat, they'll laugh at your jokes even if they're not funny, they'll politely listen when you pontificate. And even when you know they disagree with what you're saying, they never really tell you they disagree. Believe me, being a U.S. Congressman and working in Washington D.C. is a great job. But if you want to get things done for people, it can be a frustrating job.

Don't get me wrong. If you have the right kind of patience and are willing to run a marathon, you can be in a position to make an impact and do meaningful things for your country. And even as a junior member of Congress, you can find your spots and do good things. And, in the modern Congress, you can bypass some of the old seniority system by being a fundraising machine and raising money for your party's congressional campaign fund. That's how my successor, Rahm Emanuel, rose so quickly and in only a couple of terms joined the leadership team. He raised a boatload of money. And I am absolutely certain that I would have obtained any committee I wanted and rose through the ranks like Rahm Emanuel did, if only I wanted to spend my time in Congress raising money for the Democratic Congressional campaign committee. And by the way, I would have been good at it and would have succeeded. And it's what my top Washington D.C. staff hoped I would do.

But I decided not to do it.

Right after my election to Congress, I weighed my options and what career path I was going to take in my congressional career. I didn't want to just spend my time raising money for the Democratic Party. It didn't seem right to just do that. When I ran for Congress, I didn't promise the voters that if they send me to Washington I would work tirelessly, day and night and around the clock, to raise money for the Democratic Congressional campaign committee. I know I'm right when I say I wasn't elected by the people to do that. Though again, that is a practical way to work where, over time, a Congressman can do more for his constituents because he or she will be rewarded by the party leadership with a good committee that could lead to a lot of good things for the people back home. Still, it was not the path I wanted to take. I did help some of my colleagues raise money for their races, and of course I raised money for mine too. But I felt from the very beginning that if I ever had a chance to serve the public in a place where I could have a bigger impact, and do it sooner rather than later, I would take it. If an opportunity presented itself where I could make a more meaningful contribution, like my heroes in history, I wouldn't hesitate to seize the moment and go for it.

And if I bet wrong and lost, so what. I had already gone farther and faster than anyone would have predicted. And I didn't want to become one of those politicians who is afraid to lose what he has. Unless I kept moving forward, I was afraid I could become like a lot of others who make careers in Congress. They settle in and get comfortable with the lifestyle and the routine that they've grown accustomed to: go to the office, go to caucus, vote, go to the office, vote, go to the office, vote, go to the house gym, vote, go to the office, stop by the reception hosted by the pharmaceutical industry, and, since you're in the area, you might as well stop by the one hosted by the sugar beet industry, and then go to dinner, gratis, to one of the many fancy steak joints some lobbyist wants to take you to. And you do it, day in and day out, week after week, month after month, year after year. And then, before long, before you know it, my God, where has the time gone? And you find yourself sitting in your office with your Chief of Staff calculating your pension. Believe me, there are a lot worse things than that. Yet the vision of me becoming that kind of person scared the you know what out of me. That's not what I wanted to be. I was afraid I could become that. And far worse than that, I was afraid of becoming one of those politicians who was *afraid*. Afraid to lose what he's got. Afraid to fight for what he believed in. Afraid to stand up. Afraid to keep moving forward. You will never win what you want if you're afraid to lose what you have.

And I wanted to become governor. I'm not a patient man. In many ways, that's a fault. In other ways, it's a virtue. I don't like just waiting around and not doing anything. And a lot of what is the inherent role of the legislative branch is to check and balance what the executive branch wants to accomplish. My nature is more suited to drive, to do something rather than check and stop it. And while holding executive office puts you directly on the firing line, if you're tired of the gridlock, the excessive partisanship and the posturing of the legislative process, then the executive branch is the place to be. I was impatient and wanted to do things. Get things done for people. I wanted to be where the action was; where you can be the one to drive an agenda you believe in. That's what presidents do. It's what governors do. It's what mayors do. The executive branch of government is where things get done.

The Democratic primary for governor in 2002 was very competitive and hotly contested. When the field was set, there were three of us who ran. Roland Burris, who had strong support in the African-American community and held statewide office before, began the race as the front runner. Former Chicago public school CEO Paul Vallas, who had developed a national reputation as having fixed a broken Chicago school system, was also in the race. He was a very formidable opponent. Our internal polling showed that education was the most important issue that voters cared about. In addition to that, Paul Vallas was a bit of a media darling. He spent years cultivating the Chicago media when he was the head of the Chicago schools. In fact, I was told that starting in the mid-1990s, he had received more media hits than anybody in the Chicagoland area with the exception of Michael Jordan. The smart money was on him to win.

I was the third candidate in the field. I began the race with the broadest and most diverse political coalition of the three candidates. I had raised the most money and had the most campaign contributions on hand when the race began. I had spent the previous two years quietly building support around the state among Democratic political organizations. Especially among Democratic Party chairmen in downstate Illinois—the areas outside of the Chicagoland area. My father-in-law, who is a Democratic committeeman in Chicago, helped me build support among other Democratic political leaders in the city. And as the field began to take shape, I was able to win the support of most of the labor organizations in the state. And even though the first major poll taken about two months before the primary showed Roland Burris with 30% of the vote, Paul Vallas with 23%, and me with 17%, my campaign team and I believed I was well-positioned to make a run and have a chance to win. The key was for me to win the downstate vote.

In fact, my only chance of winning was to win the downstate vote. And win it big. Anything short of that meant I would lose. Generally speaking, two thirds of the Democratic primary vote comes out of the Chicagoland area—that includes the city of Chicago itself, as well as the surrounding suburbs. All three of us had our own base of support within Chicago. Roland Burris had overwhelming support in the African-American community. Paul Vallas had the support of good government, reform-minded voters. I had a strong base of support among Chicago's white ethnic working class, the Latino community and many of the Democratic political organizations in the city.

Because of his base of support in the African-American community, Roland Burris was strongest in the city. Because of his reputation and work in the Chicago schools, Paul Vallas was strongest in the surrounding suburbs. He was also the candidate of the elites. I believe he won the endorsement of every major newspaper across the state except for the *Chicago*

Sun-Times, who endorsed me. Because all three of us were candidates who lived in Chicago, none of us were very strong downstate. Roland Burris had the edge starting out because he had run statewide so many times before, and he was actually raised in downstate Centralia, Illinois. But our polling showed that the vast majority of voters downstate were open to persuasion. And even though I began the race with 8% of the downstate vote, my pollster, Fred Yang, predicted that with my personal story and the right message, we had the potential to not only win but actually dominate the downstate vote.

Now that's a remarkable prediction. At the time I ran, most of the so-called political experts thought I had no chance downstate. I was born and raised and lived in the city of Chicago. There's a great deal of distrust among downstate voters for people from the city. I had a record as both a Congressman and a state legislator of pushing what I considered to be common sense gun legislation like banning assault weapons. But the issue of gun control is considered a death knell for anyone wanting to win votes downstate. And lastly, my last name was viewed by many as a major stumbling block to winning votes in places like Southern or Central Illinois.

In July of 2001, before the race began, I was running last with about 13% of the vote. Fred's polling showed exactly what would happen if we executed our game plan, and Paul Vallas executed his. When Vallas reminded voters of his record on education, he soared in the city and in the surrounding suburbs. There was nothing we could do about it. That issue and his association with it gave him a powerful advantage. So our goal was to do the best we could and to stay as close as we could in the Chicagoland area. Run second to Vallas in the suburbs, and with the strong support of the Latino community, and the support of much of the Chicago Democratic political organizations, try to run a competitive second or third in the city. If we could do those two things, then the road to victory traveled through downstate. But according to Fred Yang, and incidentally, every one of his predictions proved right, for me to win the primary I would have to win right around 50% of the downstate vote in a three-person race. That's a tall order. But as events would play out, that's exactly what happened.

In spite of the naysayers and the pundits, I always knew I would do well among downstate voters. I shared the same values and the same life experience as most of them. It wasn't an issue of geography—big city versus small town or urban versus rural. And it wasn't about the polarizing social issues that politicians use to divide people, like gun control and abortion. The common bond I believed I had with downstate voters was bigger, more basic, and more real. The values I'm talking about are the values that really matter to people. Does the guy seeking my vote understand what's important to me? Does he understand my life experience? Does he know or even have an idea of what I want out of life? And what's holding me back? Did he share the same struggles in life? Does he believe in the same priorities? Does he want the same things? Is this the kind of guy who will be on my side?

I liked to say when I was in Southern Illinois speaking to families who worked in the coal mines that had my father emigrated to the southern part of our state instead of the northern part, he would have worked in a coal mine instead of a steel factory. Whether it's Northern Illinois or Southern Illinois, whether he worked as a steel worker or a coal miner, it's the same life experience. My family knew the same struggles their families knew. They took pride in and viewed hard work as a virtue, just as they did. They loved their country, they believed in God, and their sons and daughters served in the military when their country called. They had the same fears, faced the same challenges, and had the same hopes and dreams for their children. Their life story and the things they cared about were the same as mine. Don't give me something for free, just give me an opportunity. An opportunity to work, to get ahead, to provide for my family, and to build a better life for my children. And don't make me be the one who has to keep paying for the politicians and government who are making the decisions.

I really believed that if given the chance, once I began to communicate to them, it would be the hard-working people in downstate Illinois who would be the reason I would win the Democratic primary.

And they were.

I won the Democratic primary by two percentage points statewide because I won better than 50% of the downstate vote. The final totals came in showing I received 36% of the vote, Paul Vallas received 34%, and Roland Burris, 30%. Just as we had anticipated, Vallas was a big winner in the suburban areas, but I achieved my goal of running second there. Roland Burris took the city on the strength of winning around 85% of the African-American vote. Vallas and I essentially tied in the city. He outpolled me by a half of a percentage point. In fact, I was told of an exit poll that had me winning about two thirds of the Hispanic vote in the city, which is why I essentially tied for second.

But it was the downstate vote that decided the election. All of the hard work campaigning under the radar screen in small counties in southern and central and northwestern Illinois paid off. Of the 96 downstate counties in Illinois, I won every one except two. And I was winning them by big margins. Some by better than 70% of the vote. And in Washington County, where people for generations worked in the coal mines, I received 77% of the vote.

I was now the Democratic nominee for governor ready to run against the Republican nominee, the current Illinois Attorney General Jim Ryan. Two years before I began the journey to run for governor, Jim Ryan was considered by the political establishment as unbeatable. He had an approval rating of better than 70%. And he had shown great courage and had rightly earned the sympathy of people across Illinois by the way he handled the loss of his daughter to cancer. His presence as the likely Republican nominee for governor is what kept more prominent, bigger-named Democrats from running. I always knew, for example, that our senior senator in Illinois, Dick Durbin, was unlikely to be willing to risk losing his Senate seat by running against Jim Ryan for governor. Durbin had too much to lose. He's an effective United States senator, and he was rising in the Senate leadership structure and was in a good place to deliver for Illinois. His aversion to risk losing what he had and where he was going paved the way for me. Because had Durbin decided to run, the Democratic Party establishment in the state would have quickly coalesced behind him. And I would have been without oxygen, unable to breathe. I wouldn't have been capable of building the coalition I built, or raise the money I raised.

After twenty-six years in the wilderness, Democratic activists and most, but not every, Democratic political leader throughout Illinois was hungry for a Democratic governor. Winning a tough and competitive primary put me in a strong position to compete in the general election. And notwithstanding Jim Ryan's personal approval rating, he was on the wrong side of history. Slowly but inexorably, the state of Illinois had been drifting more Democratic. The incumbent Republican Governor, who shared the same last name as the Republican nominee, was under criminal investigation and was unpopular. But Jim Ryan's biggest problem, and my biggest advantage, was that voters wanted change. This was going to be a change election. And when you're on the right side of change and the other guy is not, it is hard to swim against those currents. He was a current statewide office holder, the standard bearer of the party in power, with the last name of Ryan. He was the status quo. I never held statewide office, I was the nominee of the party out of power, and my last name was Blagojevich. Nobody with a name like that ever won statewide office before. You can't get much more change than that.

Unlike the primary race, the polls showed that I began the general election ahead. In fact, the first public poll immediately after the primary had me winning 52% to 34%. I never looked back, and I never trailed in the general election. I worked and campaigned around the clock as I always did in my elections. I took nothing for granted and respected my opponent. And as I always did, I refused to talk about, much less even consider, anything having to do with setting up an administration. I believe in karma, and I wasn't about to disrespect the fates or, for that matter, the people. Polls are just polls. Until the people decide, I wasn't going to take anything for granted. So when my opponent announced that Jim Edgar, a former Republican governor, had agreed to serve as the head of his transition team after the election, I spurned suggestions that I should make a similar announcement. I wouldn't hear of any talk about who might be appointed to what if I was fortunate enough to be elected governor. I approached every day in that campaign focused solely and exclusively on winning the election.

As it turned out, the night of the general election was the opposite of primary night. On primary night, Paul Vallas took a huge lead early and looked like he was going to win. In fact, CNN projected him the winner. But as the night grew older, and the downstate votes were being counted, sometime after 11 p.m., I had taken the lead, and it wasn't until before midnight that I was declared the winner.

On the night of the general election, I did some last minute campaigning at a busy subway station in the African-American community. As I was climbing the steps to my home, my neighbor who lived across the street shouted his congratulations to me. I thanked him and said I was cautiously optimistic. But his congratulations were premature. According to my watch, it was only three minutes to seven. That meant the polls hadn't yet closed. And I didn't want to jinx anything. Whether my watch was running three minutes slow, or the networks were racing to be the first ones to call it, my neighbor insisted that his congratulations were warranted. He heard on the radio that CBS had projected me the winner.

I held my victory party at the Finkl Steel Company where I announced my candidacy for governor. My media team purposely scheduled my appearance onstage for 10 p.m., timed so I could speak at the top of the live local news. The crowd at the Finkl Steel Company was huge. There must've been more than 10,000 people there. Again, this was pre-Obama. Up to that time in Illinois, the crowd at Finkl Steel that night was unprecedented. No one ever saw anything like it before. And I'm sure Obama hadn't either. But he too saw that crowd. How do I know? Because he was there.

After I gave my victory speech and jumped off the stage to shake hands with supporters, I worked my way along the rope line and saw state Senator Barack Obama. All by himself. Waiting patiently in the crowd to congratulate me and shake my hand. When I saw him, I invited him over the rope line to say hello to Patti. Little did I know, and I don't even think he knew, that in six short years the huge crowd celebrating my victory that night would by his standards be considered modest. And that in six short years Barack Obama would be elected President of the United States.

And me? I would be arrested, locked up, and charged with crimes I didn't commit.

I gave my victory speech as planned. Pat Quinn introduced me. I climbed the stage to the remix of the Elvis song, "A Little Less Conversation, a Little More Action." And when I saw for the first time the size of the crowd, and that they were there celebrating my election as governor, I got caught up in the moment. The first words out of my mouth were, "I'm all shook up." And then, keeping with the Elvis theme and staying off script, I told my supporters, that "my heart was full, and that I had nothing but a whole bunch of Hunka Hunka Burnin' love for each and every one of you."

It has always been my custom to get up early the morning after I won an election and thank the voters for electing me. To personally and directly thank them for the trust and confidence they placed in me. For years, my mother worked as a ticket agent for the Chicago transit Authority at the Jefferson Park train station. It was my practice to go there to thank the commuters for their support. Going on two hours of sleep, I arrived at a little after 6 a.m. and spent the next two and a half hours shaking hands, thanking voters, and talking to people. Among the hands I shook that morning belonged to a guy on his way to work who had some simple advice. He said, "Just do the right thing." That's a simple thing to say. *Just do the right thing.* It's not a fancy way to put it. But it is eloquent in its simplicity.

Because that is what you should do when the people elect you to an office like governor. And that is what I believe I always tried to do. Throughout my six years as governor, I would think about that guy from time to time and what he said to me. It would help me keep my eye on the ball and not lose sight of the things I wanted to do for people as their governor.

I still think about him. I wonder what he thinks now. It pains and hurts me that he might think I let him down. I sure hope he doesn't think that. Because I didn't. I took the trust and confidence the people placed in me both times they elected me their governor and worked as purposefully as I could to do the right thing for them.

I hope and pray that guy is keeping an open mind. Because it's hard-working, decent people like him who I fought for and had in mind when I made decisions as governor. I could give you all kinds of reasons why I must be vindicated, and not letting that guy down is near the top of the list.

CHAPTER SIX

LIFE FOR MY MOTHER AND FATHER WAS FILLED WITH HARDSHIP AND STRUGGLE. They worked long and hard but never complained. They never owned a home of their own. They didn't take vacations. They never knew how to relax. They never had fancy clothes or owned an expensive car. We were a one-car family. When they bought a car, they had it until it broke down. They didn't eat at fancy restaurants. In fact, they hardly ate out at all. We ate at home. That was the most economical. On those rare occasions when we did have dinner at a restaurant, it was a big event, and you better be sure you ate everything and didn't waste anything, because as my mother would say, "This is costing us money." They scrimped and saved wherever they could. When my brother and I outgrew our old clothes, my mother would, out of necessity, mostly buy my older brother new ones. I wouldn't get many. I was the younger child; I got the hand-me-downs. My parents paid their taxes. They paid their bills. They helped others. They were honest people. And above all, they sacrificed for their children. What they deprived themselves, they gave to their children. Their lives were all about giving their sons the kinds of opportunities they never had or could ever dream of having.

My parents were like most parents. They wanted life to be better for their kids than it had been for themselves. And their story isn't unusual. It's the story of hard-working people everywhere, who struggle and sacrifice for their children in the same way my parents sacrificed for me. And those are the people and those are the families that I dedicated myself to when I became governor of Illinois.

Shortly after I was first elected governor, I began to really start thinking about what I wanted to do with the office. I ran a campaign based on a platform of creating opportunity for families. If I was elected governor, I would work to create opportunity for people across Illinois. In fact, one of our campaign taglines was "Blagojevich means Opportunity." But now that I was governor, I began to ask myself, what did that really mean? Opportunity for whom? Well, I knew the answer to that. I wanted to create opportunity for people like my parents. People who were willing to work hard and were willing to sacrifice but all too often weren't given a chance to do it. And opportunity for what? Well, that's easy too. An opportunity to build a better life. The basic and obvious things like a good job where you can get ahead. Good schools where your kids can learn the things they'll need so they can have a good education and a passport to a better future. Healthcare for your children and for you. You can't pursue happiness if you're not healthy. And of course a lot of other things. I knew who I wanted to help but the real question was how do you do it? What can government do to help people create opportunities that they otherwise wouldn't have?

So here I am, on November 5, 2002, elected governor of Illinois, the fifth largest state in the United States. Here I am, the son of an immigrant factory worker and a working mother. Here I am, the product of a public school education. I got my first job when I was nine years old shining shoes, and I never stopped working. Through the years growing up, I worked in factories and I worked construction. I worked in a meatpacking plant and washed pots and pans and swept floors on the Alaskan pipeline. I delivered pizzas and, for a while, sold World Book encyclopedias over the telephone. I had a lot of other jobs, and now, suddenly, I have a new job. I'm the governor of Illinois.

After I was elected, I thought about my life and everything that came before. I thought about my parents and their hard work and sacrifice. I thought about my upbringing and the things I saw growing up. And I was under no illusions. I realized probably better than anybody how improbable my journey was. A journey that lead me to become the governor of Illinois. Nobody in my family ever did it. Nobody in the neighborhood I grew up in ever had an opportunity like this. I was in a rare and unique position that few people are ever in, much less someone who came from where I did. So I was determined to do something with it. To help people. To get things done for people. To help people and their families not have to go through some of the things I saw growing up. To ease their burdens and lessen their hardships. Help them get access to affordable healthcare, for example. But where you can't help them, at least protect them. Protect them from things like higher taxes, for example. To shake up a system that served itself at the expense of the people. To change that system and make it work for the people. I wasn't going to play it safe. I wasn't going to just go along and get along. I was going to play it tough and fight to get results for the people. And if that meant I would ruffle feathers and make some enemies and have fewer friends, then so be it. I wasn't going to just give lip service to the sacrifice of my parents. I was going to sacrifice to help people like my parents. And I wasn't going to squander this unique opportunity. I was of the people, and I was going to be for the people.

There's nothing complicated about my governing philosophy. It's not the product of the Harvard School of Public Policy. Nor is it the product of years studying the writings of the great political philosophers. After I was elected, I resolved to use the power of the position to simply "do unto others as you would have others do unto you." That was my philosophy. The simple lesson that I learned in Sunday school called the Golden Rule. My purpose as governor was to do for people what I would want done for me and for my family. And to give to the people the same kinds of opportunities that those of us who make the rules give to ourselves. And I wasn't going to forget where I came from. I was determined to push policies and set priorities that would help people like my parents and the families I grew up with. People without lobbyists. People without a voice. People who do most of the work and pay most of the taxes but are too busy raising their families to know what their elected officials in state government are doing to them, or even who their elected officials in state government are.

Perhaps the most significant way a governor can do the most good for the most people is through the state budget. Unlike the federal government, the Constitution in Illinois requires that every year the state operates under a balanced budget. The spending side has to match the revenue side. When I was a candidate for governor and running on a platform to create opportunity for families, I would say over and over again that I wasn't running to be the chief accountant of the state. I was running to be its chief executive. I was going to use the more than $50 billion state budget to help people. I was going to end business as usual and the old way of doing things. And I was going to change the way the state budget was used. I would balance the state budget, but use more of it as a vehicle to help the people rather than have it be something the taxpayers had to help balance. I was going to reorder the spending priorities of the state and help create opportunities for families that they otherwise wouldn't have. And I was going to do it without raising taxes on the people.

This is a very important point. A budget is about setting priorities. It's about where the money *should* be spent, and who should pay for the spending. In the halls of state government where the lobbyists work and reign supreme, way too much of the state budget is invested to advance their interests, and it's done on the backs of the people. It's the people who get stuck paying for the priorities the lobbyists want and that they get the lawmakers to pass. And it's the people who get stuck doing it through higher taxes and higher fees. The lawmakers usually pass those things late at night, when the fewest people are watching.

In his book *God's Politics*, Jim Wallis writes about the biblical prophet Isaiah and what he offered as God's vision of a good society. That vision for a good society was all about giving the people the opportunity for basic things that included fair and good wages, housing and healthcare, safety and security. Isaiah's platform, Wallis writes, links religious values with economic justice, and moral behavior with political commitment. And he calls government budgets, moral documents. He writes that "a budget shows what we most care about and how that compares to other things we care about. So when politicians present their budgets, they are really presenting their priorities."

There is something immoral, that's right, immoral, when the people who make the rules can give themselves and their families the best of everything but either oppose or don't try to do the same thing for the families who elected them. Politicians give phony speeches saying they support expanding healthcare, but as soon as they're elected, it's all talk, no action. They don't even try to pass it. Or they vote against it when they're told to. Or they never even intended to vote for it. It was just something they said in a television commercial because the issue polled well.

I believe healthcare is a fundamental right. It's an issue that, obviously, can literally be about life or death. And I have met too many people over the years who have suffered because they didn't have it. The life, the well-being, the health of your children, your loved ones, your family–the opportunity and the chance to get well if you're sick is, I believe, a fundamental human right. And it is therefore a moral issue. It's the Golden rule. And lawmakers know how important it is because they give it to themselves. They give it to themselves but all too often they don't give it to others. And when the men and women who are elected to make the laws and make the rules give themselves and their children the best healthcare available, and they then oppose it for others, or are indifferent and sit on the sidelines while others go without, I believe they are immoral hypocrites. They are immoral, selfish, phony, hypocritical politicians who look after themselves and their own interests but don't do anything to help others. And there's a lot of that immorality going around these days.

Today in America, the richest and most powerful country in the world, more than 45 million Americans don't have access to healthcare despite the constant talk of politicians in election after election. The men and women who make the rules have it. But more than 45 million of their fellow citizens don't.

Giving people healthcare, making it affordable, making it accessible and comprehensive, giving people the opportunity to see a doctor if they're sick or to keep them from getting sick, was my single biggest priority when I was governor. And I did it. Better than any other governor in America. Better than any one of my predecessors in Illinois. It is the issue I fought the most for. And it is the area where I did the most. I am most proud of what I've been able to do in expanding access to healthcare for people in Illinois. In the six years I was governor, I expanded access to comprehensive healthcare to more than one million people. That's better than any other state in America.

Illinois became the only state in America to give all uninsured women access to routine mammograms and Pap smears that could help detect, treat, and cure breast and cervical cancer. I created the All Kids program in Illinois, the first program in our nation's history that guaranteed access to comprehensive healthcare to every child in our state. And hundreds of thousands of kids have benefited from the program. And children who might have otherwise died are now alive and have been cured of their illnesses because of the medical care they have received.

I can't say for sure when my interest in fighting to expand healthcare began. Maybe it came from what I saw and lived when I was growing up. I was ten years old on October 14, 1966, when my 12-year-old cousin Eli died of leukemia. It was a Saturday night. My mother and father and my brother and I were just walking into our apartment after an event in our church, and the telephone was ringing. Before my mother answered, I had a bad feeling. My cousin had been ill for over a year and had recently been hospitalized at the Children's Memorial Hospital in Chicago. When my mother answered the telephone, and I heard her gasp and then start to cry, I knew my cousin had died.

My cousin Eli was a very intelligent, good-natured, and good-hearted child. In some ways, he was like another older brother to me. He was the only child of my aunt Violet and uncle Willie. He was no stranger to illness. He was a special needs child who went to a public school with other special needs children. He was born with hydrocephalus, a condition that caused his head to be a lot larger than those of other children. He also suffered from the physical impairment of his left arm and left leg which caused him to walk with a noticeable limp. His physical impairments left him the object of other children's ridicule. Children can be cruel. And as I recall, the cruelty came mostly from other, older boys. I can't say that I ever remember him being teased or tormented by any girls. But my cousin Eli was a boy with great character. He concealed whatever hurt he felt from the teasing. And despite his physical infirmity, he played sports and was, all things considered, a very good athlete. And his father taught him to stand up for himself. He would stand up to bullies who picked on him because of his disability. And because he was smarter and wittier than they were, he would verbally get the best of them. But then it would turn physical. And he would courageously fight back even though he never had a chance. He would invariably get hurt and have to endure the mockery of the other boys who wanted to curry favor with the big stupid bully who picked on a disabled kid. But my cousin never flinched and never complained. And he never bore a grudge. He had no malice for the others who treated him so maliciously. And moments before he died, he told his father he wasn't afraid.

My aunt and uncle lost their only child. As a parent, I cannot imagine how unbearable a loss like that could be. When they lost their son, they lost everything in life that was important to them. But they also lost their small business and the building they owned. They couldn't afford all the medical bills. And because of their son's catastrophic illness, they went bankrupt.

A lot has changed in America since the 1960s. But unfortunately, what happened to my aunt and uncle is still happening to millions of families across America today. The number one cause of personal bankruptcies in America is unpaid medical bills. Millions of families are one illness away from losing everything. Decent, hard-working Americans like my aunt and uncle who are trying to get ahead in order to build a better life for their children shouldn't be in a position to lose everything if a loved one gets sick. And when the middle class and working people can't afford the high cost of healthcare, something is wrong. That is not the place America is supposed to be. It's a broken promise. And it breaks the very promise our forefathers made more than 250 years ago.

We hold these truths to be self-evident that all men are created equal. That they are endowed by their Creator with certain unalienable rights–the right to life, liberty, and the pursuit of happiness. That is the promise of the American dream. It's right there, written in the Declaration of Independence. It held out the promise to all the people that they had a right to an equal opportunity to live, to be free, and to try to find happiness. It was the original idea behind the Declaration of Independence. It's what is behind our nation's struggle for freedom. It's the unifying principle of our democracy. And it is for that principle that our founding fathers risked their lives when they formed a more perfect union. It's what Abraham Lincoln fought to preserve and expand during the Civil War. It's what he died for. It's the ideal that Franklin Roosevelt rallied a nation behind during the depths of the Great Depression. It's the principle that Dr. Martin Luther King marched for and so eloquently repeated in his "I Have a Dream" speech where, on the steps of the Lincoln Memorial, he said, "We hold these truths to be self-evident that all men are created equal...." It is that unifying principle that spurred the civil rights movement, and it was that principle that Dr. King, like Lincoln, gave his life for. And it is that promise and that principle that millions of brave men and women were told they were fighting to preserve when they gave their lives in our nation's wars.

I read the history of the United States as the constant struggle to make the promise of the Declaration of Independence available to everyone. The progress we've made in America to expand opportunities for people since the founding of our country is all about making the words in the Declaration of Independence something more than merely a lofty, poetic dream. The right to pursue happiness has real meaning. How can you be happy if you're not healthy? And if you're sick, or a loved one is sick, how can you even pursue trying to be happy if you can't afford a doctor who can make you healthy? Thomas Jefferson, Abraham Lincoln, Franklin Roosevelt, and Dr. Martin Luther King were all right when they insisted that the promise made in the Declaration of Independence had to be redeemed by a real, achievable purpose where everyone has an equal chance in the race of life.

Well, if you're sick, and you can't treat your illness, but your friend on the other side of the tracks can, then you don't have an equal chance in the race of life to pursue, or much less be, happy.

So what can government do about it? What is the proper role of government in healthcare? How much can government do for people that they can't do for themselves? Or how much should people do for themselves, that they shouldn't expect from government?

Good citizens must take personal responsibility and not expect government to solve all of their problems. That is certainly true. And yet there are a lot of good citizens who can't get their problems solved without government to help them. How active should government be? And in what areas should government be active in?

Those are the questions that the best and the brightest in America have been debating since the beginning of our Republic. They are important questions. Abraham Lincoln had an answer for them. Lincoln said, "The legitimate object of government is to do for a community of people whatever they need to have done, but cannot do, at all, or cannot, so well do, for themselves–in their separate, and individual capacities.

What more can you ask of someone if they are responsible and go to work or run a small business and pay their taxes and raise their children but through no fault of their own are not earning enough money to afford the right kind of health insurance policies for their family? So they go about meeting their responsibilities, but they are vulnerable if, God forbid, they get sick or one of their children gets sick. They not only can't afford to get well, but if they do get medical care, they could end up losing everything they spent their lives working for.

Access to affordable, comprehensive healthcare is something I believe Abraham Lincoln would acknowledge the people need to have done. But with the healthcare system in America today, and the power of the insurance industry and their lobbyists, it is also something they cannot do, at all, or cannot by themselves do so well, without the help of government to provide the opportunities to get healthcare where they otherwise don't exist.

When we allow a system where some of our citizens can have the best medical care available, and others can't get any, we are breaking the promise of the Declaration of Independence.

I believe expanding access to healthcare for all Americans is the civil rights issue of our time. And when I was elected, I was most excited by the prospect that I could, as the governor of the fifth biggest state in the United States, expand healthcare for people in ways that other states would emulate. That is what happened. A number of states, including Massachusetts, Pennsylvania, and California followed my lead and have provided or are trying to provide access to healthcare for all children. I was the first governor in the United States to defy the FDA and go to Canada to get the same medicine made by the same companies, but for up to 50% less for our senior citizens, who now no longer have to choose between whether they can afford their medicines or their groceries. Three other states followed my lead. Illinois became the first state in the nation to provide routine breast and cervical cancer screenings to all uninsured women. Other states are looking to do the same.

Some of the great change in American history starts at the state level. Today it's hard to imagine there was ever a time when children in our country were not guaranteed a free public education. But it wasn't until the 1840s that the state of Massachusetts became the first state in the United States to do so. Other states followed, and now it would be unthinkable if it were any other way. I hope there will be a time in America when our children, or our children's children, will look back and say with incredulity, "You know, there was a time in America where people didn't have a chance to see a doctor." And I believe that so much of the progress that's been made, and will be made, in the area of expanding healthcare will be because of initiatives that start at the state level.

If a woman is diagnosed with breast cancer, but her breast cancer is detected early enough, she has better than a 95% chance of surviving. Conversely, if that same breast cancer is diagnosed late, then that woman's chance of surviving drops to as low as 26%. It is undeniable; early detection of breast cancer saves lives. And early detection is possible if women have access to periodic and routine mammograms.

Women who have comprehensive health insurance coverage can get those mammograms. But women who don't have health insurance, or have inadequate insurance, are forced to go without the necessary screenings that could detect breast cancer early. There's a reason why more African-American women die of breast cancer than white women, even though there is proportionately a higher incidence of breast cancer among white women. There is a higher proportion of African-American women who are uninsured, and, as a result, their breast cancer is discovered too late to cure it. This inequity in opportunity is something I saw growing up. I bet almost every family has seen it too.

My cousin Carol was a beautiful young mother who died of cancer nearly a dozen years after my cousin Eli passed away. She was in her late twenties when she died. She left behind her husband and two young children. Back in the 1970s, breast cancer awareness was not what it is today. Nor was the quality of medical care as good. But in the case of my cousin Carol and her older sister Patsy, who would die of breast cancer as well, had their cancer been detected early I believe things would have been different for them. And whether it wasn't detected because of a lack of health insurance or because routine mammography was not something women did back then, the fight to give access to regular breast cancer screenings to every woman in the state of Illinois was inspired by what happened to my cousins.

Among the reasons cited by the Legislature to unconstitutionally remove me from office was that I used the executive powers of the governor to find ways around the gridlock of the Legislature to get things done to help people. I couldn't get the Illinois House to pass the bill to provide routine mammograms to uninsured women. Speaker Michael Madigan wouldn't call the bill for a vote. When I found a way around the Legislature to get it done, both Speaker Madigan and his daughter Attorney General Lisa Madigan worked with Republican business leaders to sue me and take me to court to try to undo some of my successful efforts to give people healthcare who otherwise wouldn't get it.

What kind of Democrats are those two Madigans when they can work behind the scenes, in a sneaky and dishonest way, where lawsuits are drafted by Mike Madigan's lawyer, and he persuades two wealthy Republican businessmen to file lawsuits to use the courts to keep poor people from being able to see a doctor? The two Madigans have the best healthcare money can buy. They have it for themselves, and they have it for their kids. They dress up as Democrats but they remind me of wolves dressed in sheep's clothing. To use the courts to keep poor people from receiving healthcare, while they give speeches and send out political advertisements claiming to support expanding healthcare, is worse than cynical. When two people can single-handedly prevent tens of thousands of people from getting healthcare, and some of those people may ultimately die because they couldn't get the medical treatment they need, then something is wrong. It's immoral. And what really makes it immoral is their motivation.

I'm convinced that both Mike and Lisa Madigan decided to work against my healthcare initiatives after I turned them down when they asked me for nearly $400,000 in campaign contributions. At a meeting in my campaign office at 2 p.m. on January 14, 2006, Mike Madigan asked me for two and a half percent of the campaign funds I currently had on hand. I was running for reelection and facing a Democratic primary challenge. I was also facing a general election opponent who was a popular state treasurer and had never lost an election.

Mike Madigan requested the meeting. The purpose was to raise money for what he calls his coordinated campaign. In addition to Mike and Lisa Madigan, also present at the meeting was Illinois Secretary of State Jesse White, the president of the Illinois state Senate Emil Jones, and some staff members.

I remember this meeting like it was yesterday. I was being double teamed by the two Madigans. Mike Madigan sat to my left. Lisa Madigan sat to my right. For Lisa Madigan to even be at my campaign office as part of an effort to muscle me for nearly $400,000 in campaign funds was incredibly unethical. Nearly a year before, she had subpoenaed campaign fundraising records from the very office she was now sitting in. For her to attend a meeting at that very office, working with her father who is asking me for two and a half percent of those very campaign funds she was investigating, was both blatantly hypocritical and grossly unethical. It was designed by the Madigans as a subtle threat. While dear old dad is literally and figuratively putting the arm on me from my left side, she is subtly holding a gun to my head from the right. Their message was easily interpreted. If I didn't fork over two and half percent of my campaign fund, which at the time was exactly $396,491.25, then they were both going to make trouble for me. It was subtle but purposeful. And that's what they intended and that's what they did. And it made me feel like I was being shaken down. I told an aide before the meeting that if I didn't give the Madigans the money, there was no doubt they would retaliate against me politically and, even worse, punish the people I was working to help. I believed that if I turned them down they both would make me pay. Not the next day or the next week, but over time. It was very predictable. It's how they operate. And I was right. Payback came. And it came from both of them.

Lisa waited to strike and began to pay me back for not giving her father the money they asked for by using her office of the Attorney General to investigate me. A few months later, her office leaked the news that she issued subpoenas looking into the hiring practices of my administration. She leaked that news to the *Chicago Tribune* and waited to do so until my campaign for reelection was in full swing. It was during the Fourth of July weekend, while all of us were campaigning at parades.

Then later during the summer, on Democratic Day at the Illinois State Fair, she announced that as the Democratic Attorney General she would not be endorsing me for Governor. I never asked for her endorsement. She just acted unilaterally to cause me some political embarrassment. She gave as the reason the fact that she had a conflict of interest due to her investigation into my office. But only a few months before, she had no problem and obviously no conflict when she and her father were double teaming me for the campaign cash they wanted. At the time they wanted the money, Lisa Madigan was already using her office to investigate how my campaign raised money. But back then, she saw no conflict being in my office and playing her part in an effort to get me to give her father hundreds of thousands of dollars in campaign contributions.

And as for Mike Madigan, his payback came in the form of blocking my initiatives to expand healthcare, create jobs, and anything else I proposed to try and help people. Only his payback wasn't hurting me. His victims were working people and the poor. He was hurting women who sweep floors by blocking my efforts to give them access to healthcare. These are the same women who sweep floors in some of those downtown office buildings he makes millions of dollars representing.

But politics is a funny business. I believe the two Madigans are not the people they pretend to be. Both of them are surrounded by conflicts of interest and indiscretions in their public and private lives. And while those conflicts and those indiscretions can be chalked up to the kinds of secrets a lot of phony politicians like to hide, what makes their actions so repugnant is that real people get hurt. If the people only knew the real story behind the Madigans and their public and private cynicism, they would recoil.

Hubert Humphrey said that you could judge the quality of a society by how it treats those in the dawn of life, its children. How it treats those in the autumn of life, its elderly. And how it treats those in the shadows of life, its most vulnerable. When I unilaterally rewrote a bill that the legislature passed to give every senior citizen in the state of Illinois access to free public transportation, the uproar from lawmakers and even politicians like Mayor Daley was shocking. Giving senior citizens the chance to take public transportation for free is not only putting into action some of Hubert Humphrey's vision for a good society, but also making real one of the many values my mother taught me to believe in. My mother used to tell my brother and me when we were growing up to always "respect your elders." In fact, we took public transportation a lot when we were growing up. And we always did as my mother taught us to do. We gave up our seat on a bus or subway train to people who were elderly.

And I also remember when my father was well into his seventies. And while he didn't admit it, he was losing his confidence in his ability to drive. So he took public transportation more often than he had before. He was so proud of the discount card that allowed him to pay less to take a bus because he was a senior citizen. So when the legislature, at the urging of Mayor Daley, raised the sales tax to pay for the Chicago Transit Authority, they passed a regressive tax that disproportionately hurts people who live on fixed incomes. It hurts the poor. And it hurts the elderly. And after a lifetime of working hard, paying their taxes, and raising their kids—in short, a lifetime where they contributed significantly to their community—their lives should get easier, not harder as they grow older and more vulnerable. The legislature made their lives harder by raising the sales tax. I made their lives easier by giving them free public transportation. And Illinois is the only state in America where our senior citizens can take a bus or ride a subway train for free.

And after I did that, a law was passed that I proudly signed that gave all disabled people in Illinois the same access to free public transportation that we now give to our senior citizens. Healthcare for all of our children, free public transportation to all of our seniors and to the disabled—I like to think this is the kind of society Hubert Humphrey had in mind.

CHAPTER SEVEN

SO WHAT'S IT LIKE BEING A GOVERNOR? FOR ME THERE ISN'T A SIMPLE ANSWER. I guess the answer depends on why you wanted to be governor in the first place and what you wanted to do with it, if and when, you were elected. There really are several layers to that question. Did you become governor for only personal reasons? To hold a high office with all the trappings that go along with it? Did you run for governor because you saw it as a stepping stone to an even higher office? Or was being governor a way to achieve real and meaningful things for people? Is it a combination of all three, or a combination of two of the three, or parts of all three with different weights attached to each?

And is there a metaphysical component to that question? How much of your personal happiness are you willing to sacrifice to help other people achieve happiness or at least alleviate some of their unhappiness? And what about the moral universe? What is your responsibility to it? How much of your personal happiness would you sacrifice to bend that moral universe towards justice?

So, for example, if an angel came down from heaven and offered you a deal where you would have to sacrifice your personal happiness but in exchange for that you would be able to give every child healthcare and a better chance at a healthy life, what would your moral responsibility be? And what choice would you make?

If the question is solely and exclusively whether being a governor was a fun job that brought personal happiness, then my answer is easy and obvious. It didn't. For the six years I was governor, and long before our whole world changed with my arrest, our once happy family was torn apart due to conflicting expectations between my father-in-law and me. It would soon blow up in a very public way. My mother-in-law, a beautiful and wonderful person, contracted a rare neurological disease that little by little stole her motor skills from her and would eventually take her life a month after I was reelected. Friends whom I relied on and trusted turned out not to be the friends I thought they were, or even the people I thought they were. Taking on what I believed, and still believe, to be a corrupt status quo, and ruffling all kinds of feathers to change it, and creating all kinds of enemies, would soon lead to investigations into my own administration alleging practices that I find abhorrent yet would dog me, and some people close to me, for most of my time as governor. My naïve belief in an honest, inquiring, hard-working and objective press would soon be shattered. And on the night I was overwhelmingly reelected governor, both Patti and I did our duty and smiled and waved all the while hiding what for us was a joyless election night. We now were facing another four years of what we had just lived through.

And what we had just lived through was a personal tragedy. A story that has elements found in some of Shakespeare's tragedies. I see my political rise with the help of my father-in-law as having elements of *Henry IV, Part Two* and *Henry V* and culminating with my own personal battle of Agincourt: winning the gubernatorial election. What happened after I became governor is a story filled with elements from *Othello*, *King Lear,* and *Julius Caesar*; a story of intrigue, of jealousy, of manipulation, of unnatural familial behavior, and of betrayal. And while you're at it, you might as well throw in a little *Richard the Third*. Because when the story of my years as governor ends, I was left with neither a kingdom nor a horse. Or for that matter, even a car.

I would probably never have had a start in politics if it wasn't for my father-in-law. He is a powerful Chicago Democratic ward boss who, back in 1992, was recruiting candidates to run for the state legislature. I was one of the candidates he recruited. And it was the beginning of what became somewhat of a symbiotic political relationship between the two of us. One that proved to be successful. We both had our roles to play. We complemented each other. I was the candidate running for the office. I would campaign, give the speeches, debate my opponents, raise money—I was the guy who kissed the babies. His role was the inside political game. With the support of his successful political organization, he would expand my base of support by drawing on political relationships he had developed over nearly 30 years. He would build coalitions with other ward bosses and political leaders. And he was great at it. He would persuade and leverage and sometimes even threaten political retribution to get support for me. He would also help to raise money. But he was better at, and much preferred, to run the field operation in my elections.

My father-in-law has a great personality. The Chicago media calls him *colorful*. I don't disagree. But more than being colorful, he is a natural-born salesman. He has what they call the gift of gab. He's funny. He has big dreams and the vision to see the possibility of things. I love that about him. Those two qualities were among the things that brought us together and, for a long time, made us so close. He's good-hearted and genuinely likes to help people. And over the years, he has helped a lot of people. He sometimes puffs and exaggerates. But that's part of his skill as a salesman. And he's a hustler. I mean that in the good sense of the term. Part of the story of the American dream is the guy who starts out with nothing but because he works hard and hustles and sells he becomes a big success. Some of the greatest success stories in America today are by people who started out like that. Take Jerry Jones, the owner of the Dallas Cowboys, for example. He was a self-made man who started out with little or nothing only to sell and hustle his way to being the owner of what is probably the most successful sports franchise in America.

My father-in-law has a lot of great qualities. He's a self-made man who is successful in both business and politics. Perhaps his greatest skill is his ability to get other people motivated to do a lot of the hard work that's necessary for success in both business and politics. But like all of us, he has some bad qualities too. Those qualities manifested themselves in some of the bad things he did to me. And by hurting me, he indirectly hurt my wife and children.

Richard Mell started out with nothing. He grew up in Muskegon, Michigan, and was raised by his grandparents after his mother left and his father died. He moved to Chicago in the early 1960s after he met my mother-in-law walking along the North Avenue beach. He was captivated by her good looks. He never looked back. One of my favorite stories about him happened on his wedding day. My in-laws were married the day after President Kennedy's assassination. Mell didn't know anybody in Chicago, and he didn't have anyone to stand up for him at his wedding. His future brother-in-law and a husband of his wife's best friend agreed to act as groomsmen. But he was still one groomsman short (or there was one bridesmaid too many). Whatever the reason, he remedied the problem. He gave his barber fifty bucks to agree to close his shop, even though it was a Saturday, and the barber stood to lose a lot of business. In exchange for the fifty bucks, his barber, a guy he hardly knew, agreed to be one of his groomsmen and stand up at his wedding. I love that story about my father-in-law because it illustrates so much of who he is.

I love my father-in-law. We don't have a relationship anymore. And it makes me very sad. But in spite of everything that's happened to us, I love him. I don't know how it starts. You fall in love and marry a guy's daughter. You love her. It's immaterial whether you love him, much less like him. You're not marrying him, you're marrying her. At some point, you become part of the same family so I suppose it's natural to begin to love your in-laws. I love mine. I certainly loved my mother-in-law. She was, in so many ways, a saint. She was beautiful and intelligent. She was quiet, not very assertive, thoughtful of others, and devoted to her family. She was a very capable person, competent in all things she undertook. My father-in-law tells the story of how he started the family business, a spring manufacturing company. Because of his scattered and inattentive approach, he almost ran the company into the ground. My mother-in-law took over, and it didn't take long for her to turn what was a failed concern that was losing money into a successful business. Patti is a lot like her mom. A more assertive version.

Mell and I were a great team. Working together, we never lost an election. The only time I won an election without his help was my reelection for governor in 2006. My father-in-law was by then working against me behind the scenes. At my mother-in-law's wake, a month after winning reelection, my sister-in-law told me that after she thanked my Republican opponent, Judy Baar Topinka, for paying her respects, Ms. Topinka responded by pointing toward my father-in-law and saying, "Oh, he was a big help to me in the last election." I was amused when my sister-in-law told me that story. And while I would never work against him, it didn't bother me. By then, it had long been known that he and I had a broken relationship. I didn't begrudge him working against me politically. That's just politics, and if he doesn't like mine or felt I wasn't good enough to him, he has every right to vote for whomever he wants. But what is a lot harder to forget and to forgive are the things he was knowingly doing to me that I believe led to some of the very accusations I have to face today. And some of those things are unconscionable.

The greater the political challenge we faced, the better we got along. Yet the greater the political success, the worse our relationship became. He expected things. And he demanded a lot. I could never please him. The bigger the office I held, the more he wanted and the more he believed I could give. Perhaps the seeds of our separation were sown at the very beginning, in my first race for state representative. It established the nature of our relationship; more political partnership than family business. It was based on political expediency. He needed a candidate to run for state representative because of his politics. I was eager to run for state representative because I saw it as a way to get into politics. Instead of a relationship between a father-in-law and son-in-law, one that developed on a foundation of mutual love and affection, our relationship started to grow and develop almost unwittingly by each of our own mercenary political interests. I like to say that we were unlike the many other political families in Chicago—the Daleys, the Madigans, the Hynes, the Stroegers, and even the Jacksons—where the offspring are carefully groomed, nurtured, and protected by the patriarch. Where Mike Madigan, for example, protects his daughter, and even though they're closely working together, he's the one who takes the hits. With Mell and me, it was different.

From the beginning, he wouldn't hesitate to throw me under the bus. He never groomed me for politics. He helped me, and we fought side by side. But there was no preparation. No careful planning or training. I was just thrown into it because he needed a candidate. I was thrown into the rough and tumble world of Chicago politics in much the same way 12th-century Scottish Highlanders groomed West Highland terriers to become hunting dogs. There was no time for training. They either had it, or they didn't. The Scots would throw the young puppies into vats filled with rats. If the puppy was strong enough to fight his way out of that, he was worthy to be a hunting dog. That's how I was groomed. Just thrown into the fray, and let's see if you're strong enough to survive. But don't get me wrong, I loved every minute of it.

It wasn't long after I was elected governor that our relationship began to unravel. There is no one reason why it happened. There is no single event that caused it. It was a lot of things. Over the past six years, I have agonized and asked myself over and over again what I could have done differently to prevent it. I still torment myself with these questions.

As the gulf that separated us grew wider, and we no longer had a relationship, I would ask people close to me who had first-hand knowledge of some of the issues that caused the rift whether I was too hard on him. I felt bad for him. I missed him. I missed how it used to be when we were one close family.

Did I become too uncompromising, too unrelenting, and too unforgiving? They would always assure me that I had not. That a lot of the things he was doing to me weren't just unforgivable, but that they were sure to continue the next time there was a rupture, which inevitably would occur. I would listen to their assessment then, but maybe I shouldn't have. Maybe they were the wrong ones to ask.

In the final analysis, I could no longer trust him. I could forgive him. I tried and I did. But I couldn't trust him. Some of the things he did over the years, the false public accusations, the use of third parties to start untrue whispering campaigns against me, things that would hurt his daughter and his grandchildren, these were terrible things to do. Okay, you hate your son-in-law and want to hurt him. Fine. But when you strike out to hurt him, you're hurting your daughter and granddaughters too. Manipulating to hurt your family because of power, greed, and ego. These were the kind of unnatural things Shakespeare wrote about in *King Lear*. Only in our tragedy, it wasn't the daughter betraying the father, it was the father betraying the daughter.

Life is complex. People are complex. And there are reasons why he did some of the things he did. And I could forgive even the worst of them. But as long as I was still governor and facing criminal investigations that he had a hand in creating, it was more out of self-defense than anything else that led me to keep my distance from him. I feared him, and I feared his manipulative ways of getting back at me and hurting me.

While I wasn't going to help my father-in-law in his schemes to, in his words, "get my big score," I was early on doing whatever I could to help him in ways that were appropriate. As we were building our administration and filling positions in state government, we hired dozens of people who he recommended or came out of his political organization. As long as they were qualified, their backgrounds properly vetted, and the law allowed them to be hired, his people were getting jobs.

In addition to the jobs, I asked some of my supporters to help my father-in-law raise money. And we did. We raised him something like $300,000 for a fundraiser in December 2003. That's an amazing amount of money to raise for an alderman and ward committeeman. I am absolutely certain that in the nearly thirty years he was in politics, no one ever remotely matched the amount of money we raised for him that night. But he still wasn't satisfied.

And when he wasn't satisfied, nothing would stop him. He would persist. He would enlist the help of others to push what he wanted. And in the pursuit of getting me to do what he wanted, nothing was sacred. Not even his family.

My first budget as governor was passed at the end of May 2003. Naturally, I was in Springfield working to get it passed. The work spilled into the weekend. The budget passed on a Saturday. My family came down to Springfield to spend the weekend with me: Patti, Amy, one-month old Annie, and my mother-in-law, Marge. My mother-in-law joined us in Springfield that weekend because she had a quarrel with my father-in-law over issues of politics and government that he was upset at me about. When she wouldn't take his side, he stormed out and without telling her, went to Florida. She was alone that weekend, so she came to Springfield with us.

He would do these kinds of things. It was this practice, his constant use of our family, of my mother-in-law and my sister-in-law and brother-in-law too, involving them in issues involving my administration, that he and I had differences over. It was manipulative. At first, I asked him to stop doing it. In a nice way, I told him that if we were going to continue working together politically, then we needed to set some ground rules. Keep the family out of our politics and my decisions as governor. We can disagree, we can have our differences, we can argue over things, just as we did in our campaigns together. Sometimes I can help. Sometimes I can't or I won't. But let us keep it between ourselves. Let us have not a separation of church and state, but in our case, a separation of family and state. Let's protect the sanctity of the family. I pleaded with him to keep our family out of our politics.

When that didn't work, I began to warn him. And I would warn him, over and over again, that if he didn't stop involving other members of our family in our political differences, then I was going to sever any political relationship I had with him. I told him it wasn't worth it. He was going to ruin our family if he kept dragging them into our disagreements.

It was ridiculous too. Think about it. I'm the governor of a big state. And I have a situation where if, hypothetically, my father-in-law wants me to hire Chucky Lomanto's cousin and I don't, my father-in-law will run to my mother-in-law, tell her all about it and convince her I was a big ingrate who wasn't helping him. He would work to turn her against me. And I loved my mother-in-law. I wanted her to love me. I didn't want her to think ill of me.

It was incredibly childish. On the one hand, it is so absurd that it's funny. On the other hand, it's very serious because it was messing with my family. It caused hard feelings and strained relationships with all of my in-laws. Never mind all the things I had done and was still doing for him. He would complain to her that he wasn't getting anything. And then my poor and devoted mother-in-law would feel obligated to call

Patti and try to get her to work on me. And then they would quarrel. Mother and daughter now divided; both of them naturally supporting their husbands. And arguing over issues like what precinct captain didn't get a job. How dysfunctional was this? It was tailor-made for a reality TV show.

I hated it when he did that. I absolutely hated it. To involve my mother-in-law and drag her into arguments with her daughter over my decisions as the governor was disgusting. And what made it even worse was that my mother-in-law's health was beginning to deteriorate. And he knew, as we all knew, that the rare disease she had meant that she didn't have a lot of time left. But that didn't stop him. In an effort to protect her mother from the stress of these situations, my sister-in-law asked her father why he was using her mother over differences he had with me. His simple answer: "I'll use anyone to get to him."

As time passed, our relationship was gradually getting worse. Periodically we would get together and try to work things out. We would literally sit around the dining room table in my home talking about our problems. Patti and Marge would participate. That was a concession on my part. Again, from my point of view, my wife and his wife had nothing to do with my decisions as governor. How does that warrant a family conference? That was the thing he always tried to do, have these so-called family conferences to iron out our differences. That was how he operated. He would purposefully set a fire and create a crisis in the family. My mother-in-law, wanting to be a peacemaker, tried to work it out. But I knew what his motivations were. And I resented how he was manipulating our family and causing hard feelings between us because I wasn't doing everything he wanted me to do. He used them like arbitration in a dispute between labor and management. But they were just more of his manipulative tactics to get things out of me. But I suffered through a couple of them out of respect for my mother-in-law.

I acted in good faith to try to do some of the things he wanted to try to have peace in our family. After a couple of those, it was obvious to me that these conferences were just other ways for him to get things out of me. He was clever that way. And we would adjourn those meetings with his promise that he would mend his ways and respect the proper boundaries. The irony wasn't lost on me when, at these family conferences, he would promise to stop dragging our family into his political differences with me when those very conferences were the epitome of dragging the family into our political disagreements.

As time went by, our relationship got worse. He began to take our disagreements outside of the family and into the press. I'm getting pissed off just writing this. And I haven't said any of these things publicly. I just took it. I allowed my father-in-law to do the things he was doing and say the things he was saying without fighting back. I was determined to keep it private. That's how I was raised by my parents. You put your family first. And what happens in the family, stays in the family. My mother always taught my brother and me to never tell anyone about any arguments my parents might have in our home. Those things were private. They were between my mother and father and my brother and me. We kept it in the home.

And I hope my mother forgives me. But now I'm breaking my silence. Because I believe that I wouldn't be facing criminal charges today if my father-in-law didn't do the things he did to me. If I wasn't so preoccupied worrying about his efforts to use me to get his "big score" as he would call it, my judgment in other people would have been better. And I would have seen things and learned things about them sooner than I did. And I would have made changes. And I wouldn't be where I am now.

I'm writing about some of the things that my father-in-law did to provide some context to the environment I was operating in.

The first story I recall seeing was in the *Reader* newspaper. I think the title was "Mell Gets The Shaft." It would prove to be the first of many I would see where he was violating a cardinal rule I was raised to believe in. When Mell began to engineer stories in the press about our problems, I was outraged. I felt violated. I felt betrayed. Who goes to the press about his own family? How could you ever trust a guy who does that?

I could fill a book with all of the different things he wanted me to do for him after I became governor. I knew, based on my experience with him as a congressman and state representative, that he would expect and demand certain things. I also knew that he had great expectations for himself if I ever became governor. He used to say, "If you run for the Senate, I'll work my ward for you. But that's all. You can't do anything for me as a senator." But if I ran for governor, he promised to pull out all the stops.

I remember having one of those conversations with him. It was long before I was elected governor, even before I formally declared my intention to run. When he said that, I asked him, "Just what is it that you expect if I win?" I remember telling him that maybe he ought to lay all his cards out on the table now. Before we get started. Because I was running for governor to be the best governor I could be. And of course I would help him however or wherever I legally and ethically could. But what else did he expect? Did he expect more than that? If so, maybe we shouldn't do this. Or maybe, he doesn't have to help me. He never directly answered those questions.

I wasn't surprised that I was having all kinds of problems with my father-in-law. And that they started almost immediately. That's how it always was with him. Those were predictable. When my first Chief of Staff Lon Monk told me early on, based on conversations he was having with my father-in-law, that some of his expectations were so outlandish they could never be met, he wasn't telling me anything I didn't expect. I knew there were going to be problems. And that inevitably there were going to be times when he would be angry at me. And do all of the things he would always do to get his way.

But I never dreamed that he would make it a purpose in his life to hurt me or try to destroy me. Or that he would orchestrate third parties to attack me and investigate me. Or that he would actively participate in, as well as conduct, nasty and ugly and untrue whispering campaigns against me.

I attended the 2004 Democratic National Convention in Boston. My father-in-law was there as well. In fact, I made sure he traveled around the convention sites with me because when you're a governor and have a security detail, you can get around the crowded city hosting a national convention more conveniently. So Mell traveled with me and it was nice. But it wasn't the same. And it was sad. I had been governor for less than two years, but our relationship was seriously strained.

I remember a specific telephone conversation I had with Patti from Los Angeles, where I went after the convention to raise money. She had just attended a family counseling session with her parents. And she was alarmed. Even though my mother-in-law was very sick, there were marital issues she wanted resolved with the help of a professional marriage counselor. Originally, Mell agreed to go but on only one condition. And that condition, oddly enough, was that I attend. Here again is an example of the dysfunction he was manufacturing. Mell is having problems in his marriage with his wife. She is sick and dying but wants to work things out with him. But initially he takes the position that he will only participate if his son-in-law, the governor, participates. What do I have to do with his marriage? Why is it a precondition with him that I attend a counseling session to address personal issues with his wife? So when Patti raised the subject with me, I declined to attend. It wasn't my place. And besides, here he goes again. Bringing me and the differences he and I had into a counseling session about his marriage and family was wrong. So I did not participate. And apparently that enraged Mell.

On the telephone call from Los Angeles, Patti told me that she believed her father was so angry at me and hated me so much, she was afraid he was going to kill me. It sounded crazy and I told her that. But she kept on. She insisted that she was serious. She told me that after listening to her father at that counseling session, she was actually afraid of what he might do to me. I dismissed what she told me. I laughed and said she was crazy to even think that. And of course, I never thought he would kill me. I thought the idea of it was both ludicrous and laughable. But I also never thought he would do some of the things I would learn he was doing. And then the issue of the landfill exploded. And he did something I feared he was capable of, but that in the end he wouldn't be able to bring himself to do. As events would prove, I was wrong.

It ended with the closing of a landfill but it started with some kind of toll card he wanted the tollway to buy. He came to my house and pitched me on it. He had a third-party front to hide behind. But he told me his cut could be five million dollars. I was incredulous. I asked him if he was out of his mind. Not only did I not want him to bring things like that to me, we had set up a system where I would stay away from those decisions. What was he thinking? He knew I had a policy that stated while I was governor, no one in my immediate family should do business with the state of Illinois. That policy also applied to two of my political supporters, Chris Kelly and Tony Rezko. That policy applied to them because they were going to play prominent roles on the political side raising campaign funds. Their advice and input was also something I sought when it came to making appointments to positions in state government. Because of their roles, and in an effort to avoid even the appearance of impropriety, they both agreed to forgo doing any business directly with the state.

And then there was a company by the name of Employ On. The company supposedly attempted to match the unemployed with jobs. Mell wanted the state to engage their services. Presumably, there would be some financial compensation for him. Out of respect for my father-in-law, my Chief of Staff took the meeting he asked for. But the company wasn't hired. We didn't need their services. It would have wasted taxpayer money. And again, I did not want members of my immediate family using their connections to get business from my administration for their financial benefit.

When your public responsibilities collide with the private interests of your family, what are you supposed to do? Let me put it another way. A member of your family is involved in an enterprise that you have information to believe is operating in violation of the law, and you're the governor, and your environmental protection agency is responsible to enforce that law. What do you do?

a) look the other way and pretend you don't know about it
b) reach out to the relevant member or members of your family and try to get a piece of the action
c) warn the relevant family member that rules are being broken, and they better be careful before somebody else catches them
d) do your duty, protect the public, enforce the law and act within the law.

Those were some of the choices I had when I learned that a landfill my father-in-law was involved in was violating environmental regulations.

My father-in-law suddenly became interested in the landfill business after I became governor. I'm not aware that he was ever in that business before. Early in my first term, he was courted by a family that owned a successful waste company. He would brag about how they would fly him around on their private jet. He told me they wanted to do business in Illinois. They were here once before but had apparently signed a five-year non-compete with another company. Their five-year non-compete was about to expire, and they wanted to get back into Illinois. They befriended the governor's father-in-law and supposedly wanted to cut him in on some of the opportunities. I couldn't understand why. I asked my father-in-law if he was an investor. Was that why they wanted him? He told me he wasn't investing any money. I asked my father-in-law what skill or expertise he brought to this business. He acknowledged he didn't have any. When I then asked why they would want to partner with him, he told me his value was that he could bring all kinds of waste disposal business to this company. Not knowing anything about that industry, his answer sounded plausible. Still, I knew my father-in-law, and I didn't trust him. There was something else in this deal that he wasn't telling me. I had a strong suspicion that for this deal to work, they needed something from me. And whatever it was, it wouldn't pass the smell test.

And I was right. Notwithstanding his repeated denials, the landfill they identified as the one they wanted to purchase had pending environmental violations, including the presence of kiln dust at the site. And for them to move forward, they would need those violations lifted. Otherwise, it would cost them too much money to fix.

Of course, he never told me any of this. He purposely kept that information from me. And he was never going to tell me. I know how he operates. It is my belief that he was selling the waste disposal magnates on his ability to lift the environmental restrictions by leading them to believe he could get me to do it. He knew I wouldn't do it, so his plan was to quietly get it done through the bureaucracy at the Environmental Protection Agency by using the many contacts he had in politics and government who could help him. If all went as planned, the company would get its landfill, he would get a part of the deal, and I would never know that an environmental hazard like kiln dust would be, figuratively speaking, swept under the rug.

But I did know. I found out. Because I didn't trust him and knew he wasn't telling me the whole story, I instructed my Chief of Staff to look into the matter. Again, I had reason to believe that the public interest could be compromised if I was right about my father-in-law's scheme. But I hoped I was wrong. I hoped our due diligence would discover that my father-in-law wasn't trying to personally benefit behind my back at my expense and at the expense of the public.

Unfortunately, I was right. We obtained the relevant information. Not only were there environmental violations on the landfill, but there also was a pending lawsuit. Imagine if that lawsuit was somehow dismissed because somebody at the EPA erroneously thought they were doing me a favor because my father-in-law or one of his designated third parties gave them that impression. The air quality in the area where the landfill in question was located could have been compromised. But because we acted, the environment was protected. And it's funny, once it was made clear that the environmental violations and the lawsuit were going to be pursued, that particular deal just faded away.

I dispatched a friend to talk to my father-in-law about what we discovered. I told him to tell my father-in-law that I learned of the environmental violations. That we were going to monitor the situation to make sure the normal process went forward without any disruption. And that included allowing the pending lawsuit to play itself out to its natural conclusion. There would be absolutely no intervention from me. If anything, I was going to direct the EPA to vigorously pursue the matter.

Now why didn't I tell my father-in-law myself? Maybe I should have. But by then, I was getting tired of him lying to me. When I learned about the environmental violation that he purposely wasn't telling me about, I again felt betrayed. He is my father-in-law. You don't lie to your family. You don't knowingly conceal things from members of your family that, if discovered, could get that family member in hot water. I was both angry and hurt. I was angry at the deceit and hurt that he would try to manipulate a situation where he would stand to gain financially even though it might bring harm to me or the environment.

But I wasn't the only one who was angry. He was angry too. Angry that the deal he was counting on wasn't going to happen. So he came to our house when I wasn't there and dropped off a colored brochure of a house he wanted to buy in Sanibel Island, Florida. The purpose of his visit was to tell his daughter that I killed his deal. And he wanted to know what our plans were to help him afford to purchase that house.

This was yet another episode in what was becoming a cascading deterioration of our relationship. The more I learned about the things he was doing or trying to do in some of his business deals, the more I distrusted and feared him. The more he tried to trade on his relationship with me and maneuver but then became thwarted, the more he would resent me. The people around me would increasingly warn that he was using me, that he was dangerous, and that he couldn't be trusted. The people around him were most likely telling him that his son-in-law was ungrateful, that I wouldn't help him or worse, I used him to get where I was, and now I was screwing him over. As if things weren't bad enough between us—the mistrust, the misunderstanding, the mutual feelings of resentment—I honestly believe that he felt I was betraying him by not just going along with what he wanted. I honestly felt and feared he was betraying me by trying to pursue some of his schemes. And the people around both of us only served to fan those flames. And widen the breach.

We were both in our respective camps. Growing further and further apart; talking to each other less and less frequently. How did this happen? How did it come to this? Am I seeing it all clearly enough? Are the people who are giving me information about him acting in good faith and with the right motives? Or did they have motives of their own? Had I become Othello, unduly influenced by the Iagos who were advising me? These are the kinds of things I would ask myself as my relationship with my father-in-law was rapidly getting worse. So I decided to do something about it. I called him up to have a talk with him over the phone.

This telephone conversation between us took place during the 2003 Christmas holidays at the end of my first year as governor. I called him to have a heart to heart talk, just the two of us, to explain my position and see if there was a way where I could legally and ethically help him and make him happy. The call lasted longer than most of our phone conversations. I didn't want to dwell on the past so I engaged him in a discussion about what I could do to help him. The gist of the conversation was that somehow he and I got along best when we were working together against a common adversary; when we were focused on the same object. Why couldn't we be focused like that now? And work together like we did in my campaigns for a common purpose. I reiterated to him how grateful I was for all of his help. And I proposed that we simulate how we worked together in my campaigns for my political advancement and that we do it now to help him, in a legal and ethical way, build some kind of a business. I asked him to think about starting up a consulting business where I could help him open doors in Washington, D.C. As long as his business didn't involve lobbying for the state government, I was prepared to work as hard as possible to help him. I suggested that he might want to consider bringing his son into the business with him. My brother-in-law has a winning personality and is very smart. Why not have a business where father is the senior partner and son does all the work?

And I pledged to help them and work directly with my father-in-law on a daily basis, just as we would in my campaigns, to see that they become successful. The only caveat was they couldn't do business with any state agency under my control.

The conversation was friendly, but for whatever reason he wasn't interested in my idea. I would discover later that he still had his mind set on the landfill business. And a year would go by before that issue exploded in a very public way.

Our family was together on Christmas Eve 2004. It would be the last time we were together like that. My father-in-law and I were polite to each other. But sadly, strains in our relationship were apparent. For the previous several months, an ugly and false whispering campaign was being spread about me. The whispers were so nasty and untrue that even the media refused to report them. I didn't take them seriously; I was mostly amused by them. It's the sort of ugly thing that happens in politics. But when I learned from friends and other associates that my father-in-law and some of his representatives may have been part of the chorus behind these whispers, my reaction was that he had sunk to a new low. And for me to believe that he was capable of actively participating in something that could eventually harm his daughter was indicative of how bad our relationship had become.

On that Christmas Eve, I knew my father-in-law was still in the landfill business. His companion in that landfill was a nephew of my mother-in-law, my wife's cousin Frankie. Frankie is a character right out of a Damon Runyon story. My mother-in-law never trusted him and didn't like him. She would tell Patti that he was dangerous. But my father-in-law loved him. He used to say that Frankie would be the guy to make him a lot of money, since I was the one preventing him from making his "big score." And he was going to do it at the landfill.

I was aware that Mell was involved in a landfill with Frankie. It didn't smell right to me. But as long as they followed the law, it was none of my business. But it became my business shortly after that Christmas Eve, when I learned that Frankie was operating the landfill business and allegedly taking construction debris that he didn't have a state permit for. And when state inspectors from the environmental protection agency visited his landfill to inspect it, I was told by a close friend that Frankie threatened them by throwing Patti's name around. He warned the inspectors to back off because he was the cousin of the governor's wife.

When I learned of this, I was disgusted but not surprised. People throw your name around all the time. It's not something you can control. But it really didn't matter. What mattered was that a landfill was allegedly operating in violation of environmental laws. It didn't matter who it belonged to. The law had to be followed, and the process now had to play out.

But what was the process? When this landfill incident surfaced I knew virtually nothing about how landfills operate, much less how the EPA or any other state agency regulates them. This is not uncommon. In matters like this, you rely on your chief of staff or other top staff to properly advise and guide you on what appropriate course of action to take. The chief of staff presumably is advised by the director of the relevant agency or someone with expertise in the area. In ordinary circumstances, that's how I would routinely decide a course of action and then give the appropriate direction. I would rely on the experts in the area and quickly decide. There wouldn't be a lot of discussion. There didn't need to be. But this was not an ordinary circumstance. My father-in-law was heavily involved in this landfill. He bragged about it to everyone. And within the family, he would boast about all the money he expected to make. So my dilemma was, how do I handle this? I knew my father-in-law was going to hit the roof over this. In fact, shortly after the inspectors visited the landfill site, my father-in-law enlisted the help of state Senator Jimmy Deleo, a mutual friend, to call on his behalf and ask that we leave the landfill alone.

As the process continued to unfold, more calls from his surrogates started coming in. And when my mother-in-law and sister-in-law were enlisted to call my wife on behalf of that landfill, it was clear to me that before I made any final decisions on what to do and how to do it, I reached out and sought the advice of every one of my top advisers. And I reached out to my Congressman, Rahm Emanuel, to get his advice on what to do and how to handle it.

What would have been a routine, quick decision that would have taken minutes to make, now became an extraordinary circumstance with serious political and perhaps even legal consequences. There was never a question about doing my duty and acting appropriately to protect the public regarding this landfill. The only question was how to go about it. The director of the EPA gave my Chief of Staff several options on what would be the appropriate course of action to take. I would consider those options before deciding how to proceed. Again, under ordinary circumstances, this would be easy. But this wasn't ordinary. A family member of mine was involved. And he wasn't just any family member. This one was prone to fly off the handle. He was dangerous. He was hungry for his big score. And he saw this landfill as it. He was already using third parties to warn me that there would be consequences if I didn't leave the landfill alone. And when he had my mother-in-law call my wife to ask her why I was hurting my own family, I knew that whatever I did, I sure better think it through.

"Your father wants you to know that Rod's not going to be governor forever and that there's a lot of money in this landfill for the family." That's what my mother-in-law told Patti over the telephone right after New Year's 2005 as the landfill issue was percolating under the radar. I read that statement as Mell offering the carrot. I interpreted it as I could make a lot of money if I would just leave his landfill alone. I always found it interesting that for the duration of the landfill controversy, which occurred from just after Christmas to about the first week of January, my father-in-law never once called to express his views to me. It seems to me that if everything about that landfill was legitimate, the natural thing to do would be for a father-in-law to call his son-in-law to explain that nothing inappropriate was going on. I found that very strange. If the landfill was operating legitimately, why was he having third parties contact us? If the violations of the landfill were of the ordinary variety and could be easily remedied, why wouldn't he call or agree to work with the Environmental Protection Agency to cure the violation? But it was the third parties, including my own mother-in-law, who were calling and warning us about him that made me more suspicious. Was there more here than just a landfill without the proper permits?

Here's what I would learn.

The landfill was a huge canyon-like hole in the ground. The volume of waste at the site had grown dramatically from 432,000 cubic yards in October 2002 to just under five million cubic yards in August 2004. We learned that two of the partners in the venture had previously been involved in bribing Chicago aldermen in a scandal called "Operation Silver Shovel." We also learned that the landfill was purchased from the Vulcan Company for $1.2 million. Considering the size of the landfill and the possibility of all the money that could be made there, the purchase price seemed exceptionally low. Why would the Vulcan Company sell such a valuable piece of property for so little? Were they looking to make it up somewhere else? That was the most troubling question.

At the time of the sale, I also recall that the Illinois Department of Transportation was involved in a pending lawsuit against the Vulcan Company seeking $95 million in damages. And my father-in-law had approached a friend of mine urging him to intervene with me to settle the case for $25 million. Was there a connection between the two? I didn't know. But the Vulcan lawsuit now suddenly became a lot more relevant.

After I was elected governor and before I was sworn in, former Congressman Bill Lipinski met with me. Among the issues he raised was that very lawsuit. He told me the Illinois Department of Transportation was suing the Vulcan Company for damage caused by them in connection with some excavating work they did in Congressman Lipinski's district. I was at the time unaware of this lawsuit. In that meeting in late 2002 or early 2003, the Congressman told me about the pending lawsuit and he warned me not to settle the case. He was concerned because the law firm of former Governor Thompson, who was now heading my transition team, represented the Vulcan Company in that lawsuit. He was also concerned because he expressly pointed out to me that my father-in-law was interested in seeing that case settle. That was odd. Why would my father-in-law care about a lawsuit in Congressman Lipinski's district concerning an area that had to be better than forty miles away from the ward he represented as alderman? In any event, when I learned that the Vulcan Company had sold the landfill to people my father-in-law was associated with, a red flag was suddenly waved. And to complicate things, what about Winston and Strawn, the law firm where Governor Thompson was a partner? They were also now representing me. Suddenly an issue at a landfill concerning the lack of a proper permit was becoming an issue loaded with all kinds of conflicts of interest, or at least the appearance of them.

To address the issue of Winston and Strawn and the Vulcan Company, I asked David Wilhelm, one of my closest advisers at the time, to visit Governor Thompson and raise the issue with him. He reported back to me that he did. But when I asked what the former governor thought should be done about it, I was disappointed that all he had to say was something along the lines of "I hear you loud and clear." It seemed to me that he was torn between two clients and was choosing to stay out of it.

After days and countless hours discussing the proper course of action with my top advisers, I finally reached a decision. But before I did, I asked Congressman Rahm

Emanuel for his advice. He knew my father-in-law. And he was well aware of his reputation for bluff and bluster. I shared with him all the information I had. I also told him about the threats that were being communicated to me by third parties. Again, the issue wasn't whether I was going to do my duty, but only a question of how. Which of the several options at my disposal to take? Most of my top advisers urged me to take the most aggressive approach the law allowed: close the landfill down and allow a court of law to decide the issue. Another option was to refer the matter to the Attorney General and allow her to pursue it. Some of my advisers supported that idea. My concern was that the Attorney General, Lisa Madigan, while technically the governor's lawyer, had shown from the very beginning that she was, in my opinion, more interested in screwing her client politically rather than helping him legally. So I didn't trust that option. And I didn't like the feeling of reporting my father-in-law to someone who might see the political advantage of screwing with him.

Another option was to try to quietly work with Mell and Frankie to cure their violations and monitor them so they wouldn't in the future take debris they are not permitted to take. The problem with that option was obvious. I couldn't trust either one of them, and then it could be perceived that I was somehow in on the deal by winking and nodding and looking the other way.

In the end, I felt the right thing to do was to let a court of law decide. I trusted the courts to do the right thing much more than Lisa Madigan. I trusted the courts more than my father-in-law and Frankie. So I decided to take the advice of most of my advisers and close the landfill down. And I braced myself for what I was afraid was going to come. I hoped that Rahm Emanuel, who advised me to close the landfill, was right when he calculated that Mell's threats were only a bluff and that in the end, he'd accept my decision quietly.

Rahm Emanuel is probably right a lot more often than he is wrong. But he sure was wrong on this one. He was right to advise me to close the landfill down. But he was wrong when he predicted that Mell wouldn't do anything.

After I ordered the landfill closed, the media seized on the issue. And they immediately seized on the family dynamic. I was ordering the closing of a landfill my father-in-law was involved in. And Mell seized on them. He wasted no time in attacking me, in making accusations against me and specifically against Chris Kelly, who was in charge of fundraising for my campaign fund. In a tirade to the press, Mell accused me of ingratitude. He compared himself to a wife who marries a guy with nothing. The guy goes on to medical school and becomes a doctor because his wife worked to help him through medical school. After becoming successful, he dumps that wife for the second wife. That second wife, according to Mell, was Chris Kelly. And like a spurned lover, Mell lashed out and literally accused Chris of trading board and commission appointments for campaign contributions totaling $50,000. This was an outrageous accusation. It was a lie, and my father-in-law knew it. He also knew the consequences of his accusation. This was typical of him. He gets angry and it's real. He flies off the handle and hurts somebody. But then he'll apologize and hide behind his inability to keep his temper, which he knows how to keep when he has to. What he did to Chris and what he did to me with that false and malicious accusation was deliberate. And he knew that once he made the accusation, no matter what he might say later, he was unleashing the furies on me.

And it was no accident that after he did that, Attorney General Lisa Madigan pounced on the issue and publicly subpoenaed all of my fundraising records. But worse than that, I'm convinced that was the act that ultimately led to the federal prosecutor's determination to target me and relentlessly pursue and investigate me for the next three and a half years.

Mell publicly retracted his accusation against Chris Kelly under threat of a lawsuit. He admitted that he had no knowledge of any specific instance to support his wild accusation. But the damage was done, and so was my relationship with him. He was out to get his big score even if it meant hurting me. When my duties got in his way, he hit back below the belt. A seasoned Chicago politician for more than thirty years knows what federal investigators will do when someone makes an accusation like the one he made. And while time would pass, and, after my mother-in-law passed away, I could forgive and try to rebuild a family relationship with him, that still was not something he was interested in. Less than four months after her passing, he would get angry again when I issued an executive order preventing any immediate family member of mine—my wife, my brother, and my in-laws—from lobbying for contracts with my administration. Here again I had to go out of my way to protect myself from some members of my family who wanted to benefit financially. And to do so I went above and beyond what any of my predecessors had done.

One more thing happened after Mell's accusation and retraction. A Cook County grand jury was convened to investigate the landfill matter. But the grand jury was not convened to investigate the operators of the landfill or any of the circumstances concerning the transaction to obtain it. No, the grand jury was convened to investigate me and my administration on the circumstances surrounding my decision to close the landfill down and allow a court to decide the final outcome. And that investigation was joined by Lisa Madigan and the Attorney General's office. How's that for irony? The Attorney General's office represented me and the Illinois Environmental Protection Agency in court arguing successfully that the landfill should be shut down, just as I had ordered. But now she was investigating me for the very thing she had only recently represented me on.

There's one final footnote to the landfill story. I'm told the landfill was sold a few years later for several million dollars. Frankie and the others involved in that investment have, according to things said by Mell to others, made millions of dollars in profits. Is Mell exaggerating or is it the truth? The answer could be found in the public records.

And the court offered the best potential resolution of the matter. The court would be the referee. It turned out that's what happened. The court found that Frankie and the landfill was in fact guilty of taking material it didn't have a permit to take. The court sustained keeping the landfill closed until Frankie removed the debris. The Illinois Environmental Protection Agency monitored the cleanup and reported back to the court. Once that was done, the court allowed the landfill to reopen for business. All things considered, it was a fair and just resolution.

CHAPTER EIGHT

MAYBE I HAVE READ TOO MANY HISTORY BOOKS OVER THE YEARS. I read about too many great men in history who I wanted to be like. Men with high ideals who stood up and sacrificed for principle. Those were my role models. That's who I wanted to be. I saw myself as Teddy Roosevelt. The man who was in the arena—dusty and sweaty and bloody but fighting and striving to achieve things for the people and the cause he believed in. Who makes mistakes and comes up short from time to time but who never quits trying because he cares. He is devoted to the people and spends himself in the worthy cause of trying to help them. Who sometimes triumphs and sometimes fails, but even when he fails he has the courage to dare to try to do great things.

Maybe my head was so filled with wanting to be like Teddy Roosevelt and great men like him that I failed to see that some people around me were not motivated by the same things. That they had their own agendas. And were pursuing their own self-interest. The history books I read growing up and still read today don't spend a lot of time talking about the nuts and bolts of running a big government. The great leaders left those responsibilities to others. And so did I. I left it to people in whom I placed too much trust or didn't know well enough.

Less than two months into the job, I was already discovering how profoundly alone I was. Everybody wanted something, and all kinds of people had all kinds of expectations.

This was a new day in Illinois. I was the first Democrat elected governor in twenty-six years. In the minds of many of my supporters, it was out with the old and in with the new. The Democratic political establishment across Illinois had great expectations. So did the Democratic political machine in Chicago. From their perspective, a Democratic governor meant new vistas of opportunity to fill positions and give jobs to the loyalists and precinct workers from their Democratic political organizations. Democratic political leaders who supported me during a competitive Democratic primary expected to be rewarded for their support. Democratic political leaders who didn't support me in the primary hoped I would forgive and forget and expected to be rewarded because they're Democrats. Labor leaders and business leaders, community activists and religious leaders, so-called good government types and members of issue advocacy organizations, all wanted a hand in filling the positions of the new administration. And then there are your friends, and your family, and people you hardly know who claim to be your friends—they have a spouse or a son, a nephew or a neighbor, and they all want to now join state government and serve the people of Illinois.

In the first few months of his administration, Abraham Lincoln was already worn out by all the supplicants and job seekers who wanted positions in his administration. Here is Lincoln, trying to preserve the union and struggling to keep our country from tearing apart as one Southern state after another is leaving the union, and he's being overwhelmed by all the people who want positions in his administration. And he can't satisfy them all. Everyone wants something but there is not enough to go around. This was the time when an exhausted Abraham Lincoln famously lamented to a friend or an aide, that there were simply "too many pigs for the tits." I knew that Lincoln story before I became governor.

Unlike any of my predecessors, I turned down state taxpayer money to pay for the transition team and instead used my surplus campaign funds to pay for it. I was inheriting a record budget deficit, and I wanted to send a message that wherever I could, I was determined to save taxpayers' money. I promised the people of Illinois in my campaign for governor that I was not going to raise income or sales taxes on them to balance the budget and that those who run state government would lead in the shared sacrifice to balance the budget. I promised not to balance the budget on the backs of hard-working people of Illinois. I meant what I said, and I was determined, whatever the cost, to keep my word to them.

When I began the process of organizing my new administration after November 5, 2002, I sought the help of Jim Thompson, a former four-term Illinois governor and former United States attorney, and asked him to co-chair my transition team. He did, and along with his experience and knowledge, I also engaged the services of his big successful law firm, Winston and Strawn. We retained their services and paid them from campaign funds to provide legal advice and to help my new Chief of Staff and other top members of my fledgling administration establish the proper systems and methods so we could successfully and honestly operate state government. They also were retained to advise us on how to properly make appointments to a plethora of government positions that needed to be filled.

Their services were important and so was Governor Thompson's experience because I decided to choose as my Chief of Staff my former law school roommate who spent most of his adult life working as a sports agent. Lon Monk made up for his complete lack of experience by being one of my closest friends. He was someone I believed I could trust implicitly. He stood up for me at my wedding and read the 23rd Psalm. In fact, I chose Lon Monk to be my chief of staff because, next to Patti, I trusted him more than anyone else. And I believed that his complete lack of connections and relationships in Illinois, coupled with his close personal friendship to me, would help to ensure that I could build a government dedicated and loyal to our mission, not filled with people whose loyalties were with any number of political leaders who may have recommended them to their positions.

Unlike my predecessor George Ryan, I wanted to have nothing to do with issuing state contracts. In fact, I gave instructions to set up my administration in a way that would prevent the kinds of things my predecessor and the people around him did. That was among the reasons why we set up a system at the beginning of my administration to leave the operations of government in the hands of the chief of staff. He would work with one of our two deputy governors and with the agency directors to handle and administer the day-to-day running of state government. I had absolutely no interest in that. I wasn't interested in squandering my opportunity to focus on the big picture by getting caught up in the minutiae. I wanted to stay above it. I didn't want to get dragged into the petty squabbles that surround things like jobs and promotions. Nor did I want to be slowed down by having to spend my time mired in a bureaucracy that could be like quicksand that swallows you up. So while I left the operations of government to others, I worked on a daily basis with our other deputy governor whose job it was to set policy, to work on legislative strategy, and to work on communications. I was going to be a chief executive modeled more like Ronald Reagan and the opposite of Jimmy Carter. Historians have concluded that part of what held Jimmy Carter back as president was that he got himself too involved in the details of his administration. Consequently, he couldn't see the forest from the trees. President Reagan, on the other hand, was widely criticized for his lack of attention to detail and for his propensity to leave the running of things to his troika, James Baker, Mike Deaver, and Ed Meese. This freed Reagan up to go out to the public and sell his program and get it passed. Criticize or not, Reagan was a two-term president who was mostly successful in achieving his big-picture objectives.

I was also determined to have the most diverse administration in Illinois history. And while I haven't conducted a study on it, I am certain that I did. In fact, I believe my administration was, from the point of view of diversity, light-years ahead of all of my predecessors. I appointed more African-Americans to top positions than any governor in Illinois history. I'm sure I shattered the performance of my predecessors in this area. I appointed more Latinos to top positions than anyone before. My administration and its policies and initiatives were driven by women in high places. Two of the five deputy governors I appointed during my six years were women. And while I was vigilant in staying out of decisions regarding the issuance of state contracts, I made it very clear that I wanted to see my administration work within the law to provide more opportunities for minority businesses to participate and properly bid for state work. I believe my administration shattered the performance of any of my predecessors in the area of giving women-owned businesses, African-American owned businesses, Hispanic and Asian-American owned businesses an opportunity to work with state government.

When you are a brand-new governor who just got elected, and you are the first one in your political party in twenty-six years to do so, a feeding frenzy begins immediately. Everybody wants something. Especially the political leaders of your own party. Where some of them were lukewarm in their support when I began my race for governor, now they were red-hot in their supplication. And they had all kinds of ideas. But mostly, they had all kinds of recommendations of people they wanted to place in the new administration.

Now this is how it works. There's nothing unusual about it. I had been in politics long enough to know that this was coming. While I was comfortable with the idea of having an open mind to their suggestions, I mostly wanted to be sure that the top-level positions of my new administration would be loyal to me and to the things I wanted to do as governor. And I sought to find people for top positions who came from the private sector and the business community. I wanted to find people with some fresh thinking who were outsiders and not beholden to the political establishment and the special interests that make up most of the decision makers in state government.

So where do you find these people? Well, one place to start is to ask some of your most committed supporters and friends who they might know. I thought Tony Rezko was one of those supporters and friends. I sought his help and advice and asked him who he thought could do a good job for the people. I especially thought he could be helpful because of what I believed were his deep contacts in the African-American community. I was looking for highly qualified African-American men and women who could become agency directors, but I didn't want them to feel that they owed their position to another political leader who may have recommended them. So for example, when I appointed Dr. Eric Whitaker as my Director for Public Health, I was told he was recommended by then state Senator Barack Obama, who asked Tony Rezko to present his name for consideration.

I met Tony Rezko around the time I was beginning to run for Congress. I never heard of him before that. His name came to my attention when I engaged the services of a fundraising firm to help me raise money for my race for Congress in 1996. He had been a contributor to other Democratic candidates, and I would learn later to Republican candidates as well. He was helpful to me in my first race for Congress and little by little, over time and after I became a Congressman, I developed a relationship with him that I believed made him more like a friend than just a political supporter. I didn't know much about him then or even after I became governor. Some of the things I would later learn about him and about some of his business practices I didn't know then. Had I heard them back then, they would have struck me as being completely out of character with the person that I thought he was. Barack Obama probably feels the same way I do. I saw him as a successful real estate developer and a businessman who presumably had wide and varied business interests.

While I was a congressman, Patti and I took Tony and his wife Rita out to dinner one Saturday night to a place called Green Dolphin Street. It was our treat. I was grateful for his help and support, and I wanted to take him out to dinner to get to know him better. Patti, who is a licensed real estate broker and real estate appraiser, began to do some real estate deals with him. But other than going out to dinner a couple of times while I was in Congress, I didn't see much of Tony or really know much about him.

I had never been to his home before, but I was invited immediately after I was first elected governor. My recollection is that the invite was for a dinner party he was having at his home a day or two after the election. I didn't want to go. It was the last thing I wanted to do. I was exhausted from a long election campaign and was in the process of decompressing. In fact, I remember being so tired that I was slurring my words. But I went because I was told I would hurt Tony's feelings if I didn't. And looking back, with the wisdom that hindsight can bring, I now know why I was invited and why I was being so intensely pressured to attend. I now believe Tony was trying to show some people how close he was to me. In any event, Tony's home was beautiful and very impressive. When I saw his home, it only confirmed to me that he was obviously doing very well in his business ventures.

Just a couple of months or so into my new administration, Patti and I had the first of our periodic dinners with Mayor Daley and his wife Maggie. It was in a restaurant at a downtown hotel right after the mayor and I welcomed the prime minister of Canada at an official dinner in that same hotel. Don't get me wrong. We didn't eat two dinners that night. We simply participated in our official responsibilities and had dinner together afterwards. I remember that dinner because I felt I bonded with Mayor Daley when I told him that in the short time I had been governor, I was most surprised by how lonely I found the job to be. How so many people wanted so many things. And how those are the kinds of things I didn't want to have to deal with, and I wasn't quite sure whether it was even appropriate for me as governor to have to deal with them. I didn't want to be in a position where I could somehow be compromised or appear that I was involved in something that I shouldn't have been involved in. That's why you have a chief of staff. Those are the kinds of things they're supposed to deal with. It's why you have legal counsel and, presumably, the chief of staff and the top lawyer are working together to make sure things are handled properly. I told the mayor that I found I was isolating myself so that I wouldn't be approached to have to deal with those sorts of things. And I asked him how he handled it and how he protected himself from all the supplicants and others who had all kinds of requests that may or may not have been appropriate. One thing I remember him saying that night was that whenever a lawmaker wants a job for a member of his or her family, they should be required to make that request in writing. I thought that was an interesting suggestion. I'm not sure we ever adopted that practice. There are practical reasons why that would be hard to do. And notwithstanding his advice, I don't think Mayor Daley ever did either.

When I was elected governor, I promised to end business as usual. And I believe I did. My promise to end business as usual was a promise to change the priorities of state government and change how business is done. I believe that during my tenure I largely succeeded in changing the corrupt system of governing that takes care of the insiders and does it on the backs of the people.

Virtually every special interest in Springfield supports the idea of having the people pay higher taxes. So much of government is very simple. It's about where the money comes from and who gets the money after it comes in. The special interests represented by their lobbyists who hover around the halls of government and buttonhole lawmakers and contribute to their campaigns, all want more money for the causes they've been paid to promote. The more money there is in the general fund, the more money they could get for their client. If that means higher taxes on the people, from their point of view, so what. It means more money for them. I was surprised to learn that a lot of the lobbyists from the business community have no problem with the people paying higher taxes. The business community, who is represented in state government by organizations like the Illinois Chamber of Commerce, are fine with higher income taxes. As one of their top officials, Doug Whitley, recently said, everybody knows corporations don't pay taxes. The Illinois Chamber of Commerce is an organization dominated by and funded by the big corporations. They speak for the big corporations, not for small business. The Illinois Retail Merchants Association is dominated by and funded by big pharmacies like Walgreens and CVS and the big supermarket chains, not the small mom-and-pop stores or to a lesser extent, the smaller independent pharmacies. Doug Whitley was right. Most big corporations don't pay taxes. Because of corporate tax loopholes and the best accountants money can buy, most big corporations don't pay any state corporate income taxes in Illinois. People do. Small businesses do. But the big corporations don't. In fact, 20% of businesses pay 96% of corporate taxes in our state. And 12,521 of the biggest corporations with over $263 billion in annual sales in Illinois, pay on average $151 in corporate taxes while the average individual, the working man or woman, pays on average $1500 in state income taxes. So if you're a big corporation in Illinois, and you want to protect corporate loopholes like the one that allows big banks to not pay sales tax on the computer software they buy when everyone else does, you would much prefer to protect those loopholes and see a higher income tax since they don't have to pay it.

For six years I fought to change those priorities. In some cases I succeeded, and in others I did not. But there is one thing I never let them do. I never let them raise income taxes on the people. I fought them every step of the way, and while I was governor I kept them from doing it.

When I think back about the beginning of my administration and the high hopes I had to change things and shake up a system that served itself at the expense of the people, I can't believe I'm where I'm at today. I reordered the priorities of the state budget to make it work for the benefit of the people, in many cases at the expense of the special interests. And I fought for and insisted on sweeping ethics reforms that for the first time in Illinois history created an independent inspector general to police state government, including the governor's office. The new ethics law had real teeth in it and was designed to root out abuses like the ones that we learned about in the previous administration. Top legislative leaders sought to water down my tough ethics legislation. And then state Senator Barack Obama was asked to sponsor it. Only after I threatened to veto a watered-down ethics bill, and threatened to call the Legislature into special session to pass a real one, did I get the bill I asked for. Ironically, I got none of the credit for the ethics bill and all the blame for all the wrongdoing my independent inspector general turned up.

What's the old adage? No good deed goes unpunished.

I can't believe I've been charged with crimes I didn't commit. I can't believe I'm under criminal indictment for things I didn't do. I can't believe I'm in this position when all along I worked in a way that I considered was completely the opposite of my predecessor.

I consider myself the anti-George Ryan. He was the ultimate insider. A career politician who loyally worked his way up the ranks of his party's establishment. He was pals with everybody in Springfield. And everybody in Springfield loved him. Why wouldn't they? He was the consummate wheeler-dealer. He would make a deal with anybody, about anything. And dole out favors to lawmakers of both parties, but not for the purpose of promoting the common good or the general welfare of the people, but for the purpose of taking care of the insiders through backroom you wash my back/I'll wash yours kind of politics. And he was the personification of the cynical politics in Springfield I abhorred and I fought. Just as cynical and eager to deceive the people as Democratic House Speaker Michael Madigan. In fact, George Ryan used to be the Republican House Speaker. And when these guys start running out of money for the things they want to do in government, they both come up with sneaky ways to do it in the backroom, in the dead of night, and on the backs of the people.

A stark example of this happened right after I was first elected governor. During our transition period, then-Governor Ryan invited Patti and me and my father-in-law and mother-in-law down to Springfield for dinner at the governor's mansion. It was a gracious gesture. After dinner, Governor Ryan pulled me aside and offered to help me with a record five-billion dollar budget deficit I was inheriting. He told me he spoke to my father-in-law and to another prominent Chicago alderman about an idea where he could get the Legislature to approve a big income tax increase on the people immediately before I was sworn in as governor. He told me he would be prepared to take the heat for the income tax increase, and I would have all the money I needed to balance the budget and run state government. I was aware of the scheme because my father-in-law approached me with it before. He thought it was a good idea: George Ryan takes the blame for the tax increase, and I get the credit for balancing the budget. I was astonished but not surprised by the cynicism. With a handshake, a wink and a nod, the other guy raises taxes, and I get the benefit. And it's even better. I can always say I didn't break my promise to the people. Because I had just been elected governor after running for the office for more than two years, promising the people of Illinois that under no circumstances would I raise their income or sales tax.

But there was a problem. What about the people who would have to pay higher taxes? Why should they have to pay more? Less than a month before, I was telling voters I wouldn't raise their taxes. To look the other way and let the other guy do it was worse than doing it myself.

What a disgustingly dishonest hoax on the people. In that equation, the people are just there to get money from. And if you can do it in a way where they don't blame you, more power to you. You see, this is exactly the disconnect I had—and still have—with the phony, dishonest politicians who run state government in Illinois. Screw the people. Who cares if you increase their burdens by taking more of their money? Who cares if you don't ease their hardships so long as you don't kiss off the big public employees union with tens of thousands of members who are voters and hundreds of thousands of campaign contributions? Who cares if the people suffer? From their point of view, as long as I could pretend I kept my promise to the people, I would have to be crazy to turn down all that money and not go out and take credit for solving the budget deficit.

I listened politely to Governor Ryan when he suggested that scheme. Coming from him, it didn't surprise me. George Ryan never pretended to be anything but an old-school politician. From his perspective as the quintessential old pol, he was just being a nice guy. One politician helping another politician. But when I began hearing those kinds of cynical suggestions from political figures who pretend to be something more than George Ryan, then that outright makes me sick. These clever, phony politicians sell themselves like they care about the people, when in reality they just look down on the people and see them as the ones who have to bear all the burdens, while they, the politicians, use their money to take care of themselves, their families, and the insiders.

I thanked Governor Ryan for his offer but I declined. Notwithstanding the fact that he left me a budget deficit that was significantly higher than anything we were led to believe,

I had no intention of breaking my promise to the people. But it was more than that. I didn't believe that people should have to pay more in taxes. I didn't then and I don't now. I know enough about the state budget to realize that before the people should have to pay more, the state budget should be completely purged of all of the spending priorities that look after narrow special interests and do not promote the broader common good. I kept my promise to not raise taxes on people because raising taxes was the wrong thing to do.

There is a scene at the end of the classic movie *Raging Bull* where Robert De Niro, playing Jake LaMotta, is in a jail cell. The greatness and total commitment of Robert DeNiro as an actor is in full display. He worked out, got in great shape and trained and learned how to box. He looked like the real Jake LaMotta fighting Sugar Ray Robinson from those old, black-and-white films where clouds of smoke are hovering overhead. And then to capture LaMotta later in life—out of shape, overweight, and over the hill—DeNiro put on a whole bunch of weight. Playing his character that way helped him to both capture and illustrate the essence of Jake LaMotta's personal tragedy. He rose to become the middleweight champion of the world but then, because of his own demons, he loses it all: his money, his status, and most importantly, his wife and family. And there he is, at rock bottom, in a jail cell. And it's there that he has the epiphany that he brought all of this on himself. And he starts to repeatedly hit his head against the wall all the while saying over and over again, "Stupid, stupid, stupid."

I thought Tony Rezko was a completely different person. I trusted him. I thought he was a friend. And I was raised to believe that when you think someone is your friend, they deserve to be given the benefit of the doubt when others are attacking or bad mouthing them. So initially I was reluctant to believe a lot of the bad things that were being said about him. Especially when he assured me that they were not true. I didn't believe that he was a manipulative and sinister person. That was not how I saw him. But now I think may have been wrong.

Like the Pharisees in the Old Testament, "where once I was blind, now I can see." I can now see that like Robert De Niro in *Raging Bull*, I should find a wall and start beating my head against it saying, *stupid, stupid, stupid*. It is becoming very clear to me that I was stupid to trust Tony Rezko, and I was stupid for not cutting and running from him earlier. I was stupid that I did not disassociate myself from him like Barack Obama did. The President said he was a bonehead when he trusted Tony Rezko. I say I was stupid.

It's funny how life is. How one event or one person or one relationship can change everything. How one small, insignificant random act can have such monumental consequences. What if Abraham Lincoln didn't go to Ford's theater that night? Or if Mark Antony never met Cleopatra? There would have been no battle of Actium. Octavian would never have won, and Mark Antony would've ruled Rome. How different would things be? That by itself a single act, as unimportant as it may seem at the time in the big scheme of things, can have such a monumental impact that could change everything. I often wonder what if I never met Tony Rezko? What if his life never intersected with mine? How different would things be? I'm certain I would still be governor, and I wouldn't be facing what I have to face today. Take Tony Rezko out of my life, and I really believe I wouldn't be where I am right now.

I don't know how to cook. I wouldn't even know how to boil an egg properly. I never cooked a turkey in my life. I hate to say I never even carved one. But Martha Stewart and I have something in common. We have both been the targets of federal prosecutors. In Martha Stewart's case, federal prosecutors began investigating her over things she didn't do. They were so relentless in their pursuit, they made her feel as if she did something wrong when in fact she did not. They didn't rest until they put so much fear into her that she told a lie. And for that lie, not for any of the things they say she did wrong, she spent five months in federal prison.

A similar thing happened with Scooter Libby. For years, federal investigators targeted Scooter Libby. They pursued him and accused him of obstruction of justice, of making untrue statements to the FBI and of lying before a grand jury. Notwithstanding where their investigation led, they were determined to get him. It got to the point where it didn't matter what the truth was. The federal prosecutor had made such a big deal out of this investigation that the case became more about the prosecutor's own self-preservation than justice. In fact, this prosecutor is so concerned about his own standing that he willfully conducts investigations and prosecutions that cause great injustice.

This same prosecutor is prosecuting me. This same prosecutor is the one who accused me of trying to sell Barack Obama's Senate seat for personal gain. But that accusation is completely and entirely false.

CHAPTER NINE

YOU KNOW, I COULD'VE MADE MYSELF A U.S. SENATOR. The law allows it. It allows for a governor to appoint himself to the United States Senate in the case of a vacancy. Looking back, had I done that the day after Obama's election, how different would things be for me now? It's painful to think about. Had I appointed myself to the United States Senate, or even appointed my wife—which again, I could have legally done—our lives would in all probability be a lot different than they are today.

A lot of people advised and encouraged me to appoint myself senator. Deep down, it didn't feel right to me. But when you're a governor, and different people suggest different ideas, and there are a wide range of factors that go into a decision like this, you should at least have an open mind and think about them. Talk about them with people whose opinions you trust. Explore them and test them. Try to get an honest assessment from your advisers. Each adviser has their own way of looking at things. And to varying degrees, some of their advice has to be weighed by their propensity to kiss your ass and not tell you like it is.

On the other hand, some of your advisers are forthright and will tell you straight out that, for example, appointing yourself to the United States Senate would be the wrong move. But maybe they're not right. So when they express their honest opinion, you fight back and play the Devil's advocate and challenge what they're saying. Whether it's the wisdom of making yourself a U.S. Senator or the wisdom of appointing Oprah Winfrey, part of the process, at least for me, in making important decisions is to explore ideas held by the people around me whose opinions I rely on before I make them. And among the many options that I discussed and considered with my top advisers was whether it made sense to appoint myself to the United States Senate.

Appointing myself to the Senate was not something I thought I would do. We did some homework and found examples of other governors who had done so. It didn't look right. We talked about whether appointing myself to the U.S. Senate to fill out the rest of the term but announcing that I wasn't going to run for reelection might work. It would be a way where the people indirectly decide who the senator is because I was someone who was elected twice statewide in Illinois. The thinking held that these were unusual circumstances where the will of the people to choose their senator would have to wait until the next election. Hold the seat but don't run again. The people, in the next election, could express their will for an open seat that would give them the most say in the decision. Step out and allow the voters to pick their senator in the next election.

But even that, deep down, didn't feel right. I knew the people of Illinois elected me twice to be their governor. And to quit a job the people elected me to do and give myself another job just didn't feel right. On the other hand, enough people thought I should consider the option that I wanted to fully explore it, see whether I might not have thought of something, and then balance it against the other options before I ultimately rejected it and went in another direction.

And then again don't rule that option out prematurely. Keep talking about it to some in your inner circle. Keep it alive. The fear that I might appoint myself to the senate was great leverage with the national Democrats to help me get the deal I wanted: namely jobs and healthcare and no new taxes.

If I had any doubts that a United States Senate seat is something a lot of people would want, I don't anymore. It's a highly coveted position. There's a reason why it's called the most exclusive club in the world. And in so many ways, this may be the best job there is in politics. It's highly prestigious. The pay is good. You have a big staff and access to the best and brightest who want to work for you. You have influence but unlike the executive branch of government, you don't have a lot of responsibility. And you're not on the firing line. The president is. In fact, a lot of what U.S. senators do is take shots at the president. They do it in speeches on the Senate floor that hardly anyone listens to. In fact, hardly anyone's there when the senator is giving his speech. You can see the world and travel in great comfort. You have a six-year term, and if you do your politics right back home, in most cases you can keep the job for as long as you want. If you want to be happy for the rest of your life, being a U.S. Senator is one way that can help you do it. And when there's a vacancy, people want it. And so do their supporters.

Some time after the financial collapse in September 2008, when it started to become clear that Barack Obama was likely to be elected president, my Chief of Staff called me to tell me about a lunch he had with a woman by the name of Marilyn Katz. She's a political activist, and I believe she has a communications or consulting business in Chicago. John Harris told me that the purpose of the lunch was that Marilyn Katz had raised the issue of having me appoint Valerie Jarrett, a Chicago lawyer and businesswoman, to the United States Senate to succeed Barack Obama. Marilyn Katz is close to Obama's political consultant David Axelrod. John told me that she brought up the subject of my reelection for governor. She indicated that if I appointed Valerie Jarrett to the U.S. Senate, the Obama people would help me raise money from their network of contributors across the country. And that the new senator and the Obama political operatives would help to make it happen.

I didn't give much thought to it. I remember mocking it to John Harris. I may have even bemusedly asked the question, isn't that pay to play? But I put it out of my mind.

Around that time, Patti told me that she had received a call from Marilyn Katz who wanted to have lunch with her. Patti asked me if I had any idea why she was inviting her to lunch. Patti really didn't know Marilyn Katz. She thought initially that it might have something to do with the work Patti was doing for the homeless.

I told her that the lunch was probably about the Senate seat. That call, coupled with Marilyn Katz's lunch with John Harris, made me extra cautious. And I told Patti to stay one million miles away from that. In the environment I was operating in, where federal authorities were investigating me for over the last four years and were in a position where they were soon going to have to fish or cut bait, I didn't want my wife caught up in a political discussion involving a Senate seat and potential future fundraising opportunities.

Valerie Jarrett is an impressive person. To make her a senator would have been good politics for me: my African-American base would have offered support, the media elite would have applauded the pick, and, presumably, it would have made the new president happy. I knew her and I liked her. But was this the best I could do for the people of Illinois? I was concerned that a Valerie Jarrett appointment would not be supported by House Speaker Michael Madigan, who would continue to block my legislative initiatives that could bring real progress and results for the people.

Marilyn Katz's overture was one of several that were being made to me or to people close to me. State Senate President Emil Jones surprised me when he expressed an interest in the Senate seat. He'd been a strong ally of mine who helped me achieve a lot of the things I am most proud of. He is African-American and someone who took a great deal of pride in being a mentor of sorts to Barack Obama. In every consideration of mine, Emil Jones was always a possibility to be appointed. In my conversations with him about the subject, he pledged to be a helpful ally if I appointed him.

This whole story regarding the Senate seat is upside down. I never approached anyone who was interested in becoming a United States Senator or any of their representatives and asked for, or much less even raised, the subject of campaign contributions in exchange for the Senate seat. I did not do it. I would not do it. I would've considered it the wrong thing to do. But even putting aside the question of right and wrong, it would have been, considering the circumstances and the scrutiny I was under, an incredibly stupid thing to do. But the fact remains that people approached us about campaign contributions if I either appointed them or the person they were supporting to the Senate. If anyone should have been charged with a crime for this, it should have been them and not me.

Others who were interested in the Senate seat began to raise the subject with me. A close ally and a prominent state legislator spoke to me about the possibility of choosing him. His position was that if I was going to run for reelection, then I should choose an African-American to fill the seat. But if I chose to not run again, I should choose him. And that he would be helpful and loyal. He even intimated that his overflowing campaign fund might be available to me if I later changed my mind and decided to run for a third term, since the law states that campaign money raised for state elections generally can't be used in federal Senate elections. In fact, the week before my arrest, as I was getting close to a final decision, he called me at my home and asked to meet with me in person. He told me he was going to be in Chicago in the next week and wanted to set up the meeting. I knew he wanted to talk to me about the Senate seat. That's why he didn't want to talk about it over the phone.

Now, when somebody wants to meet with you to talk about something that he doesn't want to say over the telephone, that's a red flag. It means they want to talk about something that they don't want anyone else to hear. This is very common in politics. But it also raises a red flag that maybe you don't want to hear what they want to say. Still, he pressed me for a date and time to meet. He was a close friend and supporter, so I relented and agreed to meet. But I really had no intention of doing so. I knew what he wanted to talk about, and I was uncomfortable with it. I didn't want him to raise the issue of the Senate seat or any other subject related to it. I wanted to stay away from that. I wanted to avoid any conversations with anyone who could possibly be chosen as a senator who might say something that could be interpreted as improper. So when the time came for us to get together, I purposely canceled the meeting. I was unavailable to meet. He was probably angry with me for doing it. Because I believe he knew that I knew what he wanted to talk about. But in the wake of all that happened to me, it turns out I protected him from a conversation that may have ended up getting him in trouble.

It is ironic that after the shit hit the fan, my good friend who intimated that he had campaign funds that could be available to me if he was appointed a United States senator, voted to impeach me.

All kinds of offers were coming from different people in different ways. Some came directly. Others came through the use of third parties. Some appeared to be acting on behalf of the candidate they were backing while others seemed to be acting on their own. These people were not shy about approaching me and others close to me, and to varying degrees expressing what they would do if I picked the senator they wanted.

Talk about who could be Obama's successor was not uncommon before the election. But it didn't get serious or very real until after the election. That's when I began to start thinking about all the different options and the different dynamics involved. So as soon as the election was over, the discussions began. I started to talk to, seek the advice of, and test some ideas with some of my top advisers. I also began immediately to discuss the Senate appointment with people outside of my inner circle.

I spoke to Rahm Emanuel about it on the Saturday after the election. We talked about it over the telephone. I called him from home that morning to return one of his telephone calls. The day before, Rahm and I spoke about his plans and his congressional seat. He had decided, much to my surprise, to give up his congressional seat and become President Obama's Chief of Staff. I was surprised because I believed Rahm was on the fast track to one day succeed Nancy Pelosi as Speaker of the House. I couldn't see him giving that up to become the President's Chief of Staff. It turned out that I was both wrong and right. I was wrong when I predicted that reports of him taking the job as the President's Chief of Staff were erroneous. But I was right. Rahm wasn't giving up on his dream to be Speaker of the House. In fact, Rahm understandably wanted to keep his options open if he could. That's what all good politicians do. He called to let me know what he was going to do. But the real purpose of his call was to see whether or not I would be willing to work with him and appoint a successor to his congressional seat who he would have designated to be a placeholder and hold the seat for him when he sought to return to Congress in two years. Rahm asked me if I'd be willing to do it. I told him I didn't think the law gave the governor the same power to appoint a congressman as it did a senator. It was my understanding that as governor I had the power to set the dates for a special election if a vacancy materialized, but I didn't have the legal authority to actually appoint a congressman. Rahm told me that his lawyers thought there was a way where the governor might be able to make an appointment. After chiding him for not acknowledging the help I gave his brother Ari in the past to help one of his clients bring the sport of Ultimate Fighting to Illinois—an idea, incidentally, that I didn't like but nevertheless I did to help him—I told him I would talk to my legal counsel and see if there was a way where this perhaps might work. But if I did, I teased him that this time he should consider it a favor. Because if I helped appoint a congressman who was going to keep the seat warm for him, then I was going to make a lot of people who wanted to be congressmen unhappy with me. Including my own sister-in-law, who I love, who was also talking about running for Congress in what was expected to be a special election.

In those conversations with Rahm, he asked me about what I was going to do with the Senate choice. I talked about some of the potential candidates and potential scenarios. He did not lobby for anyone in particular. He asked if I was seriously considering Senate President Emil Jones. I told him I was. He told me he thought that was a very bad idea, and I would be skewered in the media if I did it.

I raised the possibility of Lisa Madigan.

Rahm was well aware of my relationship with her father. I remember saying something to him like, if I have to do something that is personally repugnant to me, and that thing is appointing Mike Madigan's daughter to the United States Senate, then the question for me is, how much do I love the people of Illinois? Do I love the people of Illinois enough to do something that is so personally distasteful to me?

I raised that question with Rahm Emanuel a month before I decided that not only could I do it, but that it was my first choice. I hoped to make it happen. And I hoped to make it happen with Rahm Emanuel's help.

CHAPTER TEN

A FEW HOURS AFTER MY ARREST ON DECEMBER 9, 2008, THE UNITED STATES ATTORNEY PATRICK FITZGERALD HELD A SENSATIONAL PRESS CONFERENCE WHERE HE ACCUSED ME OF TRYING TO SELL A UNITED STATES SENATE SEAT. He defended his action by saying he arrested me to prevent this from occurring, that he was acting to stop a crime spree before it happened. Mr. Fitzgerald was a hundred percent wrong. I never intended to sell the Senate seat. I was merely engaged in the ordinary and routine politicking that frequently accompanies a significant appointment by the governor.

How much do I love the people of Illinois? That was a question I asked myself over and over again as I considered who I should appoint to the United States Senate. For over a month I discussed possible candidates for the Senate with several people. These people included my top staff, my political advisers, as well as other friends and leaders whose opinions I valued. I would test ideas and share some of my thoughts with them. I would gauge their responses, and seek their impressions of some of the considerations I had in mind.

And when I consistently raised the name of one candidate in particular, I would ask of them the same question I'd constantly ask of myself: *How much do I love the people of Illinois?*

My first choice for the United States Senate was Lisa Madigan. I decided to choose Illinois Attorney General Lisa Madigan only on the condition that a deal could be worked out with her father, Democratic House Speaker Michael

Madigan, where he would agree to pass a public works jobs bill that he was blocking. Where he would agree to pass legislation to expand access to affordable healthcare to working and middle-class families. Where he would agree to pass a bill that would place a moratorium on mortgage foreclosures and a bill that would require insurance companies to cover the pre-existing medical conditions of people who are sick but either cannot afford or cannot obtain health insurance. I decided to appoint his daughter to the United States Senate if he would agree to pass those bills, as well as promise to join me in preventing an income tax increase on the people of Illinois for the last two years of my term.

All along, from the very beginning, and long before Barack Obama was elected president, I thought about the possibility of a deal like this. Should Obama get elected president, could I appoint the daughter of my political nemesis who was working against my efforts to create jobs, expand healthcare, and protect taxpayers? Could I appoint Mike Madigan's daughter even though both of them had spent much of the last six years working to hurt me politically? That was the question I would ask my advisers as well as other political, business, and labor leaders with whom I shared some of my thoughts. And the question almost always remained: If I could create jobs, expand healthcare, and protect taxpayers, do I love the people of Illinois enough to put aside my personal feelings and appoint Lisa Madigan to the United States Senate?

That was the question. *How much do I love the people of Illinois?* I asked that question to a lot of people. And I constantly asked that question of myself. Yet deep down, I knew that if I could get a deal like that, appointing her to the United States Senate was the right thing to do. No other choice for the Senate would allow me to achieve as much for the people of Illinois. And while the idea of handing Mike Madigan's daughter a coveted United States Senate seat was personally distasteful to me, and choosing her would be harmful to my political base in the African-American community, giving her that job meant I could give hundreds of thousands of people jobs and tens of thousands of people access to affordable healthcare. No other choice for the United States Senate could help so many people across Illinois.

So that is why I decided to appoint Lisa Madigan to the Senate. But I would only appoint her on one condition. Her father had to first pass a jobs bill, the legislation to expand healthcare, and preferably some of the other initiatives I had hoped we could successfully negotiate. Only when he passed those initiatives would I appoint his daughter to the United States Senate. I would not appoint her if that deal couldn't be made. And I would not appoint her on the promise that he would pass those initiatives later. My experience with him proved that I couldn't trust him to keep his part of the bargain. And besides, asking the Democratic House Speaker to support legislation to expand healthcare and create jobs through public works was a very easy thing for him to do. He could pass just about anything he wants. The members of his caucus do what they're told. And lifting the brick he placed on the public works bill meant that he would now be the last political leader in Illinois, Democrat and Republican, to support what had previously passed the Illinois state Senate several times before.

It's interesting how this process evolved and developed. Personally, it was a case of love and hate. On the one hand, I was repulsed by the idea of making Lisa Madigan the senator. I hated the idea. On the other hand, I wanted to put people to work, give them access to affordable healthcare, and protect them from an income tax increase. I loved that. I really wanted this deal to happen. So at the same time I was trying to come to grips with some of my own personal reservations, I was working to build a coalition of powerful Democratic leaders and other influential people who might help me. Because for this deal to work, I needed help. I believed I couldn't do it by myself because over the last year or more, Mike Madigan refused to negotiate with me on any issue. He wouldn't meet with me or the Democratic Senate President Emil Jones. He was angry because I had previously cut out of the budget funds that he had reserved for his Democratic lawmakers.

I toyed with the idea of reaching out to him directly. I thought about it. But I didn't trust it. I thought the better way to put a deal like that together was to work through third parties who also had a vested interest in the outcome of who the next senator might be. That's why I felt it was imperative to get the help of Democratic leaders like Rahm Emanuel, Senator Dick Durbin, Senator Harry Reid, and Senator Bob Menendez. And I also felt that those national Democratic leaders might be more motivated to help get a deal done, if they felt that the alternative to Lisa Madigan would be someone that they didn't want.

And who didn't they want?

Well, they didn't want state Senate President Emil Jones. He would create political problems for them that they wanted to avoid. That view was made clear to me early on. Who else didn't they want? They didn't want me. They were fearful I might appoint myself and bring with me the Rezko baggage that both the new President and I had in common. This too, was made clear to me early on. And Harry Reid and Dick Durbin didn't want Jesse Jackson Junior. And while I wasn't going to appoint him, I believed that if they feared there was a possibility I might appoint Congressman Jackson, or that I might even appoint myself, then they would work all the harder to help me get the deal done with Mike Madigan for his daughter. They needed to know that if I couldn't get the jobs and healthcare bills passed, then maybe I would be crazy enough to send myself to the Senate.

I was almost certain I was not going to run for a third term. I never saw myself as more than a two-term governor. My decision to appoint Lisa Madigan to the United States Senate had nothing to do with me removing a potential rival for governor. But it had everything to do with me loving the people of Illinois.

How much do I love the people of Illinois? Enough to appoint the daughter of my political nemesis if it meant I could achieve a lot of good things for the people.

And this deal was good for everyone. For the people of Illinois it meant more jobs, more healthcare, and preventing their taxes from going up. And while I owed the African-American community a great deal for their support, the public works bill that I wanted passed had a billion-dollar investment in it to help poor communities rebuild. Most of that billion dollars was earmarked for the African-American community. In addition to that, as the governor I would have appointed the next Attorney General to replace Lisa Madigan and that person would have been African-American.

For the Democratic Senate leadership, this was what they wanted. They would have had a U.S. Senator who was likely to be reelected and would probably attract only token opposition from the Republicans. And notwithstanding my political differences with her and her father, I viewed her as being a qualified and capable United States Senator.

Discussions to appoint Lisa Madigan to the United States Senate in exchange for those results had been ongoing from the very beginning. Illinois Senator Dick Durbin offered to help. I spoke to the Democratic Senate majority leader Harry Reid about it. He was supportive. I spoke to United States Senator Robert Menendez of New Jersey, and he agreed to help facilitate and negotiate that deal.

My Chief of Staff John Harris periodically briefed me on conversations he said he was having with President Obama's new Chief of Staff, Rahm Emanuel, on this deal. Once I reached a decision, I wanted their help. From a personal standpoint, my decision was a painful one. The idea of making Lisa Madigan a senator after she and her father had been working so hard to hurt the interests of the average ordinary family in Illinois turned my stomach. But I decided to do it. I decided to do it because the greater good would be served. I could help a lot of people if I could make the right political deal with her father. And that's the kind of thing I said in numerous conversations with people like Senator Durbin, or the owner of the Chicago White Sox Jerry Reinsdorf, or with Rahm Emanuel, with powerful labor leaders, and others. Could I put aside my personal feelings in order to pick a senator that could end up bringing the most results and doing the most good for the people of Illinois? No other potential senator could've brought those kinds of results for the people of Illinois except for Lisa Madigan if her father was willing to make the deal. If I could negotiate a deal along those lines, then Lisa Madigan would be the Senator. If that political deal couldn't be worked out, if the two Madigans were so opposed to creating jobs or expanding healthcare that they rejected the deal, then I decided that I was going to pick Congressman Danny Davis, Gery Chico, or Eric Whitaker and appoint one of them to the United States Senate.

The weekend before I was arrested I knew what I was going to do. And I was at peace. I knew it was the best I could hope for, and I believed the table was set where if this deal was ever going to happen, all the right interests were properly aligned to help. That decision was essentially finalized the Wednesday before at a meeting in Philadelphia with my Washington D.C. political consultant, my pollster, my deputy governor, and me. I knew when I left Philadelphia who my first choice would be, and if that didn't work out, who my second choice would be, and then a third and fourth choice if it ever came to that. But it wasn't going to come to that. Because there are very few people who, if offered a chance to become a United States Senator, would turn it down. I knew what I was going to do. But I wanted to take the rest of the week and the weekend to let it settle in and develop it more before I acted.

I pulled the trigger Monday morning December 8th, the day before I was arrested. In a telephone call to my Chief of Staff early that morning, I told him what I wanted to do. I decided to appoint Illinois Attorney General Lisa Madigan to the United States Senate if a deal could be worked out with her father. I told him to work out the tactics. The deal would involve passing the capital construction bill that would create 500,000 jobs, expanding healthcare to help cover between 50,000 to 300,000 people, and the agreement to pass a bill that would put a moratorium on mortgage foreclosures because every day in Illinois 400 people were being thrown out of their homes. I also wanted to pass a bill to require insurance companies to cover the pre-existing illnesses of people who otherwise are uninsurable. And I hoped to get House Speaker Madigan to also agree to pass a bill that would provide property tax relief to homeowners in Cook County. I hoped to get all of those things, but like any negotiation, I was prepared to take less. But in no event was I going to settle for anything less than a jobs bill, healthcare expansion, and a promise to hold the line on taxes.

As I mentioned, I was hoping to use this unique opportunity to finally get real and meaningful property tax relief for homeowners in Cook County. This would not have been a deal-breaker for me. It might have been one for him. But I was going to push it and see if I might be able to get it. The choice for Mike Madigan would be whether he was prepared to sacrifice his financial interests and earn less money from his lucrative law practice in order to see his daughter become a United States Senator. I wasn't sure which he would choose: making money or making his daughter a United States Senator.

My plan was to attempt to get Speaker Madigan to pass a bill that he personally and single-handedly was holding up. Over the years, Mike Madigan has had a lucrative career representing big commercial real estate properties to reduce their property taxes and, as he told me, charging a fee for the work. The complicated property tax system in Cook County is a zero-sum game. For every dollar Mike Madigan saves for his big downtown clients, that burden shifts to the homeowner, to the little guy. Here again the little guy gets screwed when big powerful people with connections make the rules and rig the system for their benefit while doing it on the backs of the average, ordinary homeowner.

Madigan, as the Speaker of the House, has the power to simply not call bills for a vote if he doesn't like them. Over the years, he has refused to call a bill for a vote that would provide property tax relief for homeowners. His daughter, who as Attorney General is supposed to be the advocate for the average consumer like the average homeowner, has rejected repeated requests to issue a legal opinion on whether her father's unilateral action preventing property tax relief for homeowners because he has a conflict of interest with his law practice is, in fact, a conflict of interest and should be barred by law. Why is it that homeowners have to pay higher property taxes because Mike Madigan can, all by himself, keep in place a system that protects his clients and the millions of dollars in fees he earns from them? How Mike Madigan gets away with this is amazing to me. In my opinion, it's a glaring conflict of interest the size of the Grand Canyon that directly costs the average homeowner hundreds, if not thousands, of dollars a year. And it allows Mike Madigan and his firm to earn an enormous amount of money per year in legal fees. He should not be allowed to single-handedly kill property tax relief for homeowners when by doing so, he benefits financially. He makes the rules that benefit him. It is incredibly unethical. It may very well be illegal. And if it isn't, I believe it certainly should be.

My thinking was, if I'm going to hand Mike Madigan's daughter a coveted United States Senate seat that she didn't work for, and appoint someone who quietly and behind the scenes has been working against the interests of the little guy—whether it be supporting efforts to take healthcare away from poor people or protecting her father's law practice and doing it on the backs of the average homeowner—then let's see if I could get her father to put his private personal interests aside and pass a bill that would bring property tax relief to homeowners.

What still remains a mystery to me is how the Chicago media has turned a blind eye to the Madigans' seemingly scandalous behavior. Why don't they—as the investigative body they purport to be—look into the issue on behalf of homeowners and expose the conflict of interest and bring about property tax reform?

I preferred to have Rahm Emanuel work as the principal third party in negotiating the deal. I expressed that preference to my Chief of Staff John Harris. He told me he spoke to Rahm Emanuel and that Rahm had suggested that Senator Durbin negotiate the deal. I responded and told John Harris to tell Rahm that I preferred he make the deal. Rahm Emanuel is a guy who knows how to get things done. And bringing with him the weight of his new position, I felt he was the right guy to make it happen. And I wanted to see that it happened. Senator Durbin wanted to help. That was good too. The only problem with Durbin was that he feared Mike Madigan.

I remember sitting in Durban's beautiful Senate office, with his great view overlooking the Washington Mall with the Washington Monument and the Lincoln Memorial in the backdrop, as he told me how hurt he was that Mike Madigan had not spoken tó him for a long period of time. I was surprised that it seemed to bother him so much. I remember asking him why he would care. "Look at you," I said. "You're a leader in the United States Senate with an office like this, why should you care about a petty, little backroom politician in Illinois? What could he ever do to you?"

I'm not sure if he ever answered me. And it really didn't matter. While Senator Durbin's help was more than welcome, I wanted Rahm Emanuel to be the lead in making this deal. Rahm is not the kind of guy who would be afraid of Mike Madigan. I believed with his help, I would have my best chance at getting the best possible deal for the people.

I spoke to Senator Durbin on November 24, 2008, at about two o'clock in the afternoon about the senate seat. I talked about the possibility of Lisa Madigan in exchange for a jobs bill and healthcare and the other things I mentioned. Senator Durbin was aware that I did not have a good relationship with the Madigans. But he and Harry Reid and Senator Menendez welcomed her appointment. They saw her as someone who could be reelected and invite little or no opposition. And it was obvious to me on that phone conversation that he wanted her. He said she used to work for Senator Paul Simon, and she would take it if asked. So he offered to be a go-between and an emissary to see if we could make a deal. I thanked him for his offer and asked him to wait a little while. Back then, I still wasn't ready to pull the trigger.

There really aren't a lot of secrets in politics. So when I spoke to Senator Durbin on that day in November, I figured the word would likely get out to the Madigans that I was honestly considering Lisa as a possible senator. I also knew that the Madigans had been hearing that I was considering her because from the very beginning of the process, I spoke to several people about the possibility of making a deal where I could appoint her to the Senate. So on the morning of December 8th, when I directed my Chief of Staff John Harris to get the ball rolling and see if we could make this deal, I believed everything was properly positioned. The bases were loaded, and now was the time to start driving in some runs.

The Madigans were probably well aware of what I wanted in return. And in my mind, I calculated that either later that week, maybe Thursday, December 12, or maybe one day the following week but well before Christmas, an agreement would have been reached, and Mike Madigan would call his members into session for one day and pass the jobs bill, the healthcare expansion, and any of the other initiatives we might have been able to agree on. I also had in mind a potential later date in early January if more time was needed to bring it all about.

During my six years as governor, Mike Madigan routinely broke his word and made promises to me and others that he didn't keep. So I was insistent that before I appoint his daughter to the Senate, he needed to act first. Once those bills were passed, I would immediately appoint Lisa Madigan to the United States Senate. I figured if all had been allowed to move forward as I thought, she could have been appointed sometime during the week before Christmas but no later than the second week of January. The people of Illinois would have had a half million jobs created, tens of thousands of people would gain access to healthcare, homeowners in Cook County could have seen property tax relief, there would be a moratorium on mortgage foreclosures, and insurance companies would have to cover people with pre-existing medical illnesses.

That would have been one great Christmas for the Madigan family. It would have been one great Christmas for a lot more families across the state of Illinois.

Before it could get done, United States Attorney Patrick Fitzgerald had me arrested.

So when Mr. Fitzgerald said at a press conference on the day of my arrest that he acted to stop a crime spree before it happened, he couldn't have been more wrong. When he arrested me and my Chief of Staff, he didn't stop a crime spree. He instead stopped the embryonic stages of a routine and lawful political deal. This deal would have created jobs, expanded healthcare, and protected taxpayers. To be more specific, he prevented a deal that would have created 500,000 jobs and expanded healthcare to 50,000 to 300,000 people. He prevented a deal that would lead to the passing of a law requiring insurance companies to cover the pre-existing illnesses of people who are sick and cannot get insurance. He stopped the possibility of passing a law that could have provided property tax relief to homeowners in Cook County. And he set in motion a foreseeable chain of events that could lead to the people of Illinois paying a higher income tax. Mr. Fitzgerald didn't stop a crime spree. He stopped me from doing a lot of good for a lot of people.

CHAPTER ELEVEN

OUR HOME WAS A MADHOUSE. The media was everywhere. I first discovered the media's presence the morning after my arrest at around 3:30 a.m. when I was awakened by an unfamiliar sound outside. An occasional beeping sound was accompanied by a constant humming. It was like the sound of a generator. When I heard it, I got out of bed and looked out the window to see what it was. What I discovered was the first of what would turn out to be numerous media trucks from every conceivable news station imaginable keeping vigil outside of our home. The first truck I saw had a long mast that reached into the sky well above our second-floor bedroom.

Soon, blinding television lights would be turned on to do live shots for the pre-dawn early morning news. I think some of them are on the air at 5:00 a.m. It wasn't long before I would hear the sound of news helicopters hovering overhead. They later followed me flying over the expressway like I was O.J. Simpson on my ride downtown to work. This was the beginning of the new reality we had to live with now. Our pleasant and quiet neighborhood was being invaded and, worse than that, occupied by a horde of media. That occupation would last for more than a month. Early every morning, and late every evening, the media was there. And while the extent and the intensity of their presence would vary, for the better part of a month, our neighbors would have to suffer the consequences of having a governor living in their neighborhood. I'm sorry they had to go through it. They didn't sign up to be governor, I did. It's too bad our neighbors had to live through it too.

Because of the events surrounding me, our quiet, residential, family-friendly, Ravenswood Manor neighborhood was turned into an occupied territory. Invaded and conquered by the media. Sometimes I wonder if instead we might have been better off being conquered and occupied by Genghis Khan and his hordes. At least then we wouldn't have to be on television.

This was a bad scene, and it was hard on our children, especially our twelve-year-old, Amy. There is a world of difference between the awareness of a twelve-year-old and that of a five-year-old. The omnipresence of the media surrounding our house—their trucks, their lights, their cameras, the reporters shouting questions, the noise, the loss of privacy—the whole thing was especially hard on Amy. It was hard for her to escape.

The day after my arrest, Patti left for work that morning before me. She was the director of development for an organization called the Chicago Christian Industrial League, a not-for-profit organization that helps the homeless. I left for my office a little later. Getting out of the house that morning wasn't so easy. My security detail had to make some logistical adjustments to establish a buffer between me and the media. It was the beginning of leaving the house out of a back door as the best way to avoid talking to the press. I wasn't in a position at that time to talk to them or to answer any questions. Everything had happened so fast, and I still knew so little about the nature and the extent of the allegations against me.

Over the next several days, I spent most of my time trying to regroup. I first had to learn more about the allegations against me. Then I had to put together a legal team to defend me. And the most immediate thing that needed to be done was to establish a new staff to fill the positions vacated by my chief of staff and my deputy governor—two people I relied on heavily in helping me run my administration.

The inevitable talk of my resignation began immediately. It was raised by a whole bunch of self-righteous politicians tripping all over each other to see which one could be the fastest and the loudest so they could see their names in the newspapers. Never mind that the allegations against me might be untrue. Never mind that they had yet to hear my side of the story. Never mind that they knew less about the allegations or any of the evidence supporting the allegations than I did. That didn't matter. For a lot of politicians, pressing for my resignation was a way to get some press.

I also expected calls for impeachment. This was nothing new. The first talk of impeachment began a year and a half earlier during the summer of 2007. Lawmakers were angry at me because I called them into a series of special legislative sessions that required their attendance. I did this to compel them to pass a state budget and keep the operations of state government from shutting down. Many lawmakers were angry at being required to be there, and, at the instigation of the House Speaker Michael Madigan, some of them began what would become an almost seasonal call for my impeachment.

When a scandal like this surfaces, rushing to judgment and political posturing is what politicians do. It's part of their makeup. It must be in their DNA. It is to be expected, especially from politicians in the other political party.

The Republicans generally opposed my policies even before they knew what they were. But that's no surprise. This comes right out of the playbook in the section on partisan politics that calls for the political party that's out of power to oppose the party that's in power.

In my years as Governor, I had to deal with those realities. And when you're facing the kinds of allegations that I was facing, it's to be expected that the Republicans would immediately pounce on the issue in order to gain political capital both at my expense and at the expense of my party.

But my biggest obstacle came from some members in my own party, especially from the Democratic House Speaker, Michael Madigan. He has been the Speaker of the Illinois House of Representatives for over twenty years and in Illinois politics for more than forty years. He also happens to be the State Democratic Party chairman; although he's not a very good one. It's widely acknowledged that he hasn't used that position to help other Democrats. The only Democratic candidates he helps are candidates to the Illinois House whose votes he needs to remain as Speaker, and he uses his position as chairman to further the political interests of his daughter, Attorney General Lisa Madigan.

So, in addition to the natural instinct of the Republicans to immediately call for my resignation, calls from Democrats started to come in too. A drumbeat was growing to remove me from office.

And it wasn't too long before a third way of removing me from office presented itself. Before the week was out, I was visited by a prominent Illinois state senator, the Reverend-Senator James Meeks, a fellow Democrat, and someone with whom I've always had a mostly good working relationship. He came to my office with an idea. He wanted me to consider a provision in the Illinois state Constitution where the Governor can voluntarily choose to step aside by claiming that he is incapacitated and therefore unable to fulfill his duties. Under this provision, I could keep my full salary for the remainder of my term as well as the security detail that had been protecting me and my family since I was first elected. I would still be Governor in name. But the Lieutenant Governor would immediately take over for as long as the incapacitation lasted.

I listened politely to his ideas. I neither indicated to him that I was interested or not interested. I just listened. And as the days and weeks unfolded, the offer to voluntarily step aside and keep my full pay and full security detail was conveyed to me again and again through the use of third-party emissaries from the new Democratic state Senate leadership.

And then there was my Lieutenant Governor, Pat Quinn. What can I say? Harry Truman once described friendship and loyalty in politics by saying, “In Washington if you want a friend, get a dog.” Well, this wasn’t Washington, but it was politics. It’s an obvious understatement to say that it didn’t take long after my arrest for Pat Quinn to immediately express his desire to be governor. He really wanted my job. And as the days and weeks transpired, he soon became one of the most vocal advocates for me to resign.

And I have a theory on why.

It’s just a theory. But knowing the business and the players as I do, I believe my theory is accurate.

The biggest casualty of my arrest was the deal to make Lisa Madigan the senator. Putting that deal together and engaging third parties like Congressman Rahm Emanuel and Senator Dick Durbin to negotiate it was hard enough before my arrest. It was now impossible. As much as I would have liked to still find a way to make it happen, it was, in the wake of my arrest, a practical impossibility. First, enlisting the help of Rahm Emanuel and Dick Durbin and other third parties to put the deal together was now out of the question. After the dramatic and sensational way I was arrested, no one in their right mind would want to get involved in that. Second, if I approached Mike Madigan directly and offered his daughter the Senate seat in exchange for him passing a jobs bill, an expansion of healthcare, and signing a promise to not raise taxes on the people, he would have run for the hills. Who knows? He would have probably thought I was setting him up.

I knew instantly upon my arrest that my deal to appoint Lisa Madigan to the Senate was dead. Because of my arrest, I was vulnerable politically; in their minds, I was a political leper. And if they came close to me, they were afraid they might catch what I had.

So, in the immediate aftermath of my arrest, I believe that a plan was hatched among top Democratic leaders in Illinois that, if successfully executed, could still lead to the appointment of Mike Madigan's daughter Lisa Madigan to succeed President-elect Barack Obama in the U.S. Senate. And it starts with the premise that the two Madigans want that Senate seat far more than they covet the Governor's office. It's very simple. If Lisa Madigan should ever become Governor, then Mike Madigan might be compelled to give up being the Speaker. The potential for glaring conflicts of interest are obvious. And the scrutiny on the two of them would magnify exponentially. Mike Madigan likes to hide in the shadows, pull strings, and use his powerful position to accumulate power and benefit himself financially. If his daughter were sent to Washington, he could remain in the shadows and continue to do the things he's been doing. If she were to become governor, all of his shady dealings would be out in the open.

And a lot of top Democrats were in on the plan. They were all on the same team. And they all had roles to play.

Who were they? In addition to the powerful House Speaker Michael Madigan, the new Senate President John Cullerton, who happens to be the godfather to Lisa Madigan's brother and Speaker Madigan's son, was in on it. Lisa Madigan was in on it. She was one of the two principal beneficiaries of the deal—the other being my Lieutenant Governor, Pat Quinn. He was in on it too.

I believe Senator Dick Durbin was in on it. His wife lobbies the Illinois legislature. He was almost certainly communicating with the United States Senate Democratic leader Harry Reid about all of this. I say this because during the weeks leading up to my arrest, I had telephone conversations with both Senators about whom I should appoint to the Senate. Some of these calls could very well be recorded. And based on those calls, and the insights I was getting from some prominent Washington political operatives, two things became abundantly clear to me.

First, the Democratic Senate leadership in Washington did not want me to choose from among the African-American candidates who had publicly expressed an interest in the Senate appointment. For example, Congressman Danny Davis and Congressman Jesse Jackson Jr. Especially Jesse Jackson Jr. Now I'm not suggesting this was motivated by racism. It wasn't. It was political. The Senate Democratic leadership led by Harry Reid just believed both Congressmen couldn't get reelected. They couldn't raise the money for a reelection campaign. Or they were too liberal. Or in the case of Jesse Jr., too polarizing. In fact, Jesse Jackson Jr. really scared them. Of all the names mentioned as possible Senate appointees, he was the one they didn't want the most. And those messages were coming to me from a lot of different places.

So it was with both a measure of bemusement and disgust that I one day vented about the transparent hypocrisy of some of the national Democratic leaders with members of my team, saying something to them like, "How do you like these hypocrites! In the 'Age of Obama,' Harry Reid and Dick Durbin don't want an African-American to replace him in the U.S. Senate."

They wanted Lisa Madigan. They wanted her because they felt she could easily win reelection and probably even avoid a serious challenge from a Republican. With her father's ability to muscle people for campaign contributions—lobbyists, state, city, and county employees, for example—and the fact that she had already had been elected to statewide office, her appointment for their purposes made a lot of sense. They would have a safe incumbent and, in all likelihood, wouldn't have to defend the seat.

So the deal was this:

First, get me to resign right away. Then Pat Quinn becomes governor, and he appoints Lisa Madigan to the Senate. Second, if I don't resign, then convince me to take the voluntary step aside with pay and the security detail. Then Pat Quinn becomes governor and appoints Lisa Madigan to the

Senate. Third, if I refuse to resign or turn down the offer to step aside with pay, then accelerate the impeachment process and hijack me from office as swiftly as possible. And do whatever it takes to keep me from appointing a U.S. Senator. If by that time I failed to make the appointment, then after I'm removed from office, Pat Quinn becomes governor and appoints Lisa Madigan to the Senate.

But first they had to play the game. And first up was Attorney General Lisa Madigan.

As calls for my resignation intensified, the Attorney General's office filed an emergency motion before the Illinois State Supreme Court. The motion sought to have me declared incapacitated and therefore unable to do my job as governor. Her motion was legally ridiculous, politically motivated, and patently self-serving. And that is exactly how the Supreme Court saw it. As soon as they heard it, they immediately threw it out of court. And after Lisa Madigan struck out, she quickly took a seat on the bench.

Now it was time for Pat Quinn to take a bat and step up to the plate. And he wasted no time swinging for the fences. There he was, my Lieutenant Governor, my running mate in the last two elections. The guy who became my Lieutenant Governor only because of my hard work, the campaign contributions I had to raise and we both accepted, and all the long and lonely hours I spent campaigning. There he is. He's turned on me. Even before I have a chance to assert my innocence, he has become the director of the marching band leading the chorus that's calling on me to resign.

At the same time he's doing this, House Speaker Mike Madigan is doing his part for the team. As Pat Quinn is leading the band, Mike Madigan is orchestrating the House to begin impeachment proceedings immediately, with a promise to continue working right through the Christmas holidays.

Their game plan was all about speed. Time was of the essence. The window to appoint Obama's successor was rapidly closing. And if Pat Quinn wasn't appointed governor soon, Lisa Madigan might not become a senator.

So their strategic imperative was plain: get me out of the way and get me out *soon*. And whatever happens before then, try to slow me down and make sure I don't appoint a senator. Create a diversion, and as the effort to get me out of the way continued, announce support for a new law that would call for a special election; a law that would allow the voters, and not the governor, to decide who should fill the vacancy left by Barack Obama.

Now, I supported that law. I believe the people should be able to vote for who they want to be their senator. If they passed it, I would have signed it. And I immediately said so publicly. But they had no intention of passing it. It was all baloney on their part. All part of the game they were playing.

Pretend to support it but only until I'm out of office. Then should that happen, withdraw your support for the idea by saying that a special election is too costly. Pat Quinn is now the governor and to save the people money, scrap the idea where the people choose the senator, and instead, close the backroom deal where the new governor appoints Lisa Madigan to the Senate.

It's a win-win for both Lisa Madigan and Pat Quinn. Dad cuts a deal that hands her a Senate seat. And Pat Quinn waltzes into the governor's office while at the same time eliminates her as an opponent a year from now. She gets to be Senator, he gets to be Governor, and neither one of them had to earn a single vote from the people. Talk about the ultimate backroom deal!

But they had a problem. And the problem was the ticking clock. The legislature had to fish or cut bait on the bill calling for a special election. The Christmas holidays were coming, and they couldn't sit in Springfield much longer. Moreover, the Republicans began calling the Democrats' bluff. Both state and national Republicans wanted the special election because they believed they had a chance to win the seat. Conversely, the Democrats believed they could lose it. It's why they never really intended to pass that bill. Their support for the bill was only tactical; it was just a diversion to buy time to execute their plan and hold in suspension the appointment of a senator until I could be removed from office, and the Madigan-Quinn cabal could put their plan in place.

As the Democrats' real intentions about a special election started to become clear, and they weren't fooling anyone anymore, they called off their charade. They publicly reversed course. In less than two weeks, the Democrats went from being the party *for* the people choosing their senator to the party *against* the people choosing their senator. And a little before the holidays, they announced they were withdrawing their support for a special election and therefore would not be calling the bill for a vote. Their new position was that the Senate vacancy should indeed be filled by the governor. It just shouldn't be filled by me.

The Madigan-Quinn plan couldn't be put in place as long as I stayed in office. And much to their chagrin, I hadn't gone anywhere yet. I was still the governor, and by this time no one really knew what I was going to do.

No one, that is, except me.

Right around the time the Democrats were abandoning their call for a special election, I had, for the most part, figured things out. I had put a legal team together and had learned a lot more about the charges against me.

I was antsy and incredibly frustrated. This was the period I refer to as the "Dark Ages." It was the ten-day interlude from the day of my arrest to the day I could finally speak to the people. I was hunkered down and feeling caged in. Our home was surrounded by the media and except for getting out for an occasional seven-mile run in the snow, I was isolated. I really missed being out among the people. I was dying to talk to them. I owed them an explanation. I was their Governor. They had a right to hear from me. And I couldn't wait to tell them that I did nothing wrong, and I didn't let them down.

It was during this "Dark Ages" period that I was catapulted on the national stage and thrust into the national and international spotlight. I became the "talk of the town." And as you can imagine, it was not a good thing.

Well, here's something I learned from this whole experience. If you're in a hurry, and you want to get famous fast, and you don't care what they say about you, so long as they say something about you, then here's some advice on how to do it. I wouldn't recommend it to anyone, but it's a surefire way of getting famous or, I should say, infamous.

Find a way to get yourself falsely accused of trying to sell a Senate seat the new president just held, and I guarantee, before you know it, everyone will know who you are. And everyone will talk about you.

You'll be talked about by David Letterman–you'll make his "Top Ten" list. And Jay Leno, you'll be in his monologue–more than once! Someone will play you on *Saturday Night Live* and *Comedy Central.* They are being funny but you're not looking so good. All the major networks–NBC, ABC, CBS–will report on you every day, around the clock. So will MSNBC, FOX, and CNN. I didn't watch any of it. That would have been too painful. I couldn't bear to hear all the terrible things being said about me, which I knew were not true. It was the kind of stuff you just didn't want to see.

So when I watched television during this dark period, I found refuge in the stations that in ordinary times dominated our home. The channels our girls love to watch. The Disney Channel, Nickelodeon, or Noggin–they were seemingly always on. I was safe there. And so were our girls. There was no need to subject them to all the terrible things being said about their father.

Or the stations I watch like *SportsCenter*, or the NFL network, or NFL games. I could be safe there too. Or so I thought.

The Sunday night after my arrest, I was watching *Sunday Night Football* on NBC. Before the featured game started, one of the broadcasters, Keith Olbermann, was describing the highlights of that day's games. As he got to the Baltimore Ravens/Pittsburgh Steelers game, he started describing Ben Roethlisberger, the Steelers' quarterback, going back to pass. As the Ravens' pass rush broke through the Steelers' offensive line and were close to sacking Roethlisberger, Keith Olbermann said something along the lines of "Ben Roethlisberger, in more trouble than Rod Blagojevich, eluding the pass rush and finds Hines Ward downfield to complete a twenty-yard pass." At least I'm pretty sure it was Hines Ward. It may have been Santonio Holmes, I can't exactly remember. The point is I was everywhere, even on *Sunday Night Football*, and now my name was becoming synonymous with somebody in a lot of trouble. I had become the poster child for someone in trouble.

Well, I may have been in trouble, but I didn't do anything wrong. And it wouldn't be long now for me to finally be able to say it. Soon, but not just yet.

The Madigan-Quinn plan couldn't succeed if I were around. And I was still around. Despite the blitz to get me to resign during the torrential storm of the first days after the arrest, I entered the second week, and I was still the Governor. That's not what they were counting on.

By the second week of the storm, everyone who was anyone had called on me to resign. From President-elect Obama to Senator Dick Durbin—a lot of powerful people were weighing in. When asked, Mayor Daley wondered aloud how I could govern. And soon a letter signed by every Democratic member of the U.S. Senate urged me not to appoint the next Senator and warned that if I did, whoever it was, he or she would not be seated.

Now stop and think about that for a second. What if, hypothetically speaking, I appointed, let's say, a modern-day Abraham Lincoln or George Washington, or a Dr. King or Franklin Roosevelt to the Senate. Are they saying they wouldn't seat them? Well I guess they wouldn't seat Lincoln, he was a Republican. But F.D.R., they wouldn't seat him? The

Senators had no idea who I might pick. It might not be unreasonable to at least wait to see who I might send before saying no. Who knows, it might have been the next Obama.

With calls for me to resign, and the start of impeachment proceedings well under way, it was time for the Madigan-Quinn cabal to try something new. For their plan to succeed, I had to go. And I had to go at all costs.

They were using a lot of stick; maybe it was now time to try a little carrot. Use the carrot, use the stick, offer an olive branch, whatever it takes—just get him out so we could get Pat Quinn and Lisa Madigan in.

So they offered me a carrot. Actually, it was more like a "karat." It was the same very generous offer made to me a week or so before by Senator Meeks and purportedly came from the new Senate President, John Cullerton. He conveyed it to one of my attorneys, Ed Genson. Earlier, the idea had been conveyed to Patti through her father who was passing along a message from the new Senate President.

If I agreed to voluntarily step aside right away, and I didn't appoint a Senator, then it might be arranged for me to keep my full pay for the remainder of my term—that's a salary of $170,000 per year for the next two years. They would see to it that the salary would be appropriated in the next two state budgets. I could keep my security detail that protected me and my family, and I could then be free to focus all of my attention on defending the criminal charges against me.

For our family, this was a great offer. It took care of our most immediate and important needs. Like a professional athlete who gets hurt during the season, I would be put on the disabled list with full pay until I can recover and come back. In the meantime, we could pay the bills and keep some semblance of financial security during what was going to be a tough road ahead.

Now I never considered resigning. Not ever. Had I done something wrong, I would have resigned immediately. I would have felt that it was my duty to the people to do so. But

I didn't do anything wrong, and I wasn't going to quit a job the people hired me to do because of false accusations and a political witch-hunt. I owed it to the people to fight.

But I must admit, there was one option I did consider. It was the voluntary step aside option. It was hard not to. The impeachment proceedings that were just beginning were most surely going to end up removing me from office. It was less a question of *if* and more a question of *when*. And of how long. But no matter how you analyzed it, barring a miracle, I was not going to be Governor much longer.

Part of the stick approach was the fast track that the impeachment proceedings were on. The House was in such a hurry they were already convening to begin impeachment hearings before Christmas. Their rush to get started was a clear message to me: if you don't get out, we're going to throw you out. So in all likelihood, I was going to be out of a job, without pay, in the very near future.

Patti very much favored me pursuing the step aside option. To her credit, the welfare of her children was the most important consideration in any decision. It far outweighed her concerns for my political situation or, for that matter, for me personally. I love that about her. It's as it should be. A mother is supposed to put the interest of her children before the interest of her husband. And she was thinking about our children when she advocated in favor of me stepping aside.

I thought about it too, but not for long.

There's a scene in the Christmas classic *It's a Wonderful Life* where the George Bailey character, played by Jimmy Stewart, is offered a prominent, high-paying position in the biggest and most influential bank in town. The bank is owned by his family's longtime rival, Mr. Potter, played by the legendary actor Lionel Barrymore. For George Bailey, it's an attractive offer, where after years of struggle and sacrifice, he can finally realize financial security for his family and gain the time that had so long eluded him to pursue some of his dreams. Somehow circumstances always seemed to stop him. So did his sense of responsibility to his late father, their family's building and loan business, their depositors, and his Bedford Falls community. So in that scene, for one instant, as he's chewing on a cigar Mr. Potter gave him, he's tempted. He's tempted to take the offer. Then reality sets in. So does his conscience. When he asks Mr. Potter what this deal would mean for his family's Bailey Building and Loan, he's told it would have to close. Hearing that, George realizes that closing the Bailey Building and Loan would eliminate the only check on the unfettered power of Mr. Potter's bank. And if Mr. Potter's bank is left without competition, the ordinary working family in Bedford Falls would be at the mercy of Mr. Potter's greed. That answer was like an awakening for George, and he immediately spurns the offer and resolves to fight on.

That's how I felt. The offer to step aside with pay for two years was sure better than being thrown out of office without pay for two years. It would maintain my income and give us some financial security. I could immediately step out of the storm that was besieging my family. This would be good for our girls and could, in a less traumatic way, ease them into the new life we were inexorably headed for. So I thought about it. And for a brief moment began weighing the pros and cons.

But then, like George Bailey, I too had an awakening. Something about this deal didn't feel right. A little voice inside of me started talking. It was my conscience. I started feeling a tinge of guilt. This was certainly a good deal for my family, but if I took it, I would have to abandon the people who elected me. To quit the job they hired me to do; to sell them out. In the final analysis, the decision had to be based on what was in the best interest of the people and what my responsibilities were to them.

I'm the Governor, not a professional athlete. This is not professional sports and the private sector; this is government and the public sector. Being an athlete on the disabled list and getting paid for it is one thing. But being a governor and being on the disabled list and getting paid is another. How could I, in good conscience, get paid as the governor without doing the job of the governor? I couldn't do it. My situation involved the taxpayer's money. I was not interested in being a "ghost pay-roller Governor."

This was exactly the kind of cynical wheeling and dealing that I decried in others. It's one thing to do it for the public good, but it's quite another when it's done for private gain. And it's so commonplace in Illinois government that sometimes you don't recognize it right away. The lines are blurred. And the political leaders who offered it were simply conducting business as usual. I'm convinced that in their minds, they thought they were being more than fair. I think it explains, in part, why some who knew of the offer felt free to vote to impeach me. In their minds, if I could blow off a sweet deal like that, then I just blew my chance to a get a fair trial at the forthcoming impeachment proceedings.

In the end, and despite my primary responsibility as a father to protect his family, I just could not do it. It didn't feel right. The playwright Lillian Hellman once said, "I will not cut my conscience to fit this year's fashions." So I decided to turn it down. It simply wasn't something I could do. My conscience wouldn't let me. My mind was made up.

And that's what I told the people at a press conference on December 19, 2008. It was the first time I officially talked to the people since my arrest ten days earlier. And for the first time I could finally assert my innocence. What a relief it was to tell the people what I knew to be true; that I did nothing wrong, and I wasn't going to quit.

I quoted the first stanza from my favorite poem, "If" by Rudyard Kipling, a poem I discovered when I was a kid in high school and was so moved by it that I memorized it back then. "If you can keep your head when all about you are losing theirs and blaming it on you, if you can trust yourself when all men doubt you but make allowance for their doubting too, if you can wait and not be tired by waiting, or being lied about, don't deal in lies."

I then asked the people of Illinois to please be patient and afford me the same rights that they would expect for themselves if they were falsely accused of something–the presumption of innocence, the right to confront your accusers, the opportunity to have your day in court.

I went on to thank the people from all over Illinois who during those difficult ten days had sent us letters and e-mails of support. They extended their prayers and good wishes and made us feel less alone. Patti and I will never forget their kindness to us.

And it was at this press conference that I told the world what I intended to do. I was going to fight, fight, and fight. Until the very end.

CHAPTER TWELVE

AFTER MY ARREST, AND AFTER IT BECAME CLEAR THE LEGISLATURE WAS NOT GOING TO PASS A LAW ALLOWING THE PEOPLE TO CHOOSE THE NEXT SENATOR IN A SPECIAL ELECTION, IT WAS MY DUTY TO APPOINT A UNITED STATES SENATOR FROM ILLINOIS. If I failed to do that, the people of Illinois would be deprived of its voice and vote in the United States Senate. The problem was the political landscape had dramatically changed after my arrest. I was almost universally condemned by the political elite in my party. Neither the presumption of innocence nor my assertion of innocence meant anything to them. Instead, powerful political leaders saw the vacuum that was created as an opportunity for them to get the senator they wanted. They didn't expect me to withstand the enormous pressure to resign. And after vilifying and condemning me the way they did, and vowing to not seat anyone I appointed, they created a political environment that made it hard for many of the would-be candidates to accept an appointment from me even though, only a couple of weeks before my arrest, they would have jumped at the chance to be a senator. So the pool of potential candidates to appoint to the United States Senate was far smaller than it had been before everything changed.

When I was arrested and accused of trying to sell a United States Senate seat for financial gain, a routine political deal that would've accomplished good things for the people of Illinois was, along with me, the biggest casualty. Because of my arrest, I now had no choice but to resort to my fallback position.

Absent a compelling reason like the creation of jobs and the expansion of healthcare that was the condition of the Lisa Madigan Senate appointment, I wanted to appoint an African-American to the United States Senate. I believed it was important to replace the first African-American elected President with another African-American. In that spirit, my first choice to appoint to the United States Senate if the Lisa Madigan deal was unable to be consummated was Congressman Danny Davis. Danny and I served together for six years in the United States Congress. He is African-American and has been active in his community since he first came to Chicago from Arkansas in the 1960s. He is a good man. He is a man with compassion. He is an eloquent speaker who possesses a deep, theatrical voice. When Danny speaks, you're not sure you're hearing him or the actor James Earl Jones.

And I offered the Senate seat to him but he turned me down. One of my attorneys, Sam Adam Jr., sat down with Danny during the Christmas holidays to convey my offer. But because of the new circumstances and the controversy that now surrounded the Senate appointment, Danny turned us down. I certainly understood his reservations and respected his decision.

We also discussed Dr. Eric Whitaker, who is one of President Obama's best friends and who did a great job as my Director of Public Health. At this stage, he was actually the candidate I preferred. He is a medical doctor. He is African-American. And he was on the frontlines in helping me expand access to healthcare to a record amount of people, which was my biggest priority and the achievement I am most proud of. In fact, at a meeting less than a week before my arrest, it was decided to add his name to the shortlist of Senate appointees. He was third on the list and would have been a surprise pick since his name was hardly, if ever, mentioned. I thought long and hard about making him a senator before my arrest. After my arrest, Dr. Whitaker's name was resurrected and discussed.

But there were practical problems with him. To begin with, we wondered how to approach him with the offer. At the time of these considerations, he was in Hawaii on vacation with the President-elect. There was no practical way to communicate with him and time was of the essence. I wanted to choose a senator before the United States Senate reconvened on January 4, 2009. I wanted the senator from Illinois to have the best possible opportunity to gain the necessary seniority over the other incoming senators from other states. So I couldn't wait for Dr. Whitaker to return. Plus, because of his close relationship with the new President, it was unlikely that under the circumstances he would accept the offer.

We discussed other prominent African-Americans in the Chicagoland area. I considered Melody Spann Cooper, the executive producer of the most historic and one of the most successful African-American radio stations in Chicago. I considered an African-American woman named Melody Hobson who made a name for herself in the investment world. But I settled on Roland Burris as the next person to ask.

Roland Burris was the first African-American elected in Illinois to a statewide office. He is originally from downstate Illinois, and I viewed him as an elder statesman in our party. He's a very nice man and a man of great self-esteem. It was that self-esteem that I was counting on to be able to withstand the storm of protest that was inevitably going to come when I announced that I was appointing him to the United States Senate.

An hour into the Dallas Cowboys/Philadelphia Eagles game to determine which team would win the last playoff spot, it was already becoming clear that the Eagles were on their way to a blow-out win and to the playoffs. It was also the time scheduled for me to call Roland Burris and formally offer him a seat in the United States Senate. A few days before, my attorney Sam Adam Jr. met privately with Mr. Burris to see whether he would accept the appointment if offered. Sam

Adam Jr. was friends with Roland's son. They went to school together so he knew the Burris family well.

After discussing the matter for a while, Roland Burris informed Sam Adam Jr. that he was interested and was inclined to accept the offer if it came. But before he did, he wanted me to personally call him to make the offer. The time was set for four o'clock on that Sunday afternoon.

I made the call at the appointed time. It was before halftime, and the Cowboys were self-destructing. Roland and I had a nice talk. Although we were rivals for Governor in a hotly contested Democratic primary back in 2002, we always had a good relationship. He asked how I was holding up. I told him I was fine. Then we got down to business. I told him I was going to appoint a senator, and I was offering it to him. Without hesitation, he accepted.

I decided on Roland Burris after spending an afternoon discussing possible Senate candidates with some members of my legal team. Because of my arrest, I could no longer consult with or seek advice from my top staff and political advisers. They were all, to varying degrees, involved in the discussions that led to my arrest. So I consulted with my lawyers. They were all I had left. There was no one else I could trust.

After my call to Roland, Patti asked me if he thanked me for making him a U.S. Senator. It hadn't dawned on me, but I told her he didn't. And that was okay. In fact, it was kind of amusing. Roland had a certain sense of entitlement about it. From his perspective, of course he should be asked. His response was more in the way of "what took you so long?" That was the beauty of Roland, and it was among the reasons why, under the circumstances, he was the right pick.

Roland's penchant to speak of himself in the third person is legendary. He does it in a colorful and charming way. And there's nothing arrogant about it. When we ran against each other for Governor in 2002, he would say things like, "the people of Illinois need Roland Burris," or "when Roland

Burris is Governor, he'll do such and such for education." He named his children after himself—his son Roland and his daughter Rolanda. And after I announced his appointment, the media reported that years before he had a mausoleum built for his final resting place that touted his public career, listed the offices he held, and highlighted what he considered were his many achievements. Here was a man who was not going to back down. And when it started heating up, he was going to want "U.S. Senator" chiseled into that stone. Roland Burris was the right man to withstand the fury that was about to come.

And Roland Burris was the right man for the moment. Whether you liked it or not, this selection was going to be historic. And Roland Burris is a historic figure in Illinois. He is the first African-American to win statewide office. He was elected state comptroller and then elected the first and only African-American Attorney General in Illinois political history. He was a candidate for governor in 1994 and ran a very close second in the Democratic primary. He was again a candidate for governor in 1998 and again ran a close second. Roland and I ran against each other in the gubernatorial Democratic primary in 2002, and he finished a very competitive third. He ran for the United States Senate in 1984 and again ran second in a competitive Democratic primary. He also ran for Mayor of Chicago in 1995.

In many ways he was a perennial candidate who represented the African-American community in election after election for high political office in Illinois. He ran so often because before Obama and Senator Carol Moseley Braun, he was the only African-American who could run competitively and win statewide.

Roland grew up in a segregated America. He is a part of a generation that wasn't allowed the opportunity to attend traditionally white colleges or universities. A graduate of the historic African-American Howard University, Roland earned his law degree. After that, he told me that he was actually a law clerk for Supreme Court Justice Thurgood Marshall, the first African-American member to sit on the United States Supreme Court.

Roland Burris' career reflected who he was. He was well-liked by members of both political parties. He was not a polarizing figure. His route to the great American success story was not as one who challenged the system from without as an activist, but instead was one where he patiently rose through the ranks, scratching and clawing his way up the ladder of success in an ever-changing white America. At the age of 71, he was an elder statesman in Illinois politics, and under the circumstances he seemed the right choice for the United States Senate.

I announced the appointment of Roland Burris to the United States Senate at a press conference on December 30, 2008. As expected, the announcement drew a storm of protest.

Actually, the protests started coming in hours before I made the announcement. The first one came from one of my attorneys, Ed Genson. Concerned about my well being, he didn't like the idea of me making an appointment. It wasn't just Burris, it was anybody. A legendary defense attorney from the old school, if he had his way, I would have resigned immediately and focused all my efforts on winning the case and clearing my name. He was very genuine in his concern for me and my family. We would talk about it a lot during this period. And when I would advance the argument that I had a responsibility to the people who elected me, he would, like the brilliant trial attorney that he is, ask me the rhetorical question of whether I believed the people I was so concerned about would support my family if, God forbid, I'm no longer around and unable to?

He was also being lobbied hard by Senate President John Cullerton whose motivation was to keep alive the Madigan-Quinn plan. Genson told me on that call that if I went through with this appointment, he was told that I would seal my fate, and this would accelerate my removal from office.

He passed along to me the warning that if I did it, I would be removed no later than Lincoln's birthday. If on the other hand I refrained, I would be allowed to stay longer, perhaps a few months, and not lose my salary. I listened to his argument and to the warning, but I wasn't going to change course or make any deals. Here again was the disconnect between me and the political establishment. It is the ultimate irony. I'm the one facing criminal charges yet time and time again my efforts to help the people and do my duty ran up against the cynical self-interest of political leaders in Springfield. It's the psychological principle known as transference. The other guy transfers to you his motives and figures you will act exactly the way he would. So when, for example, the Senate President John Cullerton continues to offer me things like delaying the impeachment proceedings in exchange for me not appointing the Senator, he is making me an offer he would take if the shoe was on the other foot.

I had a constitutional duty to appoint a United States Senator. Period. Failure to do so would be to deprive my state of its rightful representation in the United States Senate. And it would deny the citizens of Illinois its appropriate voice and vote. This was a no brainer. I felt then, and I believe now, that if they were looking for a real impeachable offense that they could use to throw me out of office, then ignoring my duty and not appointing a senator was one.

And time was of the essence. The United States Senate was reconvening on January 4th to organize itself. Seniority and committee assignments were at stake. Giving the next Illinois Senator the best shot at best representing the state meant giving him a leg up on the other freshman Senators who would be sworn in after January 20th. To wait would be to miss an opportunity to help my state. And since the Illinois state legislature refused, after all, to give the people the opportunity to elect their Senator, if I didn't do it, then Illinois wouldn't have one. So I was going to do it, and it was going to be Roland Burris.

I was excited about it. I was about to make history. No matter what else might happen, I was about to become the first Governor in modern American history to appoint an African-American to the United States Senate. I would share a slice in all the history surrounding the election of the first African-American President by replacing him with the only African-American to currently sit in that same Senate. And why shouldn't it be controversial? The very movement that struggled to overcome the racial barriers that would have made an Obama presidency unthinkable only a generation before was chock full of controversy. It was, to borrow from Abraham Lincoln, altogether fitting and proper that this should be too.

And it was fitting and proper for me to think about my late mother. Moments before stepping out to make the announcement, I thought about her. How proud she would be with what I was about to do. I grew up surrounded by racism. I witnessed first hand the tensions that existed at that time between the races. I saw it in my neighborhood. I saw it playing sports. And I grew up in an era of unprecedented racial unrest and historic social change. And now, in spite of how I got here, I was going to act and assure that the United States Senate, even with the elevation of the first African-American President, was not going to be a "whites only" club. After I took action, it would have at least one African-American member. And I felt a strong sense of personal gratification to be able to do it. In my mind, I would, in some respect, be striking a blow on behalf of the dispossessed. For all of those–black and white–who through the years, and for far too long, had unfairly been denied an equal chance in reaching for the American Dream. I was giving a voice to those who didn't have one.

What a press conference. It was wild. The national media and even some international media joined the local media to fill the room to overflowing. After Roland and I stepped before them, I announced that he was my choice to be the next United States Senator from the state of Illinois.

Roland then stepped up to the podium and gave some brief remarks. It was during the question and answer session that followed that I noticed Congressman Bobby Rush in the back of the crowd. I then invited him up to say a few words. Bobby and I served in the U.S. Congress together. A former Black Panther during the late 1960s and early 1970s and a longtime member of Congress, Bobby would soon become one of Roland Burris's most ardent advocates. And his advocacy in favor of the Burris appointment that day took center stage.

His unannounced appearance at that press conference that day was high drama with a bit of a comical element to it. Some cynical pundits suggested that I arranged the whole thing. Nothing could be farther from the truth. I was as surprised as anyone else to see Bobby there that day. Whether his appearance was arranged by the Burris people, I don't know. What I do know is that he was there and he was great. He made the case on why it was important for the United States Senate to not be without at least one African-American Senator. Even though he lost a considerable amount of weight in his fight against cancer, Bobby never appeared to be more in command. He was soft spoken, he was reasonable, and he was persuasive. And he had the standing and credibility to speak about the issue of race in a way that I never could.

As soon as we finished, Lieutenant Governor Pat Quinn held his own press conference. He was angry and decried the fact that I appointed a senator. He predicted that I would now be removed from office before Lincoln's birthday. That's the same message sent to me earlier from the President of the Senate. It sure sounded as if they were speaking from the same talking points. Moments after I was leaving my press conference, and he was presumably going to his, I bumped into him. When I saw him, I was nice and said, "Hi, Pat." He wasn't so nice. I'm not sure if he even returned the greeting. I guess he was mad because this appointment was standing in the way of the political deal he cut to become governor and appoint Speaker Madigan's daughter to the Senate.

Now why was Pat Quinn so angry after I announced my Senate choice? Again, this is just a theory; it's my own conjecture, but I believe it to be accurate. It was obvious Pat Quinn wanted to be Governor, and if he was right that I would be out by Lincoln's birthday, then why was he so angry that day? All he had to do was wait for a few short weeks and he would become Governor.

Or would he?

I believe he saw that if Burris was ultimately seated, then he was going to have to pay another price to become Governor. In order to get the two legislative leaders, Mike Madigan and John Cullerton, to follow through with the impeachment proceedings, he would have to agree to a fallback deal. And that deal meant a big tax increase on the people. Both Madigan and Cullerton supported a big tax increase for years. It never happened because I stopped them. Now, if Madigan's daughter wasn't going to the United States Senate, and if they were going to remove me from office, then they wanted something in return. With these guys it was always about the deal. Don't just do it because it's right, with Madigan especially, there always had to be something in it for him. And if he makes Quinn Governor, but his daughter isn't going to be Senator, then Quinn has to promise to do something for him. And that promise was to agree to the big tax increase I kept promising to veto for the last six years.

This was Quinn's dilemma. As my running mate in two successful races for Governor, Pat Quinn and I promised the people that we wouldn't raise the income tax. For the last six years, I opposed, and sometimes fought with, the legislative leaders in my own party and prevented big income tax increases on the people. For six years, I said no to virtually every special interest in Springfield who, year in and year out, kept pushing for a higher income tax.

Now Pat Quinn was faced with a choice. Does he promise the political bosses that in exchange for making him Governor he will agree to break his promise to the people and raise taxes on them? Or does he put aside his personal ambition and keep his word to the people?

Well, as events would soon prove, Pat Quinn made a deal with the devil. He sold out the people. It turned out the price for him to be Governor was a huge income tax increase. And it took him less than six weeks as Governor to break the promise to the people that I kept for six years. Pat Quinn proposed a 50% increase in the state income tax on the people, and he did it at a time when people are hurting, and he did it during the worst financial crisis our country has faced since the Great Depression. And then he tried to sell it in the usual way some Democrats do: by saying he was soaking the rich when in reality his tax increase disproportionately socked it to the middle class. Man, do I wish I was still Governor because that would have never happened.

The response to the Burris appointment was fast and furious. As expected, negative reactions came in from everywhere and the response from the Democratic establishment was hot and heavy. Senator Dick Durbin vowed that Burris would not be seated. Democratic Senate majority leader Harry Reid made the same promise. Illinois Secretary of State Jesse White refused to fulfill his responsibility and officially certify the Burris appointment. A letter signed by every Democratic United States Senator officially opposed seating Roland Burris in the Senate. And before the day was out, even President-elect Obama signaled that Burris should not be allowed to take his seat.

The news media weighed in too. They called my appointment an act of defiance. Calls for me to resign followed promises to not seat Roland Burris. And calls for my impeachment and removal from office intensified. Yet in spite of the uproar and all the noise that went along with it, I was at peace. I knew I was right. I may have been alone, with the entire Democratic political establishment in the country and in my own state against me, but it didn't matter. I was right, and I took to heart what Abraham Lincoln said, that right makes might. I was at peace because my belief was strong that I was doing the right thing. I was fulfilling my constitutional obligation to appoint a United States senator to protect and promote the interests of my state. And if a bunch of cackling politicians with their own agendas didn't like it, that was their problem. Let them vow and promise, posture and pontificate, trash talk and make threats—I was confident that as long as Roland Burris stood firm, he would ultimately have to be seated in the United States Senate. Everyone may have been against this, but Roland and I had the constitution and the law on our side. All that was left now was to allow for the drama to play out.

But the drama had to play out. And for the next several days it did.

I did my part. I made the appointment, and there was nothing more for me to do. It was now up to Roland Burris to see it through. And he did. He'd made the rounds on all of the relevant media outlets. He did the Sunday morning talk shows. And then he went to Washington to take his seat in the United States Senate.

The only problem was, when on a rainy day he knocked on their door, they wouldn't let him in. It was a remarkable scene. There was Roland Burris standing in the rain covered by an umbrella talking to the media after he was denied entry into the United States Senate. The paradox was striking. At a time when the American people just elected its first African-American President, the United States Senate was denying access to a man who would become the only African-American member of that body. It was reminiscent of James Meredith not being allowed to enroll in the all-white University of Mississippi during the heart of the civil rights movement. Here was the United States Senate in 2009 looking like Ole Miss in 1962 with Senators Harry Reid and Dick Durbin starting to look less like Democratic Senators of the

21st century and more like the segregationist governors of another era.

If I'm ever a governor again, and I'm called upon to appoint a United States Senator, let me make this promise. I'll jump off a bridge first. I want nothing to do with it. Just about everyone wants it, or has someone who they want to get it. And they'll seemingly stop at nothing to make it happen.

I'm convinced that the effort to keep Burris out of the Senate was still part of the same effort to make Pat Quinn the governor and Lisa Madigan the senator. The Madigan-Quinn cabal was not giving up. The House impeachment panel had quickly approved thirteen articles of impeachment against me. Among them were things like defying the FDA on behalf of our senior citizens by going to Canada to get cheaper prescription medicines for them. With the exception of the criminal charges against me, none of the articles were impeachable offenses. And many of the things I was being impeached for were things I did to help people in my first term. I was subsequently reelected because the people approved of them. And with respect to the criminal charges against me, the House rules did not require that any of them be proved. Nor did they allow me the opportunity to disprove them. So it was clear early on that the fix was in, and I wouldn't be allowed the chance to show I did nothing wrong.

Now it was a race against the clock.

Working with Dick Durbin, the Madigan-Quinn-Cullerton clique were coordinating their efforts to stop Burris and impeach me. Senator Durbin would do his part from Washington to hold up the Burris appointment. Back home, Madigan and Cullerton would work as fast as they could to remove me from office. What would decide the issue was the question of how long they could keep Burris out of the Senate.

The Roland Burris appointment was dominating the national news. And as Senators Dick Durbin and Harry Reid kept finding excuses for not seating him, leaders from the African-American community across the country started to demand that Burris be seated. The Congressional Black Caucus soon joined in. Led by Congressman Bobby Rush, they urged the Senate Democratic leaders to seat Roland Burris immediately. President-elect Obama reversed course. He now urged the Senate Democratic leaders to seat Roland Burris and get on with focusing on the multitude of problems facing the American people.

It really was remarkable. Here we are in America, beginning a new year. A new president elected on a mandate for change. An economy in crisis. Across America, people are losing their jobs. Their savings and retirement accounts are losing their value. Foreclosures are at record levels, and people are being kicked out of their homes. The brave men and women in our armed forces are still fighting wars in two places. And with all of these challenges and more facing the American people, the Senate Democratic leadership has decided to hit the ground running not by addressing or solving those problems but by maneuvering and positioning and posturing to keep Roland Burris out of the United States Senate.

And the national Democratic Party was starting to look real bad. They were spending their time and energy to keep out a qualified African-American from the United States Senate. And it didn't appear to matter to them that by doing this, they were treating their party's most reliable base of support with contempt. This was the thanks the national Democratic Party was giving to the African-American community. The 90% of the vote that the African-American community consistently gives Democratic candidates apparently wasn't enough for them to expect 1% of the membership of the United States Senate.

Roland Burris was officially sworn in as a member of the United States Senate on January 15, 2009. He entered the chamber to a standing ovation. Presumably, those same Democratic senators who all signed a letter saying that Burris would not be seated changed their minds. And evidently so did Dick Durbin. Where a day or two before he was working frantically to keep Burris from being seated, he was on this day hosting a reception for Roland Burris to celebrate his becoming a member of the United States Senate.

Professional politicians are funny people. They promise, they pander, they posture, they position, and then without batting an eye, like magic, they change their position, and they break their promises, and it's as if nothing ever happened. That's one of the lessons of the saga over Roland Burris being seated into the United States Senate. That's the major leagues of American politics, and I've learned, the hard way, just how bad some people want to join it. I'll tell you what, I hope my kids become doctors or go into business.

Roland Burris was on his way in, and I was on my way out. There was hardly any doubt now that I was going to be removed from office. The only realistic question was when. If the threats that were conveyed to me were real, then it was likely to happen soon.

Even though I knew deep down that it was going to be soon, I still held out some sliver of hope that maybe, if given a fair trial, enough lawmakers might realize that impeaching a governor who wasn't proven to have committed any impeachable offenses was a dangerous precedent. And that by doing so, it would have serious consequences on the role of future governors in Illinois, as well as around the country. If I could be thrown out of office without the House or Senate being required to prove any wrongdoing, then what governor would be willing to take on the legislature on behalf of the people, as I so often did?

Any hope I had that the fix was not in, and that at least some lawmakers would be allowed to decide for themselves, was dashed when I placed a call to state Senator Rickey Hendon, who was a friend and ally. It was a Friday night. I called to ask him a simple question: Will I get a fair trial in the state Senate? Senator Hendon's answer told me everything I needed to know. He urged me to resign immediately. He told me not to expect a single vote and that I should resign for the sake of my family so I don't lose my state pension.

Senator Hendon was part of the new Democratic leadership team. He was clearly speaking on behalf of that team, and it was now obvious to me that even before any evidence was heard, the result was predetermined. The fix was in, and the procedure to conduct the impeachment trial in the Senate was going to be designed in such a way that I wouldn't be given a fair chance to prove I did nothing wrong.

The Illinois House voted to impeach on January 9, 2009. They justified their actions of voting to impeach without proving wrongdoing or allowing me to prove I didn't do anything wrong by comparing their role in the impeachment proceedings as being like a grand jury. A grand jury takes information that isn't challenged and then brings charges. When my lawyers complained about the unfair process, the House's response was that the Senate would provide the forum to have a full trial where wrongdoing must be proven and where I would be allowed to bring in evidence and witnesses to prove my innocence.

Those assurances turned out to be nothing more than empty statements intended to fool the public. The House and Senate leadership were all in on the deal. There would be no fair trial, not in the House and not in the Senate. When my legal team got a copy of the proposed rules that would govern the impeachment trial in the Illinois state Senate, it became abundantly clear that a kangaroo court was being set up and that the impeachment was put on the fast track.

Those rules made a mockery of some of our most fundamental constitutional rights. The right to a fair trial; the right to the presumption of innocence; the right to confront witnesses; the right to bring in witnesses; and the most basic requirement of all: if you are going to find that someone did something wrong, then first you have to prove that the person accused actually did something wrong.

As unbelievable as it sounds, this Illinois state Senate enacted rules for the impeachment on a governor that did not require they prove any wrongdoing. Merely reading accusations from a report that were not cross-examined or challenged in any way was sufficient to remove me from office.

Think about it. I was elected by the people of Illinois to be their governor not once, but twice. They hired me, and if they didn't like the job I was doing then they should be the ones to fire me. But instead, a bunch of nameless and faceless lawmakers in Illinois who nobody knows joined together to thwart the will of the people and undo an election by removing a governor through a proceeding where they didn't have to prove that the accused did anything wrong.

So I had a decision to make. Hoping for a fair trial, my lawyers represented me in the House. Unfortunately, their calls for a fair trial fell on deaf ears. When we learned of the Senate's rules that deprived me of a fair trial, the question before me was whether to even participate in it. If I chose to participate in a sham impeachment trial, I would stay in office a little longer. But by participating, I would be acknowledging the validity of their proceedings. In effect, I would be participating in and becoming a party to a proceeding that was unconstitutional and that would set a dangerous precedent for any future governor in Illinois or for that matter anywhere else in the country.

If, on the other hand, I chose to boycott the proceedings and protest its violation of the Constitution and of our most basic civil liberties, then I would be thrown out of office a little sooner, but at least I would go down fighting for a large and important principle. By boycotting the proceeding I would, in some small way, be sacrificing myself on the altar of some of the most basic civil liberties we as Americans hold most dear.

I chose to boycott. And I chose to protest. I took my case to the American people. I went outside of Illinois and appeared on as many national network shows that would be willing to hear me out. As the Illinois state Senate was trampling on our most basic constitutional principles, I made the rounds on the news shows telling the American people what was happening. And I was under no illusions. Doing those shows was not going to be easy. I was going to be interviewed by some of the toughest interviewers in our country. And it wasn't like I was walking into those interviews with the image of being a choirboy. What most of the people who were interviewing me knew was that I was the guy accused of trying to sell Barack Obama's Senate seat. And while I know those allegations are not true, those national network interviewers couldn't wait to get their hands on me.

But not everyone around me thought I should do the interviews. My decision was not universally agreed to by some members of my legal team. In fact, one of my lawyers quit over my decision to take my case to the people and subject myself to interviews by television talk show hosts.

It is unconventional for someone who's been charged with crimes to do interviews. The conservative and conventional approach is to say nothing and leave the talking to your lawyers. But when you're innocent of the things that you are being accused of, it is only natural to want to tell people that. And if you know what the truth is concerning your actions, then the truth is not something to fear but is instead something to embrace and hold on to. And when you are the governor, who was twice elected by the people, and a process is being set up to undo the will of the people, and that process violates every fundamental right we as Americans have a right to expect, I felt I had a duty to take my case to the people. And I felt it was important to make the rounds on the national television programs to let the American people and the people of Illinois know what was going on. As far as I was concerned, I had a duty as a citizen of this country to tell the American people what the Illinois legislature was doing to the Constitution. And from a personal point of view, I had this need, and still have this need, to tell everyone and anyone who would listen that I didn't do anything wrong and that I am innocent of any criminal wrongdoing. When you have been falsely accused of crimes you didn't commit, and when you are an honest person and your reputation and your integrity is in question, it is unbearable to sit silently back and not assert the truth. And your innocence.

I also did the television talk shows because the United States Attorney who is accusing me of these things left me no choice. After the U.S. attorney held his press conference where he accused me of selling Barack Obama's senate seat for personal gain, and where he said that Abraham Lincoln would roll over in his grave, his headline-grabbing and highly prejudicial statements compelled me to go to the American people and tell them it was not true. Otherwise, I would be tainted with the brush of silence. And when you are an innocent man wrongfully accused of things you did not do, staying silent is the last thing you want to do. What you want to do is find the highest mountaintop and shout as loud as you can that you didn't do what they said you did.

Before leaving for the media tour in New York, we added a live radio interview with radio talk-show host Cliff Kelly at WVON, a prominent African-American radio show. WVON is located on the south side of Chicago in an African-American neighborhood. After the show was over, and we were driving home, I ordered my security detail to stop and pull over. I wanted to get out and stop by unannounced at a barbershop on 87th Street. After meeting the owner and taking pictures with the patrons, we walked down the street and stepped into a bar called the Red Pepper Lounge. It was Friday evening, and the weekend was starting. The bar was full of customers. All the people in the bar were African-American, and I have to believe, though I've done no research on it, that I'm probably the only governor in Illinois history to make an unscheduled visit to that bar. The people were warm and supportive. I shook hands, took pictures, talked to the people and answered some of their questions. As I was doing that, the six o'clock news came on, and there I was all over the TV screen behind the bar. The mood of the people started to brighten. There was a lot of energy in that bar and before long the patrons were shouting "four more years, four more years!" I listened with appreciation and gratitude, but I knew more about what was coming than they did. So I responded to the effect of, "Hey, I'll take four more days." Barring a miracle, I was entering my last weekend as governor.

And so I went to New York for a whirlwind tour of interviews. In the span of two days, I easily did over thirty interviews. I did all the major networks and all the major Cable News Networks. I was interviewed on the *Today* show. I was up early answering tough questions from Diane Sawyer on *Good Morning America*. I appeared on *The View* before a live audience being grilled by Barbara Walters from a TV screen because she was out in California and couldn't do it in person. Joy Behar messed up my hair and kept trying to get me to imitate Richard Nixon. I did a lot of the Fox News Channels and had to answer questions from their conservative commentators. I did CNN and had to answer questions from their liberal-leaning, Washington D.C. Democratic-establishment perspective. And at night, I did Larry King's show live for an hour, answering his questions and taking a couple of telephone calls.

One of the shows I did was The D.L. Hughley show on CNN. Hughley is a successful comedian who grew up in South Central Los Angeles. I took a liking to him, and since he was supportive, he urged me to take the case I was making before the American people and do it in Springfield before the very senators who were racing to throw me out of office. When I told him and others that the impeachment was a foregone conclusion, and that a political deal was struck between the legislative leaders of both parties where they agreed to require all of their members to vote for removal, so that speaking to them was a waste of time, Hughley continued to make the case that I should at least go down there.

Hughley got me thinking. While I knew that going to Springfield and speaking before the Illinois state Senate wouldn't change a single vote, I could see that he wanted me to do it. He was supportive. And he was probably indicative of a lot of other people who were supporting me and who probably wanted to see me make my case personally before the Illinois state Senate. So I changed my mind. I asked for the opportunity to speak before the Illinois state Senate to make my case as to why they shouldn't remove me from office. I did it because I believed I owed it to the many people who through all of this were still supporting me. I would go to Springfield and make my appeal in person. But I was under no illusions. No matter what I said, it wouldn't make a difference.

I spoke before the Illinois state Senate on January 29, 2009. I spoke for approximately 47 minutes. I made the case to them in person that if they were going to remove a governor twice elected by the people from office, they at least ought to give me a chance to bring in evidence and witnesses to prove that I did nothing wrong. I asked them to think about the precedent they were about to set. I asked them to think about what it would be like if they were falsely accused of something, and the job they had was being taken away from them before any wrongdoing was proven.

The Senate chamber was quiet. The Senators sat there listening politely. But it was surreal. They knew how they were going to vote, and I knew how they were going to vote and they knew that I knew how they were going to vote, and here I am doing the best I can to try to persuade them to prove us all wrong. Shakespeare wrote that the world's a stage and each must play a part. We were all playing a part, and no matter what I said, everyone knew how this play was going to end.

I flew back home to Chicago immediately after speaking to the Senate. The Senate was scheduled to vote later that day, and I joked on the plane home that some of us might have to parachute out if the impeachment vote took place while we were still in the air. Lieutenant Governor Pat Quinn had already publicly said that he was giving me one day to get out of the governor's mansion, which was not our primary residence but where we still spent a lot of time together as a family. If he became the governor while I was in mid air, it was not a stretch to think that he would immediately recall the plane back to Springfield and make me walk home.

I was home when the impeachment vote came down.

I was suddenly no longer the governor.

Exactly three minutes after the impeachment vote, my state police security detail was ordered by new Governor Pat Quinn to immediately remove the security that was protecting me and my family. This was an extremely emotional time for all of us. Patti, our girls, and I had a real bond with the members of our security detail. They were like family. They were in our lives for the past several years. We had already started saying our goodbyes to them. A few days before the impeachment vote, as one shift of the security detail was being replaced by another, I was in the family room in the back of the house watching *SportsCenter*. All of a sudden I could hear Annie crying loudly. I got up to see what it was all about. There was Annie in her mother's arms. She started crying after seeing her mother break down as they were both saying goodbye to Tony Zürich, a member of our security detail whose job was to protect our children for the past four years.

Sergeant Robert Love was in charge of the security detail the day I was hijacked from office. He was ordered by his superiors within minutes of the impeachment vote to come into our home and retrieve the security telephone that was there in case of emergency. Bob Love is a great guy who, like all the members of our security detail, was part of our extended family. To avoid the media, he knocked on our back door and asked permission to come inside our home. Bob Love is a man's man. He kind of reminds me a little bit of the actor Carl Weathers who played Apollo Creed in the Rocky movies. He had a job to do that he didn't want to do. And when he saw Patti's reaction to the news that he had just been ordered to remove the security from my family, he started crying a little bit. He was simply following his orders to disassemble the security apparatus that had been inside of our home for the past six years. He was upset because he had to give the order to take the security detail away that only ten minutes before was protecting our home and acting as a buffer between us and the media circus that was currently surrounding our house. Suddenly, with a snap of a finger, our security team was snatched away, and we had nothing between us and the throngs of people who were congregating outside of our home.

I never knew that Pat Quinn could be so petty and so vindictive. The order to immediately take security away from my family came directly from him. Being longtime friends with Patti's father, he had known my wife since she was a little girl. And for his first act as Governor of Illinois to be one where he might jeopardize the safety of our little girls was stunning.

There's an old saying, "here today, gone tomorrow." That's what it was like. One minute I was governor with a team of people assigned to protect me and my family and literally the next minute I'm not the governor, and the team of people assigned to protect us was immediately snatched away. The rest of the detail was ordered to leave right away. They never even had a chance to say goodbye.

But I still had work to do. I still had to talk to the media.

It was a cold January night, and darkness had fallen, but everything was lit up because of the bright lights of the cameras. There were people all around. Not just the press but some of our neighbors and ordinary citizens who congregated around our house to watch the scene unfold.

At a little after 6 p.m., I went outside to talk to the media. It was strange. All of a sudden, for the first time in more than six years, I was all by myself. No staff. No security detail. I was now a private citizen, and it was just me and a whole bunch of reporters and cameramen and people.

I made a brief statement to the press about how a governor twice-elected by the people had been wrongfully hijacked from office. And then I took a moment and spoke directly to the people. I told them how I loved them and how I hoped they knew I had not let them down. I expressed my gratitude to them for the opportunity they gave me to serve them for the past six years as governor. I spoke about the achievements I was most proud of. Making Illinois the first state in America where every child can have access to healthcare. Making Illinois the only state in America where all our senior citizens can take public transportation for free. Becoming the only state in America where all uninsured women have access to routine mammograms and Pap smears that could save their lives. Providing pre-school to all three and four-year-olds whose parents otherwise couldn't give their kids the chance to start school and not fall behind other kids. I spoke about the two minimum wage increases we gave to low-wage workers when the Bush administration wouldn't do it at the federal level, and how I put a record amount of money in the public education system but did so without raising taxes on working and middle-class families.

And when a reporter asked me what my plans were for the future now that I was out of a job, I said that we were now not unlike tens of thousands of people across America who were also without jobs. And that nobody needed to feel sorry for us. Patti and I would regroup and rebuild our lives to support our children. But that I intended to keep being a voice fighting for the average ordinary guy, for whom I had fought so hard while I was governor.

Then I shook some hands, hugged some of my neighbors, talked to some kids, and then climbed the steps to my house, turned around and waved, and said goodbye.

CHAPTER THIRTEEN

MY FAMILY IS GOING THROUGH A LOT. OF COURSE THE WORST PART OF IT IS THE IMPACT SOMETHING LIKE THIS HAS ON MY CHILDREN. I'm a public figure, and the false allegations have predictably created a media firestorm. Protecting our children from being burned by those flames is hard, especially when the media surrounds our home. We live in an older and established neighborhood in Chicago. Our home is not protected by gates. When the media converges outside of our house, there is no way to protect our children from that.

A couple of weeks after celebrating her sixth birthday, Annie asked her mother why birthday wishes don't come true. Annie was referring to the secret wish she made when she blew out the candles on her birthday cake. When Patti asked her what she wished for, Annie told her she wished that I would be governor again, and the reporters would leave. I was surprised to hear that story when Patti told me about it. Because for the most part as we've gotten further away from the traumatic events, I had the impression that Annie was not nearly as troubled as Amy was concerning the circumstances surrounding me. She seemed to be living comfortably in the world of a six-year-old. It may be that the periodic visits of the media to our home may have triggered her feelings. My heart sank when Patti told me that story.

The expected indictments came down right around Annie's birthday. They were inevitable. When a prosecutor orders the arrest of a sitting governor in his home and sensationally announces false accusations that lead to a chain of events that could remove that governor from office, from his point of view, there could be no turning back. Expecting another media frenzy at our home, Patti and I decided to take our girls to Disney World and get them away from the storm. It was fortunate that it so happened our kids were on spring break from school.

One of the lawyers from our legal team, Michael Ettinger, spent the day with us at Disney World. We were joined by his wife Maureen, his daughter Nicole, his son Craig, and his friend Jordan. Disney World is a world unto itself. It is gated and employs an army of security. They do not allow the media to invade the privacy of their guests. To ensure that we could protect our girls from being further traumatized by the media, it was decided that we would spend the day getting lost in the Magic Kingdom. It seemed a fitting place to be. We would spend the day in a make-believe world on a day when make-believe charges were being brought against me. But the best part of it was that we protected our children from another round of the media circus.

It's ironic, but our girls had a great time that day. Mike Ettinger's daughter Nicole was great with our daughters. She paid them a lot of attention, played with them, made them laugh, and entertained them. For most of the day, our daughters had no idea what was happening in the outside world. That changed when late in the day, after walking around for hours in the Magic Kingdom, our kids were cooling off and playing in the pool. A woman from a local Orlando, Florida TV station started asking me questions. My daughter Amy was with me at the time drinking a lemonade. This woman was videotaping me with a handheld camcorder. She snuck into Disney World and was staked out at the pool and began asking me how I felt.

Disney World is filled with a lot of characters. Of course there's Mickey Mouse and Minnie Mouse and Donald Duck. We saw a lot of them. And then there was this woman from the media. She lied to get into the world of Disney where children can find fun and thrills and excitement. A world of magic; a place where dreams come true, and where children are encouraged to "wish upon a star." And here is this character from a local television station sneaking and lying her way into that world and invading the sanctity and innocence of a place created to bring joy and happiness to children.

Patti never wanted a political life for us. She grew up in it. She knew it. She saw the effects that lifestyle had on her family. And she didn't want it. Instead she dreamed of a quiet life where she could find happiness raising her children out of the glare of the public eye. Where she could travel and see the world. If Patti had her way, her family would be a million miles away from the strife and bloodsport of politics. But it didn't turn out that way. When the call came and I answered it, she characteristically and selflessly didn't hesitate to share in and support that decision. She subordinated her dreams for mine. And long before our lives were turned upside down, I would often think about her sacrifice and feel real pangs of guilt for taking our lives in a direction different from the one she would have preferred.

And then Patti was on a reality TV show in a jungle in Costa Rica. It is one of those detours in our life's journey that neither one of us would have ever predicted. Originally I was going to do it. But once I couldn't, Patti agreed to take my place. Like millions of Americans today, Patti and I are facing hard times. Like those Americans, we aren't quitting. We are picking ourselves up and dusting ourselves off and starting over. We are rebuilding our lives. And while doing reality TV shows in the jungle wasn't something either one of us would have imagined doing, in many ways we are more fortunate than most. As unorthodox as it is, Patti and I have been given an opportunity to make a living and support our family. When I saw Patti on television in the jungle facing her challenges, I saw a loving and devoted mother doing what she must to keep things as nice as possible for her children during what are for our family difficult and changing times.

Some people ask me if I had it to do over again, what would I have done differently concerning Barack Obama's replacement to the United States Senate? Knowing what I know now, would I have handled it differently? Specifically, would I have discussed the Senate seat over the telephone in what I presumed were private conversations? Those are good questions. I suppose if I never talked about Obama's replacement, either over the phone or in person, I wouldn't be where I am now. Or if I simply appointed myself to the United States Senate the day after the election, then none of this would have happened. I suppose if I acted that way things might be a lot different.

Still, I'm not so sure that would be the case. I now believe, and it has since become clear to me, that the federal prosecutor was so determined to get me that no matter how pristine I operated, no matter how determined I was to do right by the people of Illinois, no matter the truth, he was determined to do what he did. And if his excuse to act wasn't the Senate seat, then he would've found some other issue to trump up against me. The prosecutor wronged me. And knowing what I know now, I don't think there was anything I could have done to stop him from doing so.

Most of the conversations about the Senate seat took place over my home telephone because I was trying to be extra careful to not talk about political matters at the governor's office on a government phone. This is another irony to this story. Trying to avoid even the appearance of crossing politics with government, I held a series of telephone calls to discuss routine politics, the Senate seat, and other issues from my home. The fact that the federal prosecutor wiretapped my home telephone line and listened to what I presumed were private conversations doesn't change the most basic and important fact: I didn't do anything wrong. And I never intended to do anything wrong. I was given a golden opportunity to do something with the Senate seat that could have done a lot of good for a lot of people. I was determined to consider every honest and legal idea to help me make the best decision for the people of Illinois.

There is nothing in my private conversations that would verify I was trying to sell the Senate seat. I talked, I explored, I threw out ideas. I considered a variety of alternatives and possible scenarios, and I was always mindful of my responsibility to do what was right for the people of Illinois. And after all the discussions and exploring and listening to the ideas and the advice of my top advisers, I made a decision to choose a United States senator who was personally an anathema to me, but if the routine political deal I was trying to get done was allowed to happen, it would have achieved the most good for the most people in the state of Illinois.

I was thrown out of office by a pack of self-righteous hypocritical lawmakers in a process that violated the very civil liberties and constitutional guarantees we as Americans cherish. I was denied the most elementary right to bring in witnesses and to have every single wiretapped recording heard in the Senate impeachment trial. This evidence would have shown that I did nothing wrong. But the senate rules prevented me from having this evidence heard. Why did the leadership in the state Senate deny me that most basic right? I was the anti-Nixon, and this was the opposite of Watergate. Whereas President Nixon sought to prevent his tapes from being heard, I sought the opposite. I asked only for a chance to have my taped conversations heard.

Why did the Senate leadership establish rules that prevented me and the people of Illinois from having those tapes played in the impeachment trial? Why didn't they allow me to prove my innocence?

Part of the answer is that I believe there was a deal between the new Senate leadership, Mike Madigan, and Lieutenant Governor Pat Quinn, to get me out of the way so Quinn could propose an increase in the state income tax. Another part of the reason was that the Senate leadership, through the use of emissaries, offered me the chance immediately after my arrest to step aside with full pay and security detail for the remaining two years of my term. If I rejected that offer, the message sent to me was that I would be impeached and removed from office. I rejected that offer.

And perhaps the most important reason why they prevented me from having the taped conversations heard in the Senate trial was because many of those same Senate Democrats were on some of those telephone conversations with me. They didn't want what they were saying heard. From what I recall during the time my private conversations were being recorded, I remember talking to the new Senate President John Cullerton, his good friend and business partner state Senator Jimmy Deleo, and another member of his leadership team, state Senator Rickey Hendon. All of them had conversations with me on my telephone during that time that provide insights into their thinking and how they operate.

Take the new Senate President John Cullerton, for example. He was running to be the next Senate President, and in conversations with me he boasted about all the money he raised. It is my recollection that he claimed to have raised around $400,000 and gave it out to other state senators. Senator Cullerton bragged about all the money he raised and the point he was making was that by contributing that money to his colleagues, he expected to be elected the next Senate President. Was the money he was raising and giving to his colleagues a form of buying their votes? Well, he evidently didn't want anyone asking that question, and he obviously didn't want anyone hearing those conversations.

And there were conversations with Senator DeLeo, a big supporter of Senator Cullerton for Senate President. He apparently resented the actions of some of his colleagues because in one conversation that I remember, he asked me how it was that one of his colleagues, state Senator Jeffrey Schoenberg, had raised $100,000 in campaign contributions from the powerful nursing home industry after he successfully passed a bill that taxed senior citizens in nursing homes for the benefit of that same industry? My recollection of that conversation was that Senator DeLeo asked me if I agreed with his assessment that what Senator Schoenberg did was a form of pay-to-play politics. How was that *not* pay-to-play politics, asked Senator DeLeo.

And there was a conversation with state Senator Hendon, who explained to me that he was joining another member of the Black Caucus and breaking from the unit vote the caucus was expected to make and support John Cullerton for Senate President. His explanation was that the member in question never forgave Cullerton's opponent for a previous liaison she had with him. He explained to me that she was scorned and that since she was breaking with the Black Caucus, he was going to join her. Evidently, Senator Hendon saw that personal dalliance between two senators as an opportunity. Because he soon made a deal, threw his support behind Senator Cullerton, and joined the new leadership team of the new Senate President.

Or how about the conversations I had with my staff about issues of the day? For example, a new ethics law that banned campaign contributions from contractors to the governor. I rewrote the law to expand it to include me and everyone else, including the lawmakers. Senator Don Harmon was the sponsor of the bill that only applied the limits to the governor but didn't apply those same restrictions on themselves. After meeting with my legal counsel, who on my instruction was trying to work to expand the application of that law, I was told that Senator Harmon changed subjects and asked my legal counsel in private if he could send bond work to his own law firm. I was told about this, and I would marvel with my staff about that particular senator's hypocrisy and unethical behavior. On the one hand, he is sponsoring ethics reform that, incidentally, doesn't apply to him, and then he uses his position as a state Senator to ask for bond business for his law firm. It is amazing to me how he can pretend to be a champion for ethics and then without missing a beat use his position to try to get business for his law firm. The real question here is: was he subtly suggesting to my legal counsel that if his law firm received the bond work he asked for, he might consider expanding his ethics legislation to apply to himself and other senators? Was Senator Harmon using his legislation as leverage to benefit his law firm and himself?

Several conversations with state Senators took place over my telephone. Many of those same senators who voted to impeach me knew they had those conversations. They obviously didn't want anybody to hear them. But I wanted those taped conversations heard. I argued they would show me to be the honest and committed public servant that I am. Yet the Senators did not want what they said to be heard. And they threw me out of office.

The prosecutor had me arrested and charged based on those wiretapped conversations. And at a sensational press conference he used those taped conversations as the basis for his actions. Yet at the impeachment proceedings, I, the one who was accused of wrongdoing, was the one clamoring and demanding and pleading that the Senate and the public hear every secretly recorded telephone conversation. I implored senators to hear all the evidence. I wasn't afraid of the truth. I took the position that the people had a right to hear those tapes. The people had a right to know what their Governor was saying on the telephone. And I had no problem with my fellow citizens hearing every one of them, even if they were private conversations over my home telephone. But my accusers wouldn't allow it.

It was the accusers who were afraid of the truth. Where is the justice in that? What were they afraid of? That the tapes would show I did nothing wrong?

The government invaded my privacy by secretly placing wiretaps on my home phone, and despite that intrusion I wanted all of the tapes heard. But the people who secretly recorded my conversations fought to prevent that. I was hired by the people but was fired by the politicians. When the state Senate prevented me and the people of Illinois from having every one of those taped conversations heard, they deprived the people of the whole truth. And when they acted to remove me from office after preventing the truth from being heard, those lawmakers stole from the people of Illinois the governor they chose. They hijacked from the people the Governor they elected, not unlike how terrorists hijack airplanes.

A few years ago, Patti and I took Mayor Daley and his wife Maggie out to dinner to celebrate the Christmas holidays. When I was governor we would, from time to time, get together with the Daleys. They were great company. During those dinners as Patti and Maggie would mostly talk to each other about things like family and the kids, the mayor and I would talk about politics and governing and the common challenges we both respectively faced. Among the things the mayor and I talked about that night were the ongoing federal investigations into both our administrations and about the new political reality in America today. About the proliferation of ambitious overzealous prosecutors who have used their power to conduct investigations motivated not by the pursuit of the truth, but instead by the pursuit of their prey. Too many of them have become big game hunters. Get a high-profile politician, and you can make a name for yourself and perhaps even become a high-profile politician yourself. It's scary. But it's true. I knew I was the subject of a federal investigation, but so were many others in high position: high-ranking officials in the Bush administration, President Clinton and Hillary Clinton when they were in the White House. My view was that these investigations have become part of the new political landscape today. And the unfortunate reality is that most anyone in a high position has to live with it.

In my case, because I wasn't doing anything wrong and because I never intended to violate any laws, I didn't really give any serious thought to the notion that someone might be surreptitiously listening to my private conversations. In fact, I believed that after four years of scrutiny by federal investigators into seemingly every area of our lives, that they would find Patti and I were honest people who worked, raised our kids, paid our taxes, and honestly met our responsibilities. I thought the years of scrutiny were about to come to an end. Instead what happened to us was shocking and wrong.

From the moment I took office as governor I was mindful of my predecessor's problems, and I directed my new Chief of Staff to work with a prominent Chicago law firm and create an administration that would avoid the mistakes of the previous administration. When my predecessor was charged with corruption, I directed my top staff to make sure they studied the criminal complaint to try to avoid having a repeat in my administration. I passed landmark ethics legislation at the end of my first year to put more checks and balances in my government so that people who work for me were made aware that someone was watching. While I was not naïve that, human nature being what it is, some people would transgress, I believed the systems we put in place, coupled with the new ethics laws, made our administration far more ethically and morally responsible to the taxpayers than any of the previous administrations in recent history.

At times it still feels like a dream. Like a horrible nightmare that I keep thinking I'll wake up from. How could this have happened?

I spent the last six years of my life as the governor of Illinois doing more good for more people than I ever did in my entire life. And surprisingly, I made a lot of people unhappy when I did it. And I had to fight to get it done. Almost every step of the way, it was a fight. And I didn't just fight with political leaders and the special interests. Trying to do my duty and do the right thing, I fought with my own family. With my father-in-law over a landfill I closed that was violating environmental laws. It caused a rift and a breakup that we still haven't gotten over. And then he got mad over an executive order I unilaterally issued that prevented any immediate family member of the governor from lobbying for companies who were seeking contracts with the state.

Prior to my election, the political power in the Democratic Party was divided between Mayor Daley in Chicago and Mike Madigan in Springfield. A lot of people believed that both Democrats preferred Republican governors rather than a Democratic governor who would change the power equation in the state and in the party. Much of the support that I received from the Democratic county chairman and other political leaders across the state was precisely because they felt excluded from having a say in the direction of the party in Illinois. They supported me, in part, because they wanted something different than the Democratic Party that everyone had grown used to. A party controlled by two people and to some extent two families from Chicago. My election changed that power equation. And when I turned out to be a governor who had my own ideas on how to govern, and when I proved unwilling to be a tool for the political bosses and do their bidding, the seeds were sown for those who didn't appreciate my independence to pounce on me if they were ever given an opportunity to do so. My arrest and the false charges against me gave them that opportunity.

In my six years as governor I aggressively pushed an agenda based on the principles of what the Democratic Party is supposed to stand for. I pushed and successfully enacted an agenda to help the poor, working families, and the middle class. I expanded healthcare, invested a record amount of money in public school education, increased the minimum wage for low-wage workers twice, fought the big drug companies to help our seniors afford their medicine, protected the reproductive rights of women, became the first governor in Illinois to extend domestic partnership benefits to gay and lesbian state employees, gave all of our seniors free public transportation and did the same for the disabled and men and women serving in the Armed Forces. In short, my agenda as governor was an agenda that was true to the principles of the Democratic Party. I kept my promises to the people and kept the faith with the principles of my party.

So when the intervening extraordinary actions of the United States attorney to arrest a sitting governor and level false accusations against him occurred, I should not have been abandoned by my party. They should have at the least waited for my response. But they didn't. I was abandoned by my party because of the sensation created by the way the United States attorney had me arrested. He timed my arrest and leveled false charges relating to the sale of the very Senate seat the new president was vacating at a time that new president was only beginning to put together his new administration. A scandal like this one, however untrue and coming at a time when the new president is about to take office, created a political environment where the national Democratic Party just wanted it to go away. The political environment and political expediency dictated that both the presumption of innocence and me should be sacrificed for the benefit of the new administration and the benefit of getting off to a perceived fast start. For democratic leaders in the state of Illinois, it was about a desire to get me out of the way. They were tired of me keeping them in Springfield for long special sessions to compel them to expand healthcare. They saw it as an opportunity to rid themselves of a governor who would take on the powerful insurance industry, the pharmaceutical industry, and other powerful special interests that many of the Democratic lawmakers have close relationships with. And most significantly, I believe they abandoned me because with me out of the way, they could finally hope to get the big income tax increase many of my fellow Democrats have been pushing and wanting to enact for years.

I knew I was the subject of a federal investigation. That was the reality I was living in for the better part of four years. I did not suspect my phones were tapped. But I wasn't doing anything wrong so I wasn't concerned with it. I had no reason to fear conversations over the telephone or for that matter anywhere else. I never ever intended to break any law. So whatever I might say in a private conversation either on the telephone or in person was legal and, if anything, I had a propensity to constantly check with my legal counsel Bill Quinlan to make sure that whatever I did or whatever ideas I might have would be permissible under the law. I was aware of no corruption. Nor would I tolerate any if I knew it existed. I would've acted to root it out. And I would have worked to take the appropriate measures to correct it.

Two top aides of mine have now claimed to have engaged in wrongdoing. I'm stunned and broken-hearted by the news. And I still can't believe it. Both were men I relied on heavily to run the operations of government. I relied on them to properly advise me on how to do certain things the right way. I saw them both as honest and upstanding family men.

With respect to one of those aides, from what I know about it, I still don't believe he did anything wrong, even though he said he did. Why he would claim that he did is a matter of great curiosity to me. Maybe he should get himself another lawyer to take a fresh look at his case. The only explanation I could come up with is that he is being threatened by the prosecutor with a long jail sentence because of alleged misdeeds he may have been involved in before he came to work for me and that had nothing to do with me. Perhaps he feels compelled to lie about me to get a lesser sentence.

The other man was one of my best friends. We were roommates in law school. I've known him for nearly 30 years. I trusted him more than anyone except my wife and my brother. It is alleged that he received tens of thousands of dollars in cash payments from Tony Rezko when he worked as my Chief of Staff. I never knew about it. I still can't believe it. And when I first heard of the allegation, I laughingly mocked it. It struck me as a wild accusation by a desperate man who was saying these things about my friend in order to save himself. Because the friend and law school roommate I knew would never do something like that. It was because of his honesty and integrity and our friendship that I asked him to serve as my campaign manager in my first race for governor and to be my Chief of Staff in my first administration as governor. He was someone I believed I could trust who would be loyal to me and make sure things were done right. It is beyond belief to think that he could have done what he allegedly did. And I can't believe he would betray me by doing something like that. What circumstances in his life could be so bad that he could do something seemingly so out of character with who I thought he was? I am so hurt by my friend's betrayal. And I am sad and angry too. But I am mostly hurt—very, very hurt. It kills me to think this could be true. And I don't know what to make of it.

Ironically, it is in Shakespeare's play, *Othello*, that Iago himself says, "Good name in man and woman, dear my lord, is the immediate jewel of their souls. Who steals my purse steals trash; tis something, nothing; Twas mine, tis his, and has been slave to thousands. But he that filches from me my good name robs me of that which enriches him and make me poor indeed." One of my dearest friends may have done things that I never would have thought he was capable of doing. That he could do this and jeopardize his family, betray our friendship, threaten to rob me of my good name, and risk destroying the work my administration was dedicated to on behalf of all the people we were working to help, is devastating. And something I can't even begin to comprehend.

There is a reason why in the Lord's Prayer we ask God to lead us not into temptation but deliver us from evil. If these men who served in high positions of government succumbed to temptation, then I feel sorry for them and for their families. Preachers preach from the pulpit, priests give sermons, and rabbis share the wisdom from the Talmud about the weakness and transgressions of people. We are taught to love the sinner and hate the sin. Not long ago, he was like a brother to me. Now I don't know what he is.

When I campaigned for reelection in 2006, I used to say that I had fewer friends today than I did four years ago. We even made a television commercial with me saying that. The point I was making was that when you're the governor, and you have to make decisions, you can't possibly serve the common good without making some people unhappy. Time and time again when I was confronted with the interests of some of my supporters, and they were in conflict with the general welfare of the people, I decided and pursued the course that promoted the common good and served the general welfare.

In fact, on the day before I was arrested, in spite of the erosion of support that necessarily accompanies decisions a leader has to make, I still had a lot of friends and supporters in the political world. You could say that the day before my arrest I had legions of friends, and the day after my arrest I suddenly had none. Dr. Martin Luther King said that in times like these, you'll never remember the words of your enemies, but you'll never forget the silence of your friends. That has certainly been the case with me in the political world I worked in the past sixteen years. Those friends haven't just been silent, they have run away. They've acted the way they have because whatever friendship that existed was based upon politics and not friendship. And they've run away because they're scared. They are afraid of being subjects of federal investigations, and so they stay away and hope no one remembers how close we once were.

But our real friends have been great; especially Patti's friends. These were friendships that were forged outside of politics. They were natural friendships developed between people who like each other and had things in common. When the life we knew was suddenly taken away from us, and our lives changed so dramatically for the worse, those friends have been there for us. Patti's friends have been loyal and true. They have been there for her lending moral support and offering to help in whatever way we need. The parents of our children's friends have proven to be great friends too. During these difficult times, they have sought us out to help. They have been great. They were especially helpful to me when Patti went to

Costa Rica, and I was left alone with the kids. And my old friends, friends I had outside of politics, many of whom I saw less and less of as I got busier and bigger in government, have been there for me. They have offered their help, and they have made the lives we've been living since all of this has happened a little less lonely. I know I speak for Patti when I say how grateful we are for their friendship.

And we've made some new friends. And these are relationships that are developing as Patti and I work to pick up the pieces and start over. I'm looking forward to developing these friendships. Because they are not founded on me being at the top of the mountain but are instead starting with me at the bottom of the valley.

Innocent people have gone to prison for things they did not do. I am not unaware of how powerful the federal government can be once they set their sights on you. Of course I'm afraid of this possibility. Who wouldn't be? But I try to not give it a lot of thought. I know what the truth is. I know what motivates me, what my intentions are, and how I operate. When you are falsely accused of crimes you didn't commit and are being lied about, all you can do is trust in the truth. The truth will, as it is written in the Bible, set you free. I believe that. I have to believe that. And I believe the government will not only fail to prove me guilty but far more important than that, I will prove my innocence. I will show my fellow citizens and the people who trusted me and who elected me twice as their governor that I put them first, and I did my job honestly. And I trust in my fellow citizens as I always have to see the truth for what it is.

I never lost an election. I believe it is because I trusted the people and they trusted me. Nothing has changed as far as I'm concerned. When the full story is told, and the whole truth comes out, people will see that I honestly worked to make things better for them. And that I didn't break the law. That's why I look forward to my opportunity to prove my innocence before my fellow citizens in a court of law. All I ask is that I be given a fair trial to do so. And despite all that's happened to me and to Patti and to my family, I still believe this is America, and I'll have my day in court.

But there are times when fear creeps in. And I think about the unthinkable. Sometimes I find myself stealing glimpses of my older daughter Amy as she's doing her homework or watching television. I look at her and wonder what life will be like for her in a year or two. She just finished the seventh grade. She got all As and one B+. What will it be like for her when she leaves the school she's known since she was three to begin high school? What if, God forbid, the truth doesn't prevail, and she begins that new part of her life changing schools at the same time her father has to leave and go to a place I have a hard time even saying? How hard would that be on my sweet, happy, and usually cheerful Amy? To have to deal with that kind of change at a time in her life when she is entering the difficult and life-shaping teenage years is hard enough. But having to deal with that change and at the same time being forced to carry a burden like that is extremely painful to think about.

Or I think of our little one, our daughter Annie who just graduated from kindergarten. I watched her during her graduation ceremony. There she was sitting on the floor in her classroom with her classmates. She was so sweet and so cute and so innocent. And I thought to myself how lucky I was to share that moment with her, and I wondered to myself how many more of those moments I would be able to share. I wondered whether I would be able to watch her grow or would I miss those precious years that are still ahead of her. Would my little girl be deprived of having her daddy with her on those special occasions in her life that mean so much to her? I felt a profound sense of sadness when I thought about that.

Thinking about serving time in federal prison and the effect it would have on my two little girls is almost unbearable. It is frightening and terrifying. And I have my moments when

I think about it and, of course, it scares me. And then I get angry. Because I know what the truth is. Because I know I never intended nor did I violate any laws. And I get angry that an overzealous prosecutor would do this to my family. I get angry and want to fight back. These people are threatening my family and they are threatening the well-being of my children. They have falsely accused me of things I didn't do. That's bad enough. But the worst part of it is the part that scares me the most. And that is what this might mean for my children.

A lot has happened to my family in the last six months. I worked in a job to help people. But because of false accusations that job was taken away from me. And because of those accusations, the job my wife had helping the homeless was taken away from her.

Patti and I are rebuilding our lives. So many of the things we spent our lives working for have been broken and taken away. But we aren't quitting. And we are not alone. As we work and stoop to build up our lives, millions of Americans are doing the same with theirs. And they are an inspiration to us.

I make no secret about the inspiration I draw from great people I've read about in history books. Many of them are my heroes. And they are the heroes of others. Books are written about them. Their good deeds and their exploits are tales that are talked about and passed down from one generation to the next. Statues are erected in their honor. Schools are named after them. And they deserve all the credit they are given. Their stories, their achievements, and how they got them done should be inspirational.

But you don't have to read a history book to find inspiration. You can find inspiration in how ordinary Americans face their challenges. How they confront the cards that were dealt to them. What they do when times are tough and the well-being of their families is threatened.

The year before last, on Halloween night, I met a young mother. I had just returned home after trick-or-treating with Annie, who was four years old then and dressed as a Disney Princess. There was already a crowd by our house. So as Annie joined her mother and her aunt passing out candy, I began taking pictures with some of the children and their parents. Among the parents I met that night was a young Hispanic mother who was out with her three children. I'm guessing that their ages ranged from the oldest who might have been seven or eight, to the youngest who I know was three years old because his mother told me. I took a couple of group pictures with this mom and her kids. Before we finished, she asked for a picture with just her, her three-year-old, and me. Her three-year-old was dressed in a Winnie the Pooh costume. I know this costume very well because Amy wore it years before. As the picture was being taken, I noticed that the little boy had a scar on his head. It was clear that his head had been recently shaved and his short black hair was just beginning to grow back. The scar was serpentine, four, maybe five inches long. It was obvious this little boy recently had surgery. I asked his mother about the scar. She went on to tell me that her little boy had a tumor that was recently removed. And that he was having chemotherapy and was scheduled for another treatment the next day. But she was quick to tell me that he was fine, that the doctors told her that her son's surgery was successful and that he would get well. I then asked about her insurance. Did she need some help? She told me she didn't. Her son was enrolled in All Kids, the program I created in Illinois to give every child access to healthcare.

What struck me about this conversation with the young mother was how cheerful she was and how cheerful her children were. There she was making the best of this special night with her children. Her youngest child had a brain tumor. But she wasn't complaining about her fate or the fate of her child. She wasn't sitting home wallowing or feeling sorry for herself or conveying a sense of doom to her children. She was making the best of a bad situation. And instead of appearing bitter about what had happened to her little boy, she was thankful that she had an opportunity through the All Kids program to do something about it. And for a brief moment on that Halloween night, she was doing what she could to try to carve out a little slice of happiness for her children.

It's doubtful anyone will write a book about this young mother. And I doubt if a school or a park or a street will be named after her. But she is an inspiration to me. She is facing the hardships life has thrown at her and her family with a simple purpose and an understated courage. Every day she must confront the grim reality of raising a child with cancer. Yet she didn't complain about it and instead expressed gratitude for an opportunity that was given to her to face it.

These have been tough times for Patti and me and our children. But like that mother I met on Halloween night, and like millions of ordinary people who every day go about quietly and stoically meeting their challenges, we are going to carry on. And like her, we aren't going to lose sight of the positives of the situation. We will continue to take stock of the many blessings we have. Our children, of course, being our most precious blessings. But we have a lot of others as well.

Among those blessings are the countless letters and e-mails of support we have received from people in Illinois and across America. During this trying time, Patti and I have been touched by the compassion and good wishes of people. They've mailed us letters filled with personal stories, kind words, and passages from the Bible. A few Bibles have actually been mailed to our home. And the other day, I found a cross in a chain of beads left in the mailbox.

Despite the injustice of what happened to me and my family, I am blessed. Because even in our darkest hour we have each other. Patti and I love and are devoted to one another. The trials and tribulations we are now going through only serve to make that love and devotion even stronger. We've been blessed with two wonderful little girls. They light up our lives even during the darkest times. And we believe in God. We have faith in him. And in our own way, we call on Him to help see us through this. I believe there is a purpose behind all that has happened to us. And maybe God has a plan for me to be an instrument for good. And that the troubles we are facing, the lies, the abandonment, the heartbreak, the pain, are all obstacles in the journey we must make, where like the stories in the Bible, God brings good out of bad.

Rick Warren, in his book *The Purpose Driven Life*, writes that every problem is a character-building opportunity, and the more difficult it is, the greater the potential for building spiritual muscle and moral fiber. The Greek tragedian, Aeschylus, wrote during the Golden Age of Athens, "Even in our sleep, pain that cannot forget, falls drop by drop upon the heart and in our own despair against our will comes wisdom to us by the awful grace of God." It may be that God's plan for me is to strengthen my faith and learn through suffering. Perhaps it is part of his design for me that I develop a better understanding for other people's troubles and a deeper sympathy for their suffering. Maybe this is a trial I must go through. Where my faith and the strength of my character are tested. I've entered another wilderness period in my life. I've had them before. We all have. And it has been the case that when I have suffered my own set of hardships and felt abandoned and betrayed and utterly alone, that I have learned some of life's most valuable lessons. Those lessons have made me a better man. I know I am a better husband and a better father, and I was a more compassionate Governor than I would have been had I not learned from those hard and lonely times. In the past, when I've experienced loss, when my heart has been broken, I have learned to better understand the suffering of others. And because of that understanding, I have learned to be better to others. I am sustained by the love of my family and my faith in God. And in the end, it will be the truth that will see us through in God's good time.

I am not writing myself off with respect to a future in public service. And I don't intend to just fade away. I am no less committed to the people and the causes, I fought for than I was before all this happened to me. While I may not be in the same position to help those people advance those causes, I'm still just as committed to them. In the words of Tennyson's "Ulysses," "though much has changed, much abides. And though we are not now the strength which in old days moved earth and heaven, that which we are, we are; one equal temper of heroic hearts made weak by time and by fate but strong in will; to strive, to seek, to find, and not to yield."

I am going to continue to speak out and be a voice for the little guy. And I fully intend to continue to be active in promoting the issues and causes I believe in.

The once safe and happy life of my family has been threatened by an overzealous prosecutor who knowingly brought false accusations against me. He ordered my arrest at my home where my children sleep. He did it at six o'clock in the morning. What possible purpose would that serve, to have my children awakened to see their father arrested in the early morning hours? As a former prosecutor, I know that arrests are warranted for two reasons. The first is that the one being charged is a threat to flee and the second reason is that he poses a danger to his community. I was the Governor of Illinois at the time. I wasn't a flight risk, and who was I likely to hurt? I wasn't a terrorist or a drug dealer, for God's sake. I have spent a lifetime as an honest and law abiding citizen. I have absolutely no criminal record. Why not just do what always happens in matters like this: call my lawyer and ask me to come in? To do what they did and how they did it just isn't how things are done in America. To invade my home where every American has a right to expect that he or she is safe from the intrusion of the government is one of the most basic rights that separate us from other countries. This is what they did in Soviet Russia. It's what they do in North Korea or Iran or

Castro's Cuba. It's not how it is supposed to be in George Washington's or Thomas Jefferson's America. This isn't American justice. What this prosecutor did by ordering my arrest at my home with my children there came right out of the playbook of the KGB.

This is why my father fled after World War II. This is why he fought the Nazis and spent four years in a Nazi prisoner of war camp. And why, after the war, he refused to return to his native land because the Communists took over, and it was no longer free. He wanted freedom, and he saw the United States of America as the land of the free. He wanted to come to this special and unique place where people from all over the globe can find freedom and have the opportunity to build a good life for their families.

My immigrant father loved America. He loved it because it was free and because it was a place where you could work hard and get ahead. He loved America in a way that only someone who knew what it was like to live in a place that wasn't free could appreciate. He raised my brother and me to love America too. He told us stories about the war and the old country. About what the Nazis did to people and how the communists destroyed freedom. And he drew comparisons to what it was like there and how it was here. My father believed America was the most special place on earth. A place where you could dream big dreams, and they could come true. A place where you could go as far as your talents will take you. A place where you could be almost anything you wanted to be if you worked hard and persevered long enough. A place where you could say what you want and pray where you want. That is what made America so different from other places. Freedom. The freedom of the individual. America was a place where the individual had rights guaranteed to him that protected him from the intrusion of government. The freedom of the individual was more than just some abstract concept written on a piece of paper. It was real to people from around the world who knew it. A lot of people born here take that gift of freedom for granted. My father never did. And he taught my brother and me not to take it for granted, either. He raised us to love our country and to serve our country. Like so many immigrant parents, my father had big dreams for his sons. Those dreams my father had for us came true because everything he believed about America turned out to be true.

I have lived the American dream. To rise from humble beginnings to become governor of the fifth largest state in America is the American dream. Never, not in my darkest moments, did I ever question what my father taught me to believe about America. But I never really thought about why he felt so passionately about it. That is, until I was arrested and falsely accused of things I didn't do. The shock of my arrest, the false accusations, the rush to judgment, the hypocrisy of politicians, the cynicism and lack of interest in the truth by the media, all of these things have brought disillusionment, and for the first time in my life, have led me to fully understand why my father was so passionate on the subject of freedom. He knew what it was like to live in a place without it. He saw it. He knew it existed. And I now realize that I never spent enough time thinking about how it could happen here. Now I know. It can happen here. It has happened to me. And if it could happen to a governor, it could happen to anyone.

In my darkest moments I sometimes think about those things. I think about how disillusioned I've become over the injustice of the whole experience. And then I snap out of it. I realize that what has happened to me and my family is not because America is wrong or unjust or corrupt. It's not America. America is great. As bad as it has been for me and my family, where my reputation has been falsely sullied and my rights as a citizen have been so severely trampled on, I still have the freedom to write this book and fight back. I still have the freedom to assert my innocence and work to get the truth out. You can't do that in communist China.

No, there is nothing wrong with America. What is wrong is what this prosecutor has done. He's wrong. His actions are undermining and threatening the rights we Americans expect and so often take for granted. It is not America that is wrong. His arrest, his press conference, and his false accusations are what's wrong. Not America. I believe this country and the freedoms we enjoy are worth fighting for. I believe that it is the patriotic duty of every citizen to fight for his country to protect it and the liberties that are guaranteed to us as citizens. I believe we should fight to protect our country and our freedoms from enemies abroad. And I believe that we should fight those who would take our liberties and freedoms away from within. This fight against overzealous prosecution that only furthers political purposes is just as important as the fight against a foreign enemy. Because both of them threaten the very liberties that we Americans should expect, as a free people living in a free society.

For most of my life I saw the threat to our liberties as coming from our enemies abroad. Now, for the first time in my life, I can fully appreciate and see how our liberties as citizens can be threatened from within. That is what is so shocking to me. That this could happen in America.

This prosecutor had to know what I intended to do with the Senate appointment. I wanted to consummate a routine political deal that would achieve the most good for the most people in Illinois. The next day he ordered my arrest and prevented me from doing that. What he did to me and how he did it was not an honest mistake. It was malicious and dishonest. It was unethical. As a former prosecutor, I believe he violated the canon of ethics that governs how prosecutors are required to behave by speaking at a press conference the day of my arrest and claiming that "Lincoln would roll over in his grave." And after he did it, he told the whole world I was attempting to sell a Senate seat for personal gain when I was only trying to complete a routine political deal. What this prosecutor has done to me and to my family has no place in a free country like America. Not in the land of the free and the home of the brave.

If you love America, you should be willing to fight for it.

I am fighting for the truth. I am fighting for my family. And I see this fight as a fight for my country.